Collectible Investments for the High Net Worth Investor

Quantitative Finance Series

Aims and Objectives

- Books based on the work of financial market practitioners and academics
- Presenting cutting-edge research to the professional/practitioner market
- Combining intellectual rigor and practical application
- Covering the interaction between mathematical theory and financial practice
- To improve portfolio performance, risk management and trading book performance
- Covering quantitative techniques

Market

Brokers/Traders; Actuaries; Consultants; Asset Managers; Fund Managers; Regulators; Central Bankers; Treasury Officials; Technical Analysis; and Academics for Masters in Finance and MBA market.

Series Titles

Economics for Financial Markets
Performance Measurement in Finance
Real R&D Options
Advance Trading Rules, Second Edition
Advances in Portfolio Construction and Implementation
Computational Finance
Linear Factor Models in Finance
Initial Public Offering
Funds of Hedge Funds
Venture Capital in Europe
Forecasting Volatility in the Financial Markets, Third Edition
International Mergers and Acquisitions Activity Since 1990
Corporate Governance and Regulatory Impact on Mergers and Acquisitions
Forecasting Expected Returns in the Financial Markets
The Analytics of Risk Model Validation
Computational Finance using C++ and C#

Series Editor

Dr. Stephen Satchell

Dr Satchell is the Reader in Financial Econometrics at Trinity College, Cambridge; Visiting Professor at Birkbeck College, City University Business School and University of Technology, Sydney. He also works in a consultative capacity to many firms, and edits the journal *Derivatives: Use, Trading and Regulations* and the *Journal of Asset Management.*

Collectible Investments for the High Net Worth Investor

Stephen Satchell

ELSEVIER

AMSTERDAM • BOSTON • HEIDELBERG • LONDON
NEW YORK • OXFORD • PARIS • SAN DIEGO
SAN FRANCISCO • SINGAPORE • SYDNEY • TOKYO
Academic Press is an imprint of Elsevier

Academic Press is an imprint of Elsevier
30 Corporate Drive, Suite 400
Burlington, MA 01803 USA

Linacre House, Jordan Hill
Oxford OX2 8DP
United Kingdom

Library of Congress Cataloging-in-Publication Data
Application submitted.

British Library Cataloguing-in-Publication Data
A catalogue record for this book is available from the British Library.

ISBN: 978-0-12-374522-4

For information on all Academic Press publications
visit our Web site at *www.elsevierdirect.com*

Printed and bound in the United Kingdom

Transferred to Digital Printing in 2011

Contents

Preface

The purpose of this book is to provide a resource for high net worth advisors, wealth managers, and investors on investing in collectibles as a financial activity. A collectible is any physical asset that has the potential to appreciate in value over time because it is rare or desired by many, such as stamps, coins, fine art, and wine. Many high net worth individuals are interested in diversifying their portfolios and investing in collectibles. As such, they need guidance from their financial advisors or for themselves about the financial aspects of such investing. In this book we provide guidance from 20 experts who address issues such as liquidity challenges, tax ramifications, appreciation timelines, the challenge of forecasting and measuring appreciation, the psychological component of collecting, and emotion in collectibles investing.

The topics covered in the book include investment in art, books, cars, maps, stamps, and wine. There are numerous other collectibles I've not mentioned. In an ideal world, I would have liked to include coins, antiques, dolls, and guitars. However, on reading the various contributions, I became aware that many of the issues are common to all the investment categories and that collecting coins and collecting stamps, for example, are really not all that different from one another.

One of the aspects that has made this book project so interesting to me is the psychological side to collecting. The psychological component to high net worth investment is well documented and forms the basis of various forms of psychological profiling to assess an investor's risk appetite. There is a large body of literature on the compulsive nature of collecting. The question raised by this book is whether these two strands have some common points. Put in the simplest terms, many high net worth individuals have had a compulsion to accumulate money. Does this ongoing and possibly cumulative compulsion apply also to the acquisition and accumulation of paintings or butterflies?

Many chapters deal with issues of indexation. These problems seem common, to a large extent. Discussed in various parts (see, for example, Chapters 6, 7, 8, 9, and 10) are potential indices for art, books, and stamps. The principles described here could easily be applied to any other collectible. None of the procedures we discuss is without its problems. All the indices suffer from some sort of bias, and it might be helpful to readers to understand the sources of these biases. Typically, an index is constructed by someone who wants to sell you things; in those circumstances, the index could well be very optimistic and show that, had you bought the collectible in question, you would have experienced a history of smooth outperformance relative to some other investment activity.

Another common theme is the high transaction costs associated with investment in collectibles. In many cases, these costs approach 30%. Clearly, with numbers of this magnitude, short-term investment is not really a profitable option. Collectors need to be holding for the long term. One theme barely discussed in any of the chapters is the stream of intangible consumption that collectors enjoy. This is impossible to measure, but it's a very real part of the collecting/investing decision. Some chapters hint at this obliquely, but no author, including this editor, tries to estimate this intangible dividend. Such features have implications for the management of a collectible portfolio within a larger portfolio by family offices or high net worth managers.

These issues of asset allocation and investment horizon are discussed by Daryl Roxburgh in Chapter 1. Indeed, he covers a wide range of issues dealing with the challenges facing managers and the tools available to help them.

Which leads us to Chapter 2 by Dr. Shirley Mueller; it is a study of the neuropsychology of collecting and high net worth investment. Dr. Mueller provides a very accessible treatment of neuropsychology and its relevance to collecting. This involves the identification of those parts of the brain that contribute to the collecting decision and details, through example, the way they interact. Readers might initially stumble over phrases, such as *nucleus accumbens,* but the author leads us gently through the various components of neurological decision making; I found this material to be a valuable addition to the book. Furthermore, the author argues that such understanding will aid us in making better collecting and investment decisions. As such, this is the Enlightenment, in contrast with the Gothic Romanticism of Chapter 3.

Chapter 3, by Professor David Johnstone, looks at issues of behavioral finance and behavioral economics, especially as they apply to dealers and collectors. One feels that, as a collector, one should read such material to help cure one of irrational, and presumably suboptimal, actions. However, there is a touch of the Gothic here; the bitter truth might be that recognition of one's flaws in this respect might not lead to cure.

The fourth chapter is a paper by Professor Russell Belk, first published in the *Journal of Economic Psychology*, considers collecting as luxury consumption. This material is based on surveys of collectors and develops many of the positive psychological traits of collecting. The focus is on collecting in terms of the collector's position in society and less on the compulsive and dysfunctional aspects of it.

These first four chapters constitute a part of the book devoted to general themes. The next part consists of specific types of collecting; it will soon be apparent to the reader that the study of the art market seems to dominate all other areas. We include three chapters on art, written from both a collector's and an investor's perspective.

The first art chapter, Chapter 5 by Jeffrey Horvitz, gives a very thorough overview of the art market. This covers all aspects of the art economy, including its size and the questions of what constitutes art and investible art. The chapter presents an analysis of the components of value and even a discussion of the make-up of demand and supply. Questions of costs, information, taxation, and performance are all covered here; this chapter presents a masterly treatment of a large subject.

In Chapter 6, Professor Rachel Campbell provides a detailed analysis of art as an alternative asset. This discussion involves issues such as measuring risk and return for art as well as portfolio analysis. Portfolio analysis involves looking at a collection of assets; it enables us to evaluate the contributions of assets taken co-jointly with other assets. This means that a particular asset that might not look too exciting in its own right could still be worth investing in because it reduces the overall risk of the portfolio. Modern portfolio theory is the basis of modern finance and alternative assets, which can include, besides art, forests, infrastructure, and other nonstandard assets; this has been a growth area in investment in recent years, particularly among high net worth and endowment-related investment.

The third art chapter, Chapter 7 by Anders Petterson and Dr. Oliver Williams, is a quite different form of analysis from the two preceding chapters in that it analyzes the efficacy of the capital asset pricing model and arbitrage pricing theory in the context of the art market. It includes a very sophisticated analysis of the statistical issues involved and the data problems encountered. The authors attempt to estimate global markets, including the volatile and active contemporary Chinese and Indian 20th-century painting markets. They use as an explanatory variable measures of global wealth to produce forecasts of high-net-worth wealth. This chapter is a useful contribution to the art, and the high net worth, literatures.

Chapter 8 discusses investment in rare books. It is authored by Andrew Rudd, a book collector in his own right. Andrew uses his background as one of the world's leading financial "quants" to subject book prices to a rigorous statistical analysis. As in a number of other chapters, the notion of a collectible index becomes of great importance.

Chapter 9 is written by another collector, Adam J. Apt, with a strong quant background. Adam's collecting interest is maps, and he provides a comprehensive and readable survey of the numerous issues to do with map collecting. In many ways, this is a microcosm of collecting any theme. Collectors who want to go out on their own will find this material very illuminating.

Chapter 10 is concerned with collecting and investing in stamps. I, as a veteran stamp collector, have combined to author this chapter with John Auld, a senior member of the British Stamp Trade and a stamp auctioneer with many years' experience. We look at all the complexities of price, value, indexation, and market structure. In many ways, stamps are quintessentially *the* collecting hobby. They have been collected and invested in since the penny black was issued in 1840. They have all the characteristics of opaque prices and high transaction costs and have been forged by very skilled individuals, leading to the need for expert opinion and certification. They have low storage cost and are highly portable, so they become mobile, if not liquid, assets. Those who collect them find great pleasure and possibly great profit from pursuit of the hobby.

Chapter 11 is an introduction to Chapter 12, which is about the collecting of and investment in wine. This collectible is probably second only to art as an area of popularity and interest. The investment potential of fine wines is well known, and the stream of dividends attainable from ownership and/or consumption is well documented. The chapter is by Alan Brown, a well-known and very senior asset manager. Mr. Brown is a distinguished collector of fine wines and is prominent in wine investment discussions and debates.

Chapter 12 is a reprint of a famous paper by Professor Ashenfelter and his coauthors. Their revolutionary hypothesis is that you can assess the quality of a vintage (at least of claret) by the knowledge of a small number of variables that can be used predictively as an investment tool. These variables reflect the weather conditions prior to harvest. Included in his paper is the response of the wine press, which is predictably negative. It is worth digressing to speculate as to where the negativity comes from. Part of it may be due to fears of redundancy as wine gurus are replaced by algorithms. Part of it could be due to the jealousy that quantitatively challenged practitioners feel toward those who are more quantitatively endowed. In any case, this reaction to quantitative analysis in nontraditional areas, such as collecting, is so widespread that it is worth documenting as a psychological phenomenon. The editor has no sympathy for it whatsoever. Professor Ashenfelter's work is highly regarded, and rightly so.

Chapter 13, the last chapter, deals with classic cars. The author, David Barzilay, is well placed to write this chapter since he is a classic car journalist. This chapter takes the reader through the history of collecting classic cars and communicates very effectively the pleasure of doing so.

Taken together, these 13 chapters look at the broad picture of collectible investing for the high net worth investor. In selecting this material, I have tried to cover as many aspects of this market as I can. As I mentioned, however, there is much yet to be discussed. It might well be that a further volume on this fascinating topic will be necessary.

Stephen Satchell

List of Contributors

Adam Jared Apt, CFA, is the proprietor of Peabody River Asset Management LLC, a private wealth management company in Cambridge, Massachusetts, which he founded recently after 21 years in investment management. He is secretary of the Boston Map Society and has published a number of articles on the history of the cartography of the White Mountains of New Hampshire. He received his B.A. in astronomy from Amherst College, a D. Phil. in modern history from Oxford University, and an M.B.A. from the University of Chicago.

Orley Ashenfelter is Joseph Douglas Green 1895 Professor of Economics at Princeton University and Director of the Industrial Relations Section. His areas of specialization include labor economics, econometrics, and law and economics. He is a recipient of the IZA Prize in Labor Economics; the Mincer Award for Lifetime Achievement of the Society of Labor Economists; and a Fellow of the Econometric Society, the American Academy of Arts and Sciences, and the Society of Labor Economics. He coedited the *Handbook of Labor Economics* (Elsevier Science B.V.) and is currently coeditor of the *American Law and Economics Review* and a previous editor of the *American Economic Review*.

David Ashmore is the managing editor of *Liquid Assets: The International Guide to Fine Wines*.

John Auld joined the Stamp Trade in 1973 at Stanley Gibbons. In 1978 he joined a London auction house, where he remained until the opportunity came to establish his own business. He founded Alliance Auctions in 1990. Later he took over Express Stamp Auctions and Pottergate Stamp Auctions, combining them with Alliance Auctions to form what is now one of Britain's leading auctioneers.

David Barzilay trained as a journalist before holding a number of senior positions with local, regional, and national publications. His last full-time journalistic post was as Northern Ireland correspondent of the *London Evening Standard*. He is a former Scotland Yard press spokesman and has held senior public relations positions with Good Relations, Burton Marsteller, Daniel J. Edelman, and HHCC before setting up his own consultancies. He now regularly writes for a number of motoring publications, including the *Daily Telegraph*, *The Times*, and *Octane Magazine*. He has advised a wide variety of international clients on public relations, with particular attention to media relations. His expertise ranges from motoring and motor sport to travel, IT, human resources/business management, and general business.

Russell Belk is the N. Eldon Tanner Professor of Business Administration, Graduate School, David Eccles School of Business at the University of Utah. He is widely regarded as a consumer behavior expert and has been published in numerous academic journals. A former president of the International Society for Marketing and Development and the Association for Consumer Research, Dr. Belk is also a Fellow of the Association for Consumer Research. He is an influential figure in the field of the anthropology of consumption.

Alan Brown is Group Chief Investment Officer at Schroder Investment Management and a Director of Schroders plc. With more than 34 years of experience in the industry, he served as CIO at PanAgora Asset Management and State Street Global Advisors before joining Schroders in 2005. He has a B.A. and an M.A. in natural science (physics) from Cambridge University. He is a keen and serious wine collector.

Rachel Campbell holds a Ph.D. from Erasmus University, Rotterdam. She is currently an assistant professor of finance at the University of Maastricht. Her work has been published in a number of leading journals, including the *Journal of International Money and Finance, Journal of Banking and Finance, Financial Analysts Journal, Journal of Portfolio Management, Journal of Empirical Finance, Journal of Risk,* and *Derivatives Weekly.* She teaches for Euromoney Financial Training on Art Investment and works as an independent economic advisor for The Fine Art Fund in London and for Fine Art Wealth Management in the United Kingdom.

Jeffrey Horvitz is a private investor and Vice Chair of Moreland Management Company, a family investment office based in Beverly Farms, Massachusetts. He has spoken at investment conferences and published articles on various investment topics for high net worth investors. He serves on a number of non-profit boards, including those of the Boston Museum of Fine Arts, Tufts University School of Medicine, the Beverly School for the Deaf, and Harvard University's Art Museum Visiting Committee. Mr. Horvitz's art collection is renowned, including one of the world's most extensive collections of French Old Master drawings. He has been listed as one of the top 200 art collectors in the world and as one of the top 100 art collectors in America. Mr. Horvitz holds a B.A. and an M.A. in sociology from the University of Pennsylvania and an M.A. in psychology from UCLA.

David Johnstone holds a Ph.D. from the University of Sydney. He has published on topics concerning statistical decision theory in prestigious international journals. Recent papers published in *Theory and Decision*, the *Journal of Banking and Finance*, and the *Pacific Basin Finance Journal* extended his work to include behavioral models of decision making, which underpin the emerging field of behavioral finance. His main interest in antiques is in Australian colonial (1800–1850) furniture and naïve colonial art. He has assembled collections through long-term patronage of both auction and dealer markets. His understanding of investor and dealer behavior has been sharpened by many years of observation of both market forms and their participants.

Robert LaLonde received his Ph.D. in economics from Princeton University and joined the University of Chicago in 1985, where he first taught for 10 years at both the Graduate School of Business and the Harris School. Previously, LaLonde was an associate professor of economics at Michigan State University. He has been a research fellow at the National Bureau of Economic Research (NBER) since 1986 and served as a senior staff economist at the Council of Economic Advisors during the 1987–1988 academic year. He is also a Research Fellow at NBER and the Institute for the Study of Labor (IZA). Currently he serves as a member of the Board of Directors of Public/Private Ventures, a national nonprofit organization whose mission is to improve the effectiveness of social policies, programs, and community initiatives.

Shirley M. Mueller is president and CEO of MyMoneyMD, a consulting firm that provides insights into the psychology behind investing decisions, working from Indianapolis, Indiana, and New York City. She received her M.D. and postgraduate training at the University of Iowa in Iowa City and is board certified in neurology and psychiatry. Previously a tenured professor of neurology at Indiana University, she has published over 50 scientific research papers and served as chief of neurology at Wishard Memorial Hospital in Indianapolis. She started MyMoneyMD after working for seven years as a financial advisor following her retirement from medicine in 1995. Dr. Mueller is also a collector of Chinese export porcelain. She has published six papers in vetted journals on the topic and speaks internationally regarding it. Currently she is on the board of the American Ceramic Circle based in New York City and on the Dean's Advisory Committee at the Herron School of Art in Indianapolis.

Anders Petterson is a leading expert on art market research, with particular focus on the modern and contemporary art market in Russia, China, India, the Middle East, and Southeast Asia. He is the Founder and Managing Director of ArtTactic.com, a Web-based London art market research and consultancy set up in 2001. Prior to starting ArtTactic, he worked in the debt capital markets division of JP Morgan in London. He is a frequent commentator on the art market for Bloomberg News and Bloomberg TV, CNN, and the *Wall Street Journal*, and is currently lecturing on art markets and art as an asset class at Sotheby's Institute in London and Singapore. He holds a B.Sc. and M.Sc. in

Management from London School of Economics and a CEMS (Community of European Management Schools) from Hochschule St. Gallen, Switzerland.

Daryl Roxburgh is Head of BITA Risk Solutions, a portfolio construction and risk solutions provider based in London and New York. He specializes in portfolio construction and risk analysis solutions for the quantitative, institutional, and private banking markets. He is an avid antique car collector and has advised on this topic.

Andrew Rudd is Chairman and CEO of Advisor Software, Inc., a market leader in providing solutions that enable financial institutions and investment advisors to improve the quality and delivery of investment advice. He is also the founder and former Chairman and CEO of Barra Inc. (now MSCI Barra; NYSE:MXB). Under his guidance Barra developed risk management technologies, investment portfolio analysis methods, trading technologies, and a vision for the modern management of large pools of assets that have subsequently become the professional standard on a global basis. He has written two books and numerous journal articles on a wide range of domestic and international investment practices and theories. He also acts as an Associate Editor of the *Financial Analysts Journal*, the *Journal of Portfolio Management,* and the *Journal of Investing.* From 1977 to 1982 he was a professor of Finance and Operations Research at Cornell University in Ithaca, New York. He collects financial economics and mathematics first editions.

Stephen Satchell is a Fellow of Trinity College, Reader in Financial Econometrics at the University of Cambridge, and Visiting Professor at Birkbeck College, City University Business School and University of Technology, Sydney. He provides consulting for a range of financial institutions in the broad area of quantitative finance. He has edited or authored more than 20 books on finance. Dr Satchell is the Editor of *Journal of Asset Management* and *Derivatives, Use, Trading, and Regulation.* He is a member of the Editorial Boards of *Applied Financial Economics* and *Journal of Financial Econometrics.*

Oliver Williams decided his compensation was such that he could retire from his City career at the age of 29. He is currently pursuing a Ph.D. in economics at Cambridge and is collaborating with a colleague in an art investment company.

Part One

General Themes

1 The Role of High Net Worth Investment Managers in Collectible Investing for Their Clients

Daryl Roxburgh

-BITA Risk Solutions

This chapter discusses the role of the investment advisor in working with high net worth investors who are interested in or are already investing in collectibles. We examine the relationship between the investor and the investment manager in terms of the service provided, the breadth of investment offering, and the suitability of investments. Then we discuss the management of investments and the tools used in the process of developing a client portfolio, the role performed by investment managers regarding collectible investments, and the positive side of investing in collectibles.

High Net Worth Managers and Family Offices

The terms *Private Bank* and *Family Office* have lost some of their original meaning and ability to describe the services provided as they have been hijacked by the marketing teams of the large financial institutions. At the same time, stockbrokers have become wealth managers and asset managers. However, the distinctions are important when it comes to the issue of management and advice on collectible investments, as we will discuss later.

The family office has traditionally been an organization that looks after the interests of a family, whether investment, property, legal, or succession planning. The role has very much been ensuring the coherence and sustainability of the family and its fortune as well as managing day-to-day affairs, such as travel and staffing. In this guise, the management of art, wine, antiques, and other valuable artifacts was just one aspect of managing the family assets and ensuring that they were conserved and catalogued and, as required, that collections were rejuvenated. The expertise to work on these collections would have been partially accumulated within the family office, then augmented by external experts, and perhaps finally, as scale justified, expanded internally. Often, major

Collectible Investments for the High Net Worth Investor

collections would be left to the state as a philanthropic gesture or as an action with beneficial tax consequences to the family.

Today the status of collecting and collections has expanded within the family office. Through the use of modern technology, different branches of the family can access the family collections through a family portal, and can, for example, book assets such as pieces of art or properties for their use. Fundamentally, the family office is geared to bringing experts to bear on the collecting needs of the family and thus sustain assets and wealth through generations. As such, this new technology is very well placed to facilitate the pursuit of collectible investments for high net worth family situations.

High net worth managers serve a wider set of clients with the goal of generating investment return for the client. This is in line with the investment guidelines set out by the client, including their time horizon and propensity for risk. The managers will generally employ a set of investment vehicles that meet a simple set of criteria:

- The advisor understands the investments.
- The investments can be delivered economically to the investor.
- The investments are acceptable to the wide investor base.
- The investments meet the requirements of the manager's regulator.

These criteria are often the hurdles that prevent most high net worth managers from investing in collectibles on behalf of their clients. We further discuss this idea in the section on methods of investment.

The type of service provided by the investment firm will be the most significant determinant of what the firm is willing to offer its clients in terms of advice on collectible investments. The conclusion could be drawn from the previous comments that such advice would come only from family offices; however, as the reader will see, this is not necessarily so.

The Nature of Relationships between Client and Manager

As we conducted research for this book, we spoke to many investment managers across the entire gamut of investment firms. The style of relationship differed widely among them. In this section we consider three aspects of the client/manager relationship: the service provided by the manager, how the manager determines what is suitable for the client, and where collectible investments fit in this context.

First, we consider the relationship in terms of investment service and approach. The services provided tend to fall within a matrix that can be defined by these parameters:

- First, the level of granularity of investment decision: stock picker through multimanager (fund selector) to asset allocator.
- Second, the type of authority given to the manager by the client: execution only through advisory, advisory managed to discretionary including trust status.

- Finally, the breadth of instruments used for investment: from traditional cash, bonds, and equity through to a broad asset mix.

Unfortunately, clients have not always been well served. The industry has seen a polarization of offerings, with the large investment managers moving away from direct "production" to manager and product selection.

This is sometimes in the context of a strategic asset allocation offering, with some degree of sophistication involved and that takes account of the individual clients needs. Unfortunately, often it is likely to be a model portfolio selected on the basis of a more perfunctory assessment of the client. In simple terms, this can be thought of as "one size fits all."

In contrast, a number of medium-size management firms, along with boutique firms, have sought to distinguish themselves in the marketplace through a more tailored, "bespoke" offering and/or a higher degree of investment expertise provided directly to the client. In some instances this is reflected as structuring an asset allocation to the specific needs of an investor. In many cases, the family might have a large holding of assets in something that it cannot sell—perhaps a family business or a block of shares held in an endowment. So the asset allocation needs to complement this position. In mathematical terms, this is akin to a portfolio construction with constrained weights.

In this process, the firm might well be the trusted advisor and create not only an asset allocation but also appoint managers to execute the investments within different assets—an approach very much like that of the institutional investment world. Or they could specialize in direct company investment, building a portfolio of equities for the client. These firms are the most likely investment managers to provide access to collectible investments for their clients. This can take the form of a marketing differentiator as they seek to identify the firm with a special interest set, such as the horse or motor-racing fraternities, as something that the firm has been traditionally involved with or as part of a broad service aiming to meet their clients' every requirement.

The second parameter in the relationship matrix is the type of authority given by the investor to the manager. At one end of the spectrum, "execution only" is precisely that: the manager undertakes the transaction on behalf of and on the instruction of the investor. The vast majority of collectible investment specialists work on precisely this basis because they are not authorized by a regulatory agency to give investment advice. They are willing to provide advice on providence and quality. Furthermore, they may place a potential purchase into the context of a collection, but they are unable to provide investment advice. Quite often an investor will run an execution-only portion of their collectible portfolio with an investment manager alongside the managed portion, allowing them to execute their own investment ideas.

Where an investment house has a specialty in a particular form of collectible investment, it will generally offer this as part of its advisory service, seeking the client's agreement to the investment before proceeding. Alternatively, if the investment is managed on a discretionary basis, authority would be obtained when the client signs the investment mandate.

It might seem obvious that those companies that provide the widest range of asset classes will be the ones that are most likely to offer collectible investments, but actually this tends not to be the case, since these assets are considered to be outside the usual remit of investment. For that reason, collectibles are more often offered by companies that have a narrower range of offering within which they offer a specialist service. This can also be viewed in terms of what is meant by offering collectible investments. In this instance it is considered the investment in a collectible class through some form of unit trust or investment trust.

A key regulatory issue today is whether or not an investment is deemed "suitable" or not for a client, both as an asset in its own right and in terms of the client's portfolio context. In the general course of portfolio construction, this is crudely done through presenting to a client a list of asset classes as the investment product offered by a firm and asking for restrictions. However, there is a growing trend to move toward a more sophisticated approach, with companies like Ibbotson and Risk Metrics providing a questionnaire that outputs a risk number that can be matched to a model portfolio. BITA Risk Solutions has produced a third-generation questionnaire and scoring algorithm that output a series of parameters on which portfolio construction can be based, including degrees of suitability of individual asset classes. This approach can provide a firm foundation for the relationship between the client and manager because it creates discussion around the central purpose of that relationship: investment.

Whether or not a questionnaire is used to derive the level of risk that a client is willing to sustain and to understand the suitability of investments, the investment manager must determine the purpose of the client's investment. This purpose can have many parameters and is often described as the *utility* of the investor—meaning that which, when maximized, will give the investor maximum satisfaction. Often the utility is a balance or trade-off between various factors, such as risk and return.

The investment managers in our research gave their perspectives on the investors' utilities with respect to collectibles. The following were deemed to be utilities of investing in collectibles. At the very top of the list:

- Personal control and involvement in building the collection

Then:

- Acquisition of rare artifacts that money simply cannot buy but that must be sought out and tracked down
- Ownership of a fine, exquisite, or unique item
- Completion of a series or collection
- Prestige, recognition, and sharing of the collection

- Participation in the social network of collectors and experts in the field
- Immortality through the posthumous persistence of the collection
- Acquiring an item at a good price

At the very bottom of the list:

- Seeking a commercial return over time
- Not missing out in the participation in a published rise in value

Now, remembering that these are the views of investment managers will explain the following comments on the relationship between the investment manager and the investor in terms of collectible investments.

Thus far, we have looked at the relationship between the investor and the investment manager in terms of the service provided, the breadth of investment offering, and the suitability of investments. Finally, we segment the role performed. In discussion with the investment houses, we found that this role could be placed in one of five categories:

- First, and very much in the majority, are the *supporters*. They support the client's collections in terms of, at minimum, incorporating the collection within the valuation. This might be valued according to some index or by the client or the client's external advisers, and this puts the collection on record as part of the client's investment portfolio.
- Second are the *enablers*. They get more involved through the provision of sources of finance with which the client could further build the collection. These would commonly be secured against the collection or the rest of the investment portfolio.
- Third are the *investors*. Here a more active approach is taken, with the investment manager providing access to one or more types of collectible investments through some form of fund. Typically, these could be wine, art or even classic car funds. These funds tend to be relatively small in nature in terms of sums invested and can have significant liquidity restrictions.
- *Advisers* are the fourth category. They either provide direct advice or they manage external specialists in each field, bringing their knowledge to bear on the collectible portfolio. This group is rare and generally found only within niche private banks and family offices that provide complete management services to an individual or family.
- The last category consists of *curators*, who not only provide the investment input but also structure the collection within its defined goals and seek to preserve the items within it.

Investment Methods for Collectibles Favored by Managers

We've listed general prerequisites for an asset class to be chosen by an investment manager for a client base, and it is worth repeating that list here:

- The advisor understands the investments.
- The investments can be delivered economically to the investor.
- The investments are acceptable to the wide investor base.
- The investments meet the requirements of the manager's regulator.

There are some other criteria that tend to be interconnected. These criteria are:

Liquidity, or the ease with which a collectible can be bought and sold

This is critical to an investment manager in considering the need to access client funds and trade an asset in changing markets. Ironically, rare or scarce objects might be highly liquid as they are sought after and a sale will generate interest. However, this might apply only to the top-quality items of a genre, with other items—though still being desirable—more susceptible to fashion, losing liquidity and realizable value fast as a market turns and supply exceeds demand.

With the advent of Internet and Web-based auction sites, the pricing of many collectibles has become far more transparent. Major items of value could always be followed at auction houses, but now the prices of fine wines or classic cars around the globe can be compared in minutes. This has led to more efficient markets in such collectibles but also markets that have become led by speculation rather than value.

The normal solution to this is to create a fund through which investors can participate in the fortunes of multiple assets of a type and in which the manager's need to meet cash calls is simplified through holding a broad collection of assets and a pool of cash within the fund. There are other benefits to the fund approach in that it allows diversity of investment and the pooling of invested funds, which might make the top-tier items in a collectible class accessible for investment. However, the obvious drawback is lack of ownership and control of the individual asset. The latter point is a utility issue for the collector, rather than for the investment manager. The latter is seeking return, safety, and distribution, and will therefore generally opt for the fund approach.

Rarity and homogeneity

A number of collectibles have very many similar instances of an item but are only distinguished by condition or provenance, as in the cases of wine, stamps, and classic cars. In these examples, there are still great rarities than can be sought after and command great value, but exposure can be achieved to the genre through readily tradable assets, and many similar collections can be built, allowing the creation of diversified investment funds. Correlation of price movements within a collectible genre is not a topic for this chapter, but in a moment we'll see that premium returns are generally achieved only by the top tier of items. For that reason the diversity of investability of a genre needs to be considered in the light of degrees of rarity. This can make it hard for investment managers to achieve premium returns, because the assets exhibiting them might well be beyond their reach.

Access

This picks up on the previous point. How does an investment manager achieve access to the top-performing assets in a genre? The genre will need to be seen as an exciting investment by the wider populace, with a perceived potential for gain, pulling in more speculative than collecting buyers. This will result in demand exceeding supply; the middle and lower tiers of the genre will not produce the higher returns associated with the top tier. As in any market, at this point it can become unstable.

Valuation

The valuation of collectibles falls into two groups based on the homogeneity and liquidity points we've discussed. Where there are many examples of each item, the market is now, thanks to the Internet, quite transparent, and *purchase* price comparison is easy. Having said that, the price that can be realized on sale could be very different, with the dealer taking a margin to reflect not only his costs but his perception of market direction. For individual items, their value will be based on last sale price adjusted for the movement of their peer group since that transaction. It has to be said that one only needs a single buyer to complete the transaction, but two or more significantly help the realizable price. For this reason the generation of interest by the agent undertaking the sale becomes critical.

Collectible assets can be valued on a continuous basis, but this is not really an accurate guide to performance of any single asset—more of the genre or a subgroup of it. For this reason it is hard for an investment manager to include them within their asset allocation unless investment is based on a fund. The exception, of course, would be a family office or foundation with a professionally managed collection.

All the preceding points lead to the question of how to invest in a collectible genre. Quite simply, the conclusions that can be drawn are as follows:

- If the prime reason for acquisition is the utilities ascribed to ownership, acquire individual items of the highest possible standing within a genre.
- If the prime reason for acquisition is investment and the utilities of ownership are secondary, invest through a fund or index, unless:
- If the investor has sufficient wealth to amass a number of high-quality individual items, they can enjoy the utilities of ownership and the diversity and greater liquidity of a collection. Who said money can't buy happiness?

These conclusions are borne out by the discussions we held with the various investment houses in preparation for this book. Examples we came across have included an art fund, a wine fund, a yacht finance, and a car fund.

What has to be remembered is that an asset will not necessarily perform the same as an index, nor will a fund; both are subject to the influence of the manager's or buyer's selection. This cryptic remark simply means that the returns to the collectible fund will be strongly influenced by day-to-day buy/sell decisions, and these changes in portfolio weights can move the fund's returns some distance from the index returns.

Having considered the various approaches to investing in collectibles, we next look at how these can be included with an investment portfolio and the impact they might have.

Incorporating Art Indexes into an Investment Portfolio

We first examine some characteristics of a series of collectible asset classes and then see how they can be incorporated within an investor's portfolio. The following information is based on a Sterling investor's portfolio and the returns that would accrue to it. The collectibles are predominantly art indices covering a number of genres; interestingly, they comprise the performance of the top few percent of a genre by price as well as on a broader basis. These are set out in Table 1.1, together with some key characteristics.

The indices represented in the table are described in detail in Chapter 7 of this book. The key concept to grasp is that in each case there are indices representing different bands of price—for example, the top 10% of Old Masters by sale price. This links with the comments earlier in this chapter about the different performance within a genre according to the price commanded or the market perception of quality and desirability of an asset.

The long-term return is the average return achieved over the last 10 years on an annualized basis. It has to be remembered that this figure is dependent on the start and end dates of measurement, and many of these indices had very strong performance during 2007, which will unduly influence this figure. More detail can be found in the section in which the annual returns and plots of historic performance are given.

By referencing the four numbers for each asset in the table for best and worst performance periods, we can see further indication of the nature of returns—not least that though an asset class can rise by many hundred percent in a year, it can then collapse by 50–60% the following year. This is typical of an asset class with a small number of transactions and driven by key buyers and sellers and a handful of exceptionally rare items.

In addition to the collectible assets, we've charted a "current" portfolio for the figures in this chapter. This is a well-diversified portfolio with an asset allocation as set out in Table 1.2.

The following figures are based on buying and holding the individual indices at the start date of the chart where the index is rebased to 100%. For comparison, a fully diversified portfolio managed on a buy and hold basis at the beginning of the period is shown. More information on this portfolio is given in the next section. This is identified as "Current" in the figures. For each collectible asset class we look at the periods 1995–2000 and 2000–2003, covering the rise in the financial markets and their subsequent decline. In addition, the historic annual returns for each asset class from 1994–2007 are tabulated and charted for information.

Table 1.1

Asset	Long-Term Return	Long-Term Risk	Best % of Return over X Months		Worst % of Return over X Months		Calendar Years of Loss in Past 14
			12	24	12	24	
All art, top 2%	10.8	13.7	93	132	−32	−46	6
All art, top 10%	8.4	11.0	62	129	−26	−31	5
All art	8.2	11.4	63	96	−26	−32	5
Chinese contemporary art, top 10%	29.3	35.5	287	948	−65	−65	7
Chinese contemporary art, top 80%	24.4	26.5	210	572	−32	−43	5
Contemporary art, top 2%	16.7	18.6	173	250	−34	−35	5
Contemporary art, top 10%	12.8	15.1	115	129	−23	−22	4
Contemporary art, top 80%	9.5	11.4	130	127	−21	−33	7
European Impressionist art, top 2%	4.8	19.2	108	248	−59	−58	7
European Impressionist art, top 10%	7.5	15.3	81	129	−43	−50	6
European Impressionist art, top 80%	8.9	13.1	88	118	−27	−41	5
Indian art, top 10%	16.3	19.7	166	409	−42	−41	6
Indian art, top 80%	14.9	16.1	112	297	−43	−37	5
Old Masters, top 2%	10.9	24.8	166	145	−45	−56	6
Old Masters, top 10%	7.8	16.4	94	138	−28	−39	8
Old Masters, top 80%	4.8	19.2	108	248	−58	−58	6
Stamps, top 10%	4.5	8.0	27	42	−16	−12	5
Stamps, all	3.4	7.3	20	30	−10	−15	4
Balanced portfolio	8.8	7.8	37	53	−19	−25	3
U.K. Large Co. Index	8.7	13.2	36	62	−30	−40	4

Table 1.2 Diversified Portfolio Asset Allocation

Asset	Value (GBP)	Weight (%)	Expected Return (%)	Expected Risk (%)
Cash	200,000	10.4	5.3	0.3
Government bonds	200,000	10.4	6.7	4.7
Corporate bonds	20,000	1.0	3.2	5.8
Convertible bonds	20,000	1.0	7.7	7.6
Equity—U.K.	200,000	10.4	11.0	14.5
Equity—North America	150,000	7.8	11.3	15.8
Equity—Pan-Europe	200,000	10.4	10.3	18.5
Equity—Japan	100,000	5.2	3.0	18.7
Emerging markets	25,000	1.3	10.8	22.0
Hedge funds	250,000	13.1	7.8	5.7
Private equity	100,000	5.2	16.0	29.5
General commodities	150,000	7.8	8.7	9.7
Property—U.K. commercial	150,000	7.8	10.7	3.2
Balanced fund	150,000	7.8	8.3	9.2
TOTAL	1,915,000	100.0	8.9	7.8

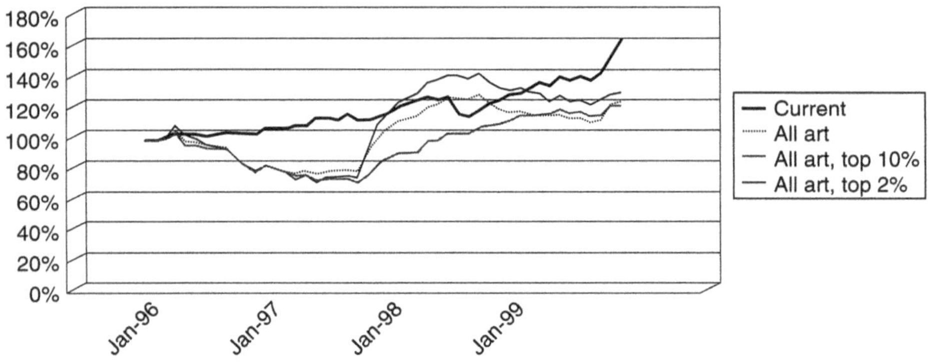

Figure 1.1 End of Fixed-Income Bull/Equity Bear Markets, January 1996–December 1999.

General Art Index

All the general art indices together fell about 30% from January 1996 to December 1997. Then, fueled by market sentiment, they rose between 50% and 100% in the following 12 months before consolidating. Again, the top 2% of the segment was the most aggressive performer by far, and interestingly, the top 10% lagged the overall index (see Figure 1.1).

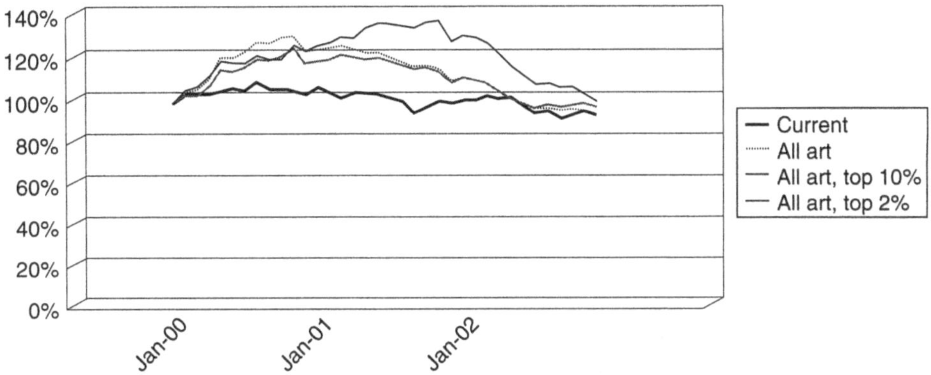

Figure 1.2 Equity Market Downturn, January 2000–December 2002.

	1994	1995	1996	1997	1998	1999	2000	2001	2002	2003	2004	2005	2006	2007	2008
All art	−18.4%	27.1%	−15.2%	25.7%	19.7%	4.0%	28.4%	−11.6%	−14.8%	−18.0%	31.7%	−1.2%	36.4%	37.5%	0.0%
All art, top 10%	−16.6%	17.3%	−17.6%	6.3%	31.5%	10.6%	19.1%	−7.4%	−10.4%	−18.4%	21.6%	3.6%	36.9%	56.2%	0.0%
All art, top 2%	−18.6%	46.6%	−15.7%	37.3%	22.6%	−2.3%	28.8%	3.7%	−22.0%	−25.3%	32.5%	−8.1%	48.0%	53.3%	0.0%
Current	4.3%	17.3%	7.2%	10.3%	10.9%	36.8%	−7.9%	−8.6%	−10.8%	13.1%	9.0%	19.0%	7.7%	4.9%	0.0%

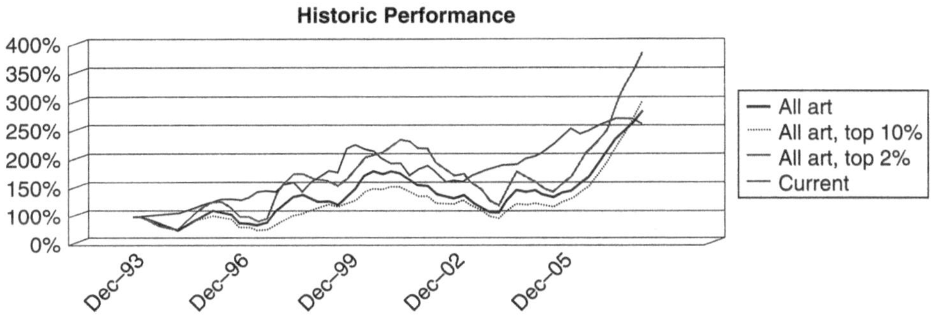

Figure 1.3 Historic Testing and Historic Performance, 1994–2008.

During the equity market downturn from 2000–2003, general art held up well, even continuing to rise in the case of the top 2%. The top 10% and the general index moved closely together and went into a gradual decline 12 months before the top 2% peaked and then went into a sharp decline. All these indices outperformed the balanced portfolio "current" through this period (see Figures 1.2 and 1.3).

Chinese Contemporary Art

During the second half of the 1990s, the top index lost about 60% of its value over four years, whereas the wider segment gained 60% (see Figure 1.4). This is explained by the fact that the top index had risen 135% the previous year

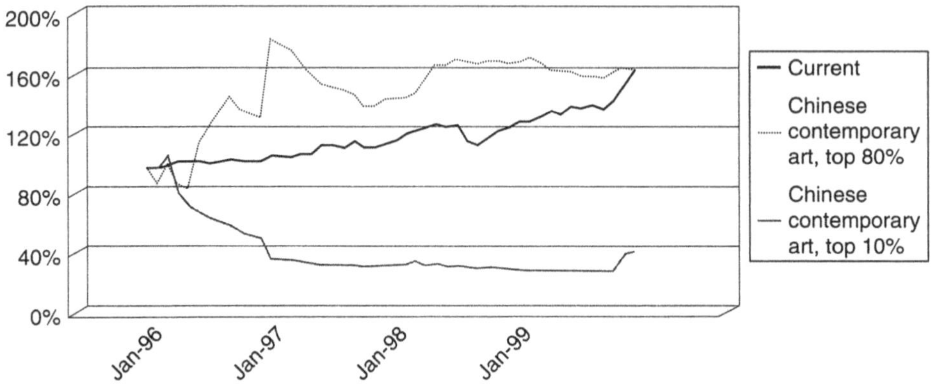

Figure 1.4 Chinese Contemporary Art, End of Fixed-Income Bull/Equity Bear Markets, January 1996–December 1999.

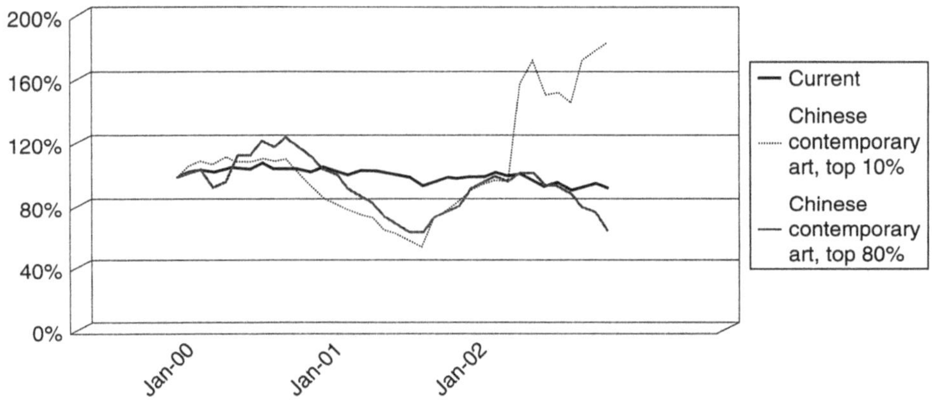

Figure 1.5 Chinese Contemporary Art, Equity Market Downturn, January 2000–December 2003.

and then drifted back from there, and the wider market had gained impetus and steadily risen on the back of that performance.

Both indices fell in aggregate during the first 18 months of the decade; there was then a dramatic split, with the top 10% index rising sharply from early 2002 (see Figure 1.5). As shown in Figure 1.6, this divergence was short lived, with the top 10% converging back to the top 80% index levels during 2005. However, from there through 2007, both achieved three-digit growth for the next three years. Interestingly, as the top 10% was falling 42% in 2003 and 10% in 2004, the top 80% was rising 18% and 59% in those years, respectively, demonstrating the pull created by top items in a genre of investors into the wider assets.

	1994	1995	1996	1997	1998	1999	2000	2001	2002	2003	2004	2005	2006	2007	2008
Chinese contemporary art, top 10%	−2.7%	136.7%	−44.3%	−34.5%	−8.2%	38.5%	2.9%	−9.6%	116.7%	−42.2%	−9.8%	146.4%	260.8%	112.7%	0.0%
Chinese contemporary art, top 80%	−18.7%	−23.5%	−26.2%	9.2%	16.7%	−2.7%	12.8%	−27.6%	−19.4%	17.6%	58.8%	107.1%	187.4%	122.4%	0.0%
Current	4.3%	17.3%	7.2%	10.3%	10.9%	36.8%	−7.9%	−8.6%	−10.8%	13.1%	9.0%	19.0%	7.7%	4.9%	0.0%

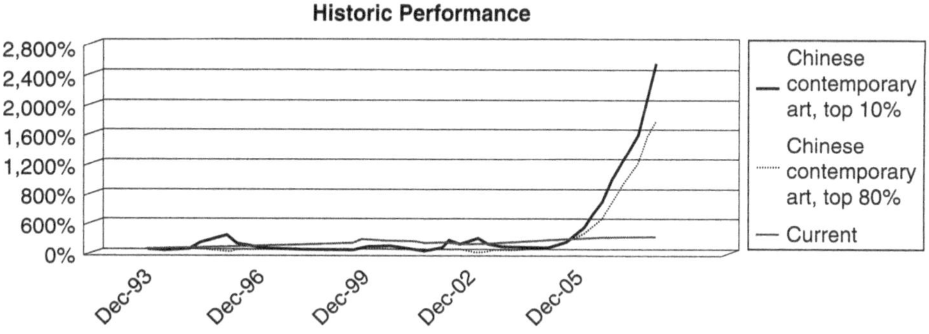

Figure 1.6 Contemporary Art, Historic Testing and Historic Performance, 1994–2008.

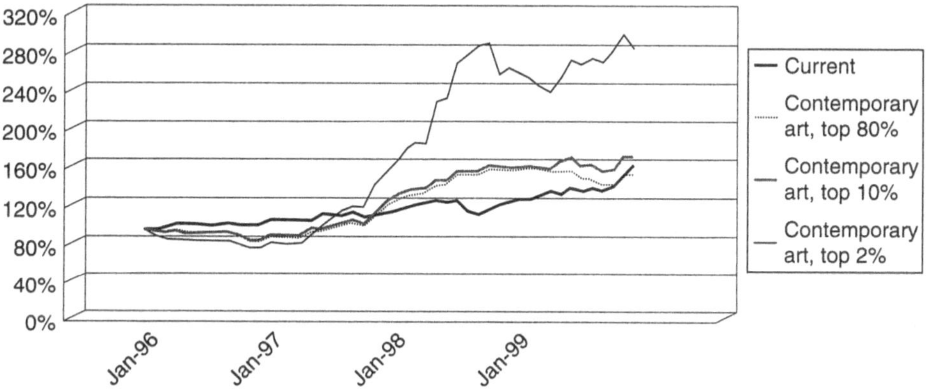

Figure 1.7 Contemporary Art, End of Fixed-Income Bull/Equity Bear Markets, January 1996–December 1999.

Contemporary Art

Again, there was a significant difference between the performance of the top index and the broader ones (see Figure 1.7). However, even these performed significantly above the diversified portfolio for periods before the broad index corrected in 2000 ahead of the top 80.

As confidence fell in 2000, the top 2 index was worst hit, with the broader indices continuing to make headway (see Figures 1.8 and 1.9). In early 2001 the top 2% index turned, and by late 2002 there was a turning point when the top 2% was accelerating away from both the top 80%, which remained flat, and the top 10%, which was performing strongly.

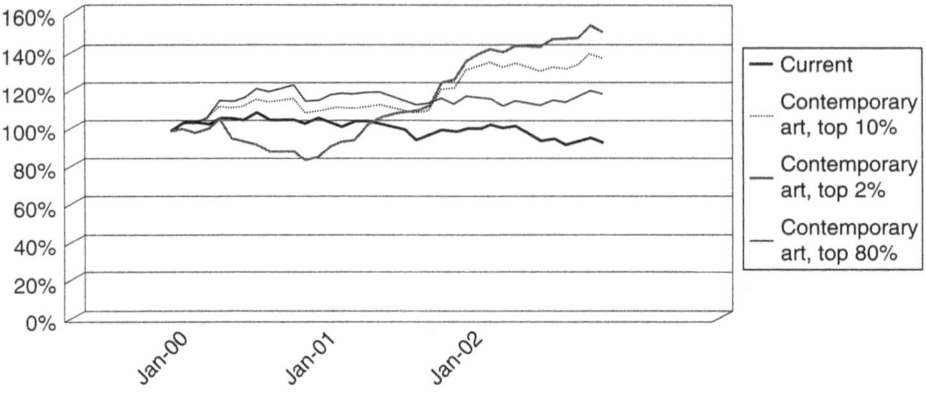

Figure 1.8 Contemporary Art, Equity Market Downturn, January 2000–December 2002.

	1994	1995	1996	1997	1998	1999	2000	2001	2002	2003	2004	2005	2006	2007	2008
Contemporary art, top 10%	7.5%	−12.9%	−10.8%	44.5%	28.9%	6.9%	11.3%	12.6%	12.5%	−9.9%	6.5%	12.2%	−8.0%	91.5%	0.0%
Contemporary art, top 2%	4.1%	−17.8%	−20.3%	95.1%	72.2%	7.6%	−15.4%	49.3%	20.0%	−21.1%	15.9%	−0.6%	−14.2%	103.8%	0.0%
Contemporary art, top 80%	−14.7%	−20.9%	−12.3%	41.2%	31.5%	−2.6%	17.0%	−1.1%	4.9%	−4.5%	8.0%	19.5%	−15.3%	119.1%	0.0%
Current	4.3%	17.3%	7.2%	10.3%	10.9%	36.8%	−7.9%	−8.6%	−10.8%	13.1%	9.0%	19.0%	7.7%	4.9%	0.0%

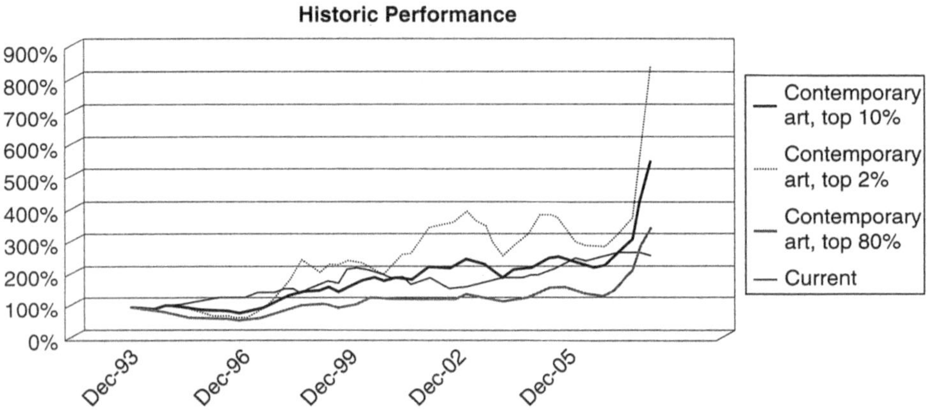

Figure 1.9 Contemporary Art, Historic Testing and Historic Performance, 1994–2008.

European Impressionist Art

During 1996 and 1997 the top 2% index had its own boom, and in 1998, a bust. It pulled the top 10% up with it during this period, but the comparison of performance is interesting (see Figure 1.10). Rebasing in 1995 at 100, the top 2% peaked at 228 and fell back to 150, and the top 10% peaked at 160 and fell back to 140, clearly illustrating the higher volatility associated with the top 2% indices.

The European Impressionist indices had an amazing rise in 2000, continuing into 2001 for the top 10% and top 80% before a steady and rapid decline into

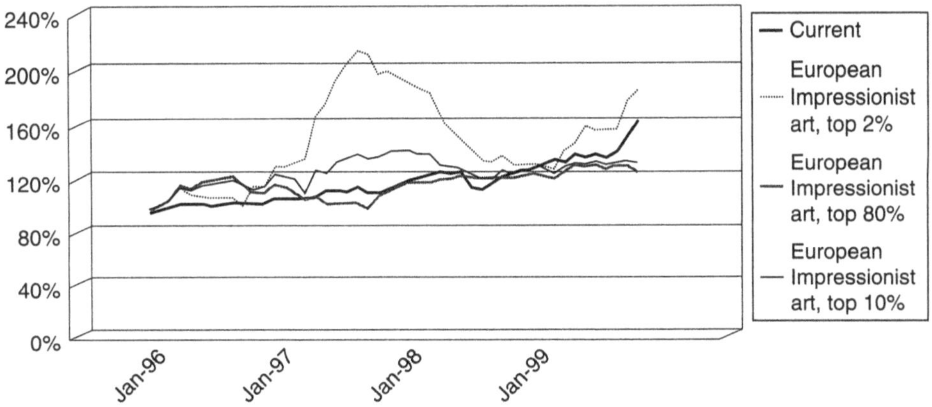

Figure 1.10 European Impressionist Art, End of Fixed-Income Bull/Equity Bear Markets, January 1996–December 1999.

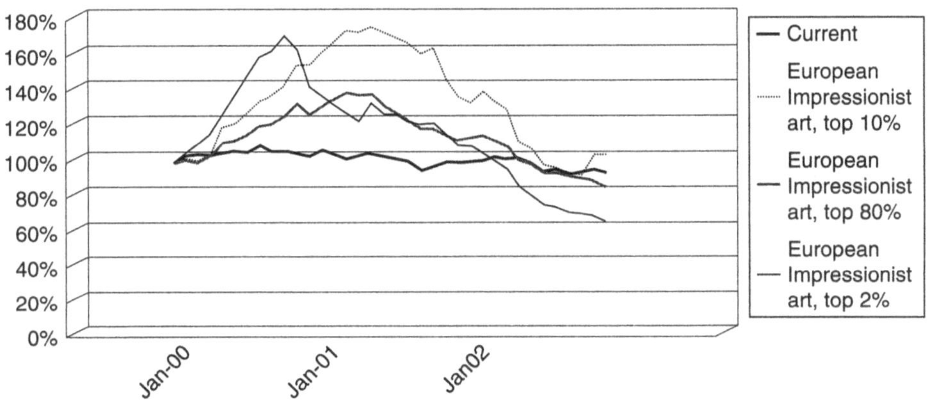

Figure 1.11 European Impressionist Art, Equity Market Downturn, January 2000–December 2002.

2003 (see Figures 1.11 and 1.12). In 2004 they all rallied, with a correction in the top 2% in 2005, before remarkable progress across the board in 2007.

Indian Art

During the late 1990s the performance of Indian art was lackluster overall though volatile on an annual basis, with annual returns between –30% and +14%. The two indices moved closely together until 1999, when the top 10% had a dramatic rise of 68% while the top 80% fell 7.3% (see Figure 1.13).

In 2000 the top 80% caught up a little, with a 20% rise, and continued to climb in 2001 while the top 10% fell; they both declined in 2002. In 2004 there was a sudden rally with near triple-digit returns. This trend continued into 2005

	1994	1995	1996	1997	1998	1999	2000	2001	2002	2003	2004	2005	2006	2007	2008
Current	4.3%	17.3%	7.2%	10.3%	10.9%	36.8%	−7.9%	−8.6%	−10.8%	13.1%	9.0%	19.0%	7.7%	4.9%	0.0%
European Impressionist art, top 10%	−22.9%	11.7%	30.3%	22.5%	−11.7%	6.9%	53.2%	−11.2%	−23.8%	−26.5%	−1.5%	9.1%	11.0%	76.9%	0.0%
European Impressionist art, top 80%	−4.4%	10.5%	21.7%	2.1%	8.3%	3.8%	24.3%	−12.0%	−22.9%	−17.8%	22.5%	16.7%	−3.4%	87.9%	0.0%
European Impressionist art, top 2%	−46.9%	0.0%	32.8%	71.8%	−34.0%	41.5%	48.8%	−23.3%	−39.4%	−4.0%	12.5%	−24.7%	23.5%	64.1%	0.0%

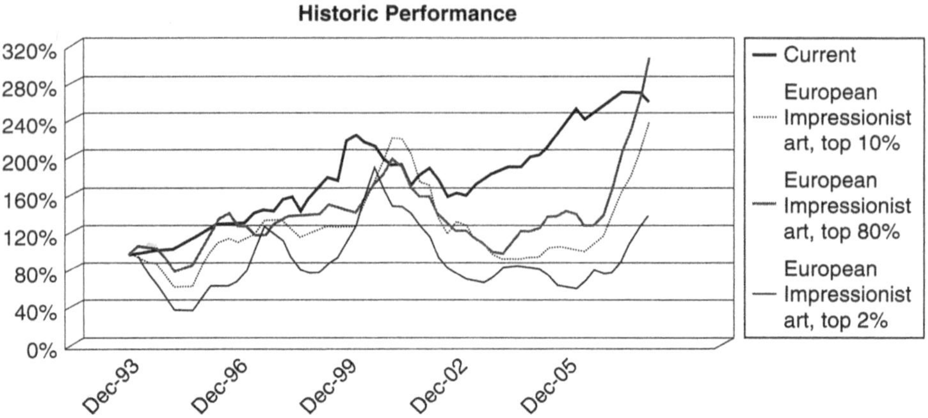

Figure 1.12 European Impressionist Art, Historic Testing and Historic Performance, 1994–2008.

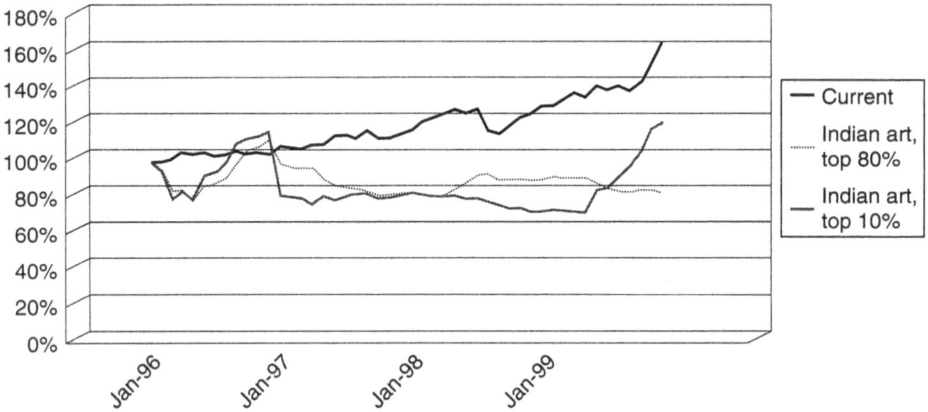

Figure 1.13 Indian Art, End of Fixed-Income Bull/Equity Bear Markets, January 1996–December 1999.

and 2006, with the top 10% strongly leading the top 80% before both crested in 2007 (see Figures 1.14 and 1.15).

Old Masters

During the late 1990s the Old Masters indices exhibited an unusual pattern, with three distinct booms and declines in each of the three indices. The top 80% led from 1997, then the top 2% from 1998 and finally the top 10% from

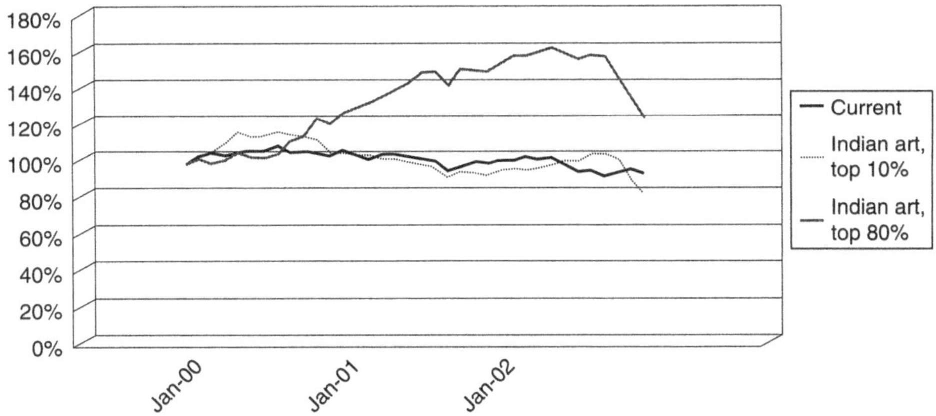

Figure 1.14 Indian Art, Equity Market Downturn, January 2000–December 2002.

	1994	1995	1996	1997	1998	1999	2000	2001	2002	2003	2004	2005	2006	2007	2008
Current	4.3%	17.3%	7.2%	10.3%	10.9%	36.8%	−7.9%	−8.6%	−10.8%	13.1%	9.0%	19.0%	7.7%	4.9%	0.0%
Indian art, top 10%	−16.8%	−6.6%	14.5%	−30.1%	−11.1%	68.2%	8.9%	−11.8%	−10.7%	2.2%	88.2%	148.9%	92.3%	3.5%	0.0%
Indian art, top 80%	11.5%	−11.6%	11.2%	−26.6%	8.3%	−7.3%	19.9%	23.3%	−16.5%	−0.6%	97.0%	96.5%	68.6%	9.9%	0.0%

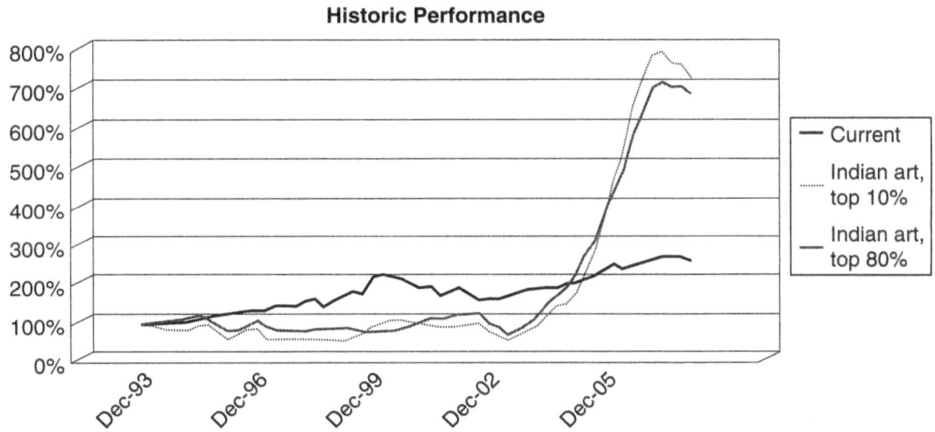

Figure 1.15 Indian Art, Historic Testing and Historic Performance, 1994–2008.

late 1998. They all then declined to meet back at the same level in early 1999 (see Figure 1.16).

Post-1999, the top 80% again led into the 2000s, peaking at the end of 2000 and going into a three-year decline. The top 10% did not do very much, but the top 2% had a volatile and exciting period with annual returns between −31% and +108%. Figures 1.17 and 1.18 show that 2005 was good for the two concentrated indices and poor for the top 80%; 2006 was the reverse. In 2007 the two broader indices were strong, and things were good for the top 2%.

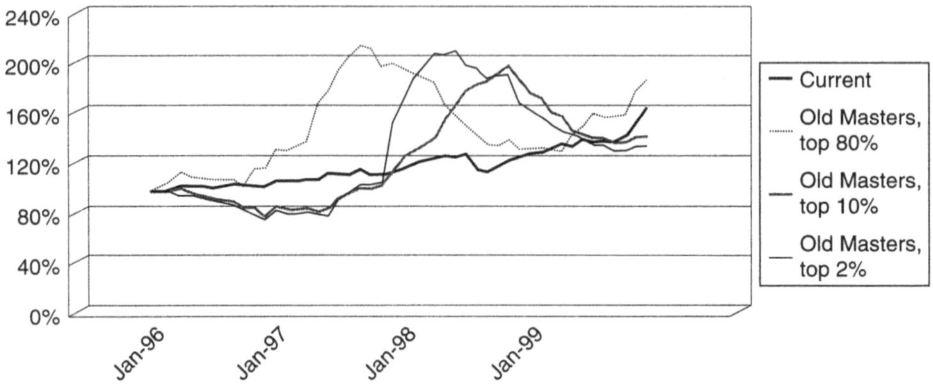

Figure 1.16 Old Masters, End of Fixed-Income Bull/Equity Bear Markets, January 1996–December 1999.

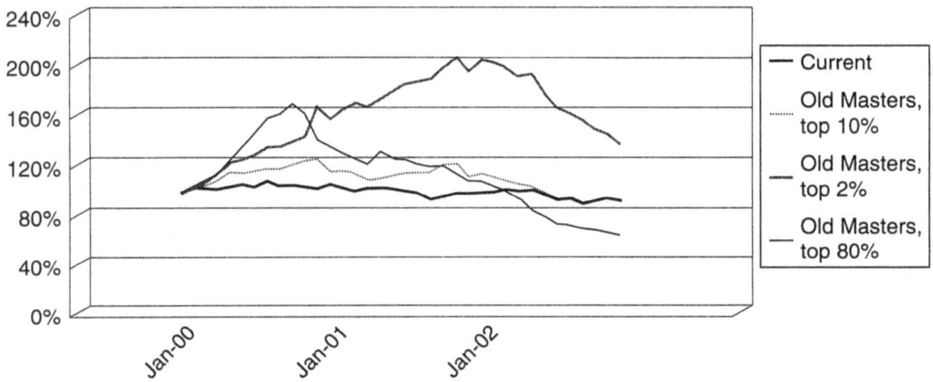

Figure 1.17 Old Masters, Equity Market Downturn, January 2000–December 2002.

Stamps

In comparison with the art indices, stamps have a much lower volatility of returns, but they are still volatile, with one year's gain very often wiped out by the next year's loss. Until 1999, the two stamps indices moved together, with the top 10% underperforming the top 80%. In 1999 the top 10% rose 24%, probably on the back of the general market euphoria (see Figure 1.19).

This upward trend continued into 2000, with a slight fall in 2001. Then there were further significant rises in 2002 and 2005 for the top 10%, but with more significant corrections in the following year. The top 100% mirrored these movements but with lower magnitudes (See Figures 1.20 and 1.21).

So, having looked at the individual asset classes, we shall now put them into the context of an investor portfolio. The investor has an interest in art, particularly art from India and China. She also has an existing portfolio; its asset allocation is set out in Table 1.3. She wants to invest £200,000 cash in art but wants to be aware of the resulting impact on the overall portfolio risk.

	1994	1995	1996	1997	1998	1999	2000	2001	2002	2003	2004	2005	2006	2007	2008
Current	4.3%	17.3%	7.2%	10.3%	10.9%	36.8%	–7.9%	–8.6%	–10.8%	13.1%	9.0%	19.0%	7.7%	4.9%	0.0%
Old Masters, top 10%	–20.8%	5.9%	–17.7%	46.2%	63.0%	–23.9%	34.2%	–11.1%	–22.2%	–12.2%	–3.1%	50.7%	–11.7%	49.0%	0.0%
Old Masters, top 2%	33.1%	–32.2%	–23.6%	100.5%	11.0%	–20.4%	91.1%	16.9%	–29.6%	–31.2%	9.2%	108.4%	–13.8%	17.3%	0.0%
Old Masters, top 80%	–46.9%	0.0%	32.8%	71.8%	–34.0%	41.5%	48.8%	–23.3%	–39.4%	–4.0%	12.5%	–24.7%	23.5%	64.1%	0.0%

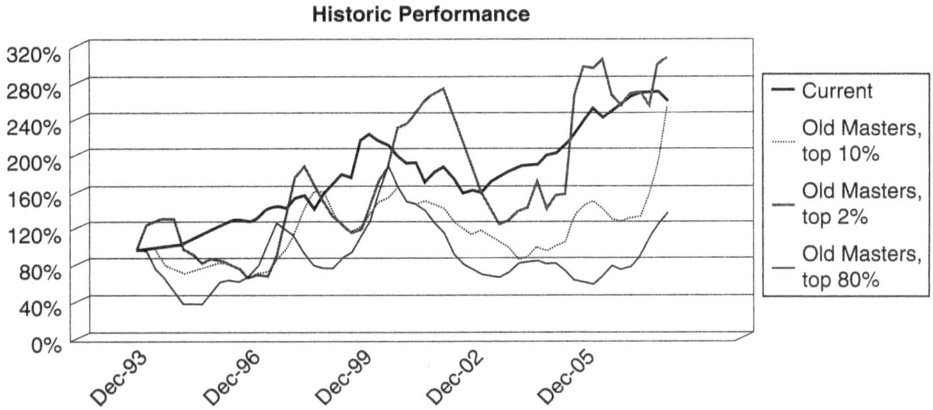

Figure 1.18 Old Masters, Historic Testing and Historic Performance, 1994–2008.

Figure 1.19 Stamps, End of Fixed-Income Bull/Equity Bear Markets, January 1996–December 1999.

Tools Used for Building High Net Worth Portfolios

Now let's look at some investment tools useful in building high net worth portfolios. Unlike institutional investment, the psychology of the individual can be used as an input to determine the investor's time horizon, risk appetite, and other pertinent characteristics. This information can be input into an asset allocation process, in which collectibles can be included as an additional asset class.

Within the area of high net worth management, much money is still run very traditionally; although in some cases this works very well, it can be also

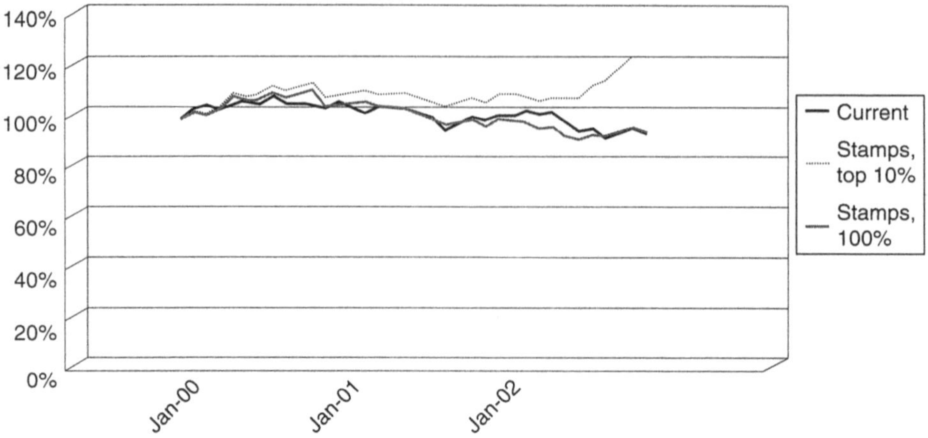

Figure 1.20 Stamps, Equity Market Downturn, January 2000–December 2002.

	1994	1995	1996	1997	1998	1999	2000	2001	2002	2003	2004	2005	2006	2007	2008
Current	4.3%	17.3%	7.2%	10.3%	10.9%	36.8%	–7.9%	–8.6%	–10.8%	13.1%	9.0%	19.0%	7.7%	4.9%	0.0%
Stamps, top 10%	–3.5%	3.9%	–5.8%	5.2%	–0.7%	24.0%	8.7%	–2.0%	17.6%	–6.8%	0.6%	24.1%	–8.3%	11.0%	0.0%
Stamps, 100%	2.9%	10.4%	–7.1%	10.1%	1.9%	4.9%	5.1%	–7.9%	–1.9%	2.0%	7.4%	20.4%	–9.4%	10.9%	0.0%

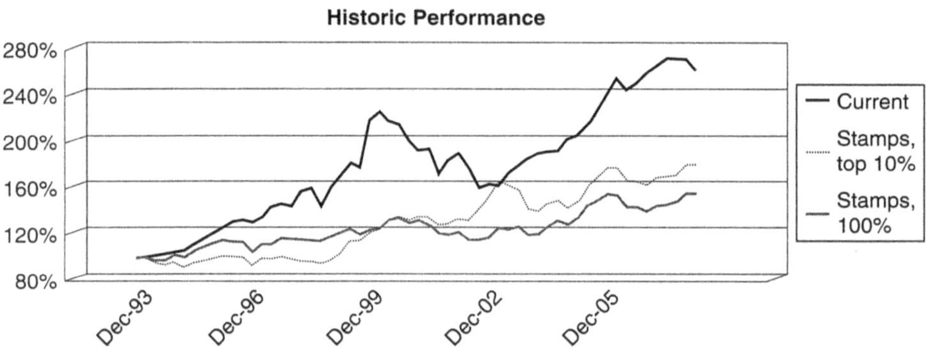

Figure 1.21 Old Masters, Historic Testing and Historic Performance, 1994–2008.

very inefficient. This inefficiency could arise from a number of sources, but a common one is the failure to take into account the correlations between the client's private holdings and his investment portfolio. Such a culture of traditional values that often pervades management in this area has an unwillingness to take on new ideas and an aversion to technical matters. Diversification from a family company or other asset should be key in constructing the portfolio. It might be the case that the collectibles are a key part of the family fortune and as such are the object that needs to be diversified away from, but more usually it will be property or company interests.

Table 1.3 Sample Investor Portfolio

Asset	Value (GBP)	Weight (%)	Expected Return (%)	Expected Risk (%)
Cash	200,000	10.4	5.3	0.3
Government bonds	200,000	10.4	6.7	4.7
Corporate bonds	20,000	1.0	3.2	5.8
Convertible bonds	20,000	1.0	7.7	7.6
Equity—U.K.	200,000	10.4	11.0	14.5
Equity—North America	150,000	7.8	11.3	15.8
Equity—Pan-Europe	200,000	10.4	10.3	18.5
Equity—Japan	100,000	5.2	3.0	18.7
Emerging markets	25,000	1.3	10.8	22.0
Hedge funds	250,000	13.1	7.8	5.7
Private equity	100,000	5.2	16.0	29.5
General commodities	150,000	7.8	8.7	9.7
Property—U.K. commercial	150,000	7.8	10.7	3.2
Balanced fund	150,000	7.8	8.3	9.2
TOTAL	1,915,000	100.0	8.9	7.8

If we break down this process, it can be considered as five steps:

1. Gather information from the client.
2. Create a suitable profile.
3. Build an asset universe.
4. Construct a portfolio.
5. Review this construction with the client.

This process has not varied much for most of the history of investment, since joint stock companies were first formed by the Dutch and shortly after, and much more famously, by John Law, who created the Mississippi bubble in the early 18th century, continuing until the mid-1980s, when it became law in the United Kingdom that clients have to be classified in terms of risk in their portfolio. This is slightly unfair, since in the 18th century the joint stock companies were created to spread the risk of funding trade expeditions across multiple investors; what John Law then demonstrated was that having too much money in a single company exposes the investor to stock-specific risk.

There is a mass of academic work on portfolio diversification and construction techniques, and we will discuss these briefly later. However, at this point the level of risk that the client is prepared to take has to be determined. The most common approach is to use a questionnaire; this can be simplistic—are you high, medium, or low risk?—and indeed this has been most investment managers' approach for many years. However, it is significantly lacking because it does not give the investor a baseline against which to measure the risk, nor does it identify in any way what the investor might be risking.

This method has developed further over the past 10 years with approaches designed to derive a score based on an investor's answers to a set of questions, the scoring of which has been calibrated in accordance with resultant portfolio characteristics. These questionnaires can approach this goal in different ways. One is psychometric, based on a set of questions that are not generally related to the topic being considered—investment—but that will elicit the individual's propensity for risk. A second approach is to look at the behavior of the investor in various investment scenarios. The aim of this exercise is to introduce the investor to the risks associated with investment and the concept that these have to be traded off against expected levels of return. There is some academic evidence, not cited here, that laboratory risk experiments do not always translate very accurately to real-world applications, so we expect the latter approach to be superior to the former. Here we look at a couple of examples of such questions.

Example 1.1

You have the choice among three investment portfolios, and the charts in Figure 1.22 illustrate the historic ranked returns, from worst year to best, and the cumulative return over the period. You will see that the portfolios with the highest historic return also had the most years of loss. Which investment portfolio would you choose?

Portfolio A: 0 years in 12 return a loss, historic return 4%
Portfolio A: 3 years in 12 return a loss, historic return 6%
Portfolio C: 4 years in 12 return a loss, historic return 8%

Example 1.2

Assuming that you were investing for the long term (eight years plus) and your portfolio underperformed your expectations for one to two years, would you:

1. Accept that this was a short-term fluctuation in long-term returns.
2. Seek a higher-risk return combination in the expectation of improved returns but higher risk.
3. Seek a lower-risk return combination in the expectation of lower, more certain returns.
4. Do nothing.

The advantage of this approach—apart from the ability to use it as an educational basis of conversation with the client—is that it has relevance to the rest of the portfolio construction process, and the impact of certain answers can be seen in the resultant portfolio.

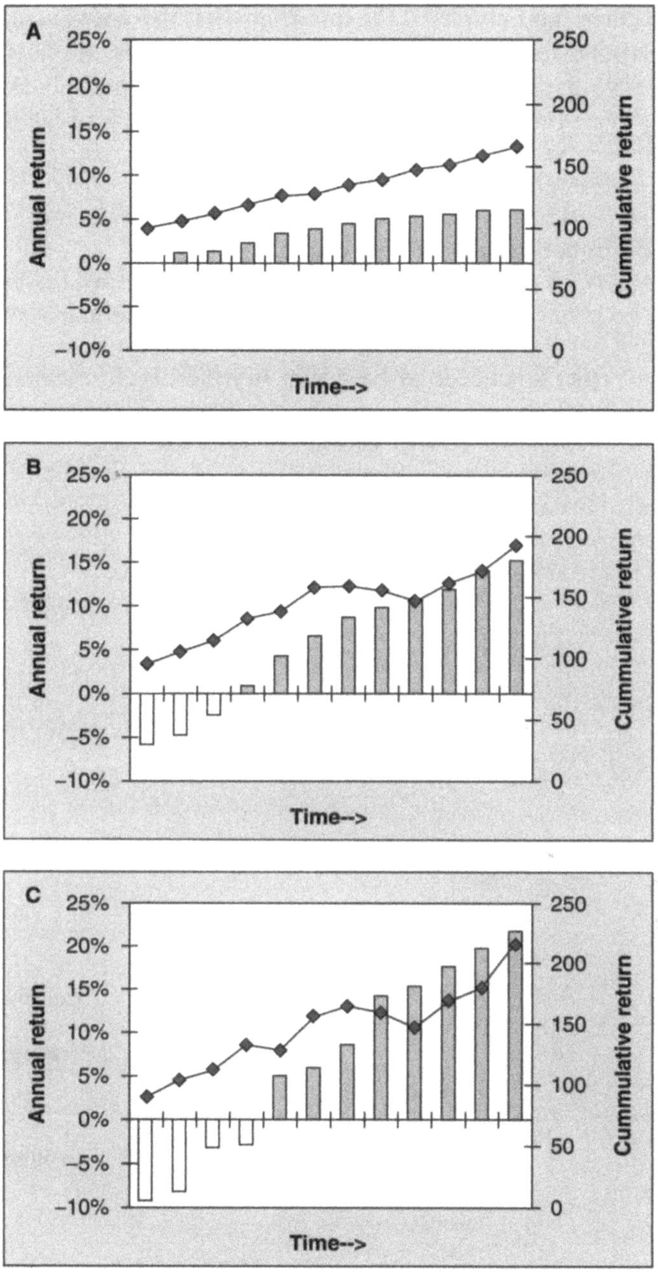

Figure 1.22 Example 1.1 sample portfolios. *Source:* BITA Risk Solutions

Once the client has completed the questionnaire, the answers must be translated into parameters for portfolio construction. Many applications simply generate a single parameter at this point; others drive multiple aspects of the portfolio construction. Our belief is that there are four sets of factors that need to be determined, as illustrated in Figure 1.23. (House asset allocation is the style of the investment house that is basically a set of constraints that ensure that the outcome portfolio represents their investment style and is dictated by the investment house rather than the client.)

The suitability of the asset classes will be determined by the experience of the investor, his propensity for the various types of risk, time horizon, and need for liquidity.

In terms of risk, this needs to be a leap beyond "high, medium, and low" and not just a value at risk (VaR) or volatility figure. This measure also needs to include the client's aversion to periods of loss, his need for stable income, his regret at not participating in upward runs in the market (if he holds a defensive portfolio) and his liquidity requirements, among other factors.

Finally, the key portfolio parameters such as base currency, geographic diversity, and absolute/relative bias need to be considered. So, it is not enough to simply complete a questionnaire; the answers require proper scoring and incorporation into the portfolio construction approach.

The construction of the portfolio needs to balance the client's conflicting requirements, as illustrated in Figure 1.24. Generally, in a multiasset class problem this is best achieved through a form of portfolio optimization that can balance the client's varying requirements.

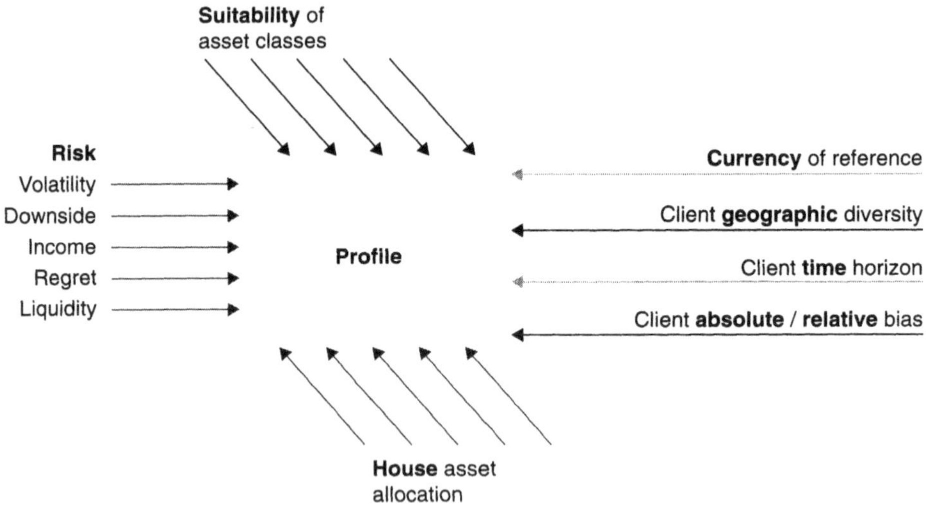

Figure 1.23 Factors to consider in client portfolio construction. *Source:* BITA Risk Solutions

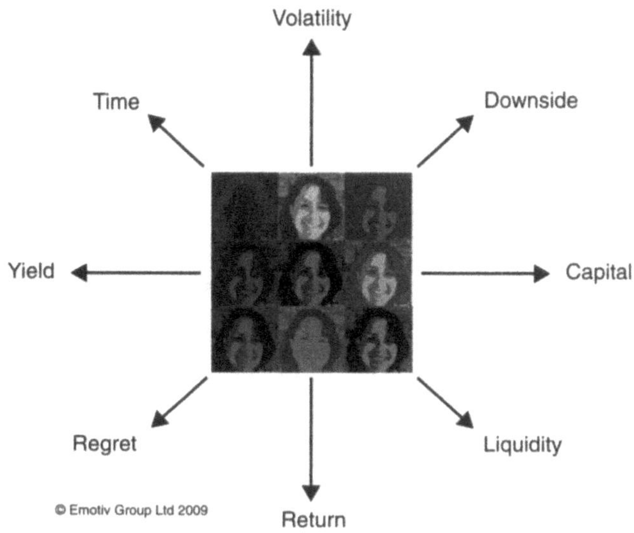

Figure 1.24 Conflicting client requirements. *Source:* BITA Risk Solutions

Having completed the portfolio optimization and come up with one or more investment approaches for the client, it is best to illustrate their different characteristics through backtesting them. Though this approach does not and should not be used to indicate how an investment proposal might behave in the future, it can be used to judge how a client would react to various events. The classic comparison is a lower-risk conservative portfolio that, if bought and held through the 1990s to the early 2000s, would have the same end value as a more volatile portfolio that had peaked with the market in 1999, assuming both had buy and hold strategies. In this case, would the client have taken the risk-averse option and not complained while it was underperforming? Of course, we could look at such strategies including collectible assets.

High Net Worth Investment Managers on the Pros and Cons of Putting Collectibles into Client Portfolios

In the course of working on this book, the authors sent a note to a number of high net worth managers, asking them to consider the following points:

1. Do you see a role for collectibles in high net worth investment?
2. If so, which ones?
3. How would you deal with distributional and storage issues?
4. Are there any other points to consider in implementation?

A number of responses were received and a particular manager was selected for interview. His vast experience in the field gave us a clear insight into the problems of implementing collectible portfolio construction at the practical level. Here we reproduce notes from the interview.

The first point our contact made was the confusion in the mind of the client between items that could be seen as investment goods versus collectible goods versus consumption goods. This is particularly a problem in the case of property, where wealthy clients might desire residences in a number of major cities. The same will apply to high-status cars. There is a strong element of collecting; there is also investment and consumption. Sometimes there are issues of status of ownership, which can seriously complicate matters. This can arise in the case of antiques illegally taken from archaeological sites and sold through reputable outlets. The problem, however, is much more general and may apply to property as well. This will allow us to assess the possibility of individuals holding collectibles.

If it is mutually agreed that collectible objects will be part of the client portfolio, the investment manager needs to give the client advice as to the value of the items. Such a step is necessary; for purposes of asset allocation, the manager needs to know the size of the collectible position. Here a cautious approach is advocated for a number of reasons. Professional integrity can be compromised if internal valuations are used. It is thus necessary to maintain a register of external experts for valuation purposes. This is costly in administrative resources for the manager and in terms of valuation fees for the client. One cannot rely on collectible indices for the purpose of valuation; their inadequacies are discussed elsewhere in a number of chapters.

Following on from this discussion on valuation, one of the big problems facing high net worth collectors is that they can become most of the market. The usual assumption of finance is that an individual will not move the market; this means that the prices are exogenous to the investor and he can take them as given. However, if one collects a particularly scarce theme, as many people do, the collector might be one of a small number of people who are prepared to pay large prices for scarce items in this area. When the buyer becomes a seller, it is very likely that prices could fall substantially. There are some splendid counterexamples to this: Paying high prices for pre-Raphaelite paintings was the preserve of one or two large collectors until recently, when their appeal spread to a much wider audience, and this has led to a continued rise in price, allowing the original collectors to sell profitably. Similar stories apply to Scottish artists who have benefited from a rise in Scottish nationalism. However, these are rare counterexamples, and these difficulties in market size and influence lead to problems in placing collectibles in a portfolio that might require valuations and use of a risk model.

Another feature of collectible investment is its role in money laundering. Though many of these items have been used by political refugees to get their assets away from oppressive regimes, there is some evidence that in recent times collecting in contemporary Eastern European art might have some very sinister connotations. To the individual collector, this could be a risk he is prepared to take, but to a high net worth manager, where reputation is probably the most valuable asset of all, this will be an unacceptable risk.

Having bought valuable items, there is an ongoing funding requirement, which means that the manager will have to ask the client for money for the following. Insurance and storage costs are two obvious costs, but some forms of maintenance and security are also necessary. In the U.K. context, one can buy properties or objects deemed to be national treasures. This will give you a tax advantage, but it then becomes a requirement to display the objects or property to the public, and this could be a source of increased insurance costs and strong psychological aversion to the general *populus*. On the plus side, national treasures can be returned to the nation in lieu of death duties at current market value, which allows for some efficient intergenerational transfer.

The auction houses can take an active role in collectible investment and currently will arrange a loan against the collateral of assets that can be kept in store by them and, when sold, will be sold through them. This activity seems to be, under some circumstances, a mutually beneficial arrangement. Clearly, there are great advantages in keeping highest-quality investables in storage, because depreciation can be taken out of the equation, and one need only worry about fluctuation in market prices.

The Positives of Collectible Investments

Much of what we've discussed so far has dealt with the problems of collectible investment; however, there are a number of pluses. Collectibles allow the investor the benefits of status and enjoyment. For the investor to achieve this status, it is necessary for the manager or his experts to define the term *quality*. This might seem self-evident to the outsider but in fact is a dynamic process, the purpose of which is the identification of signatory pieces. It would be a separate study of great interest as to how this process works. The role of the expert is obviously important, but a masterpiece is not just a masterpiece because the critic says so. In the world of stamps, for example, there are a number of unique pieces, but the market realizations that these pieces have achieved vary greatly.

There are a range of social aspects to collecting, which are the part that would be deemed to be enjoyable. Apart from the utility gained from ownership, there is the utility gained from completing—finding the missing pieces. Attendance at exhibitions provides a moneyed person with a social life and contact with creative and "interesting" people. From the perspective of the manager, encouraging a client to invest in collectibles will give them this satisfaction and takes the pressure off the manager. It is thus both a diversion and a diversification. Happiness can also be found not just by completing but the constant upgrade in quality. Through collecting, there is also the possibility of gaining national honor and forgiveness. Giving a gift to the state or bequeathing your collection to a national gallery or museum can precipitate social elevation or be a payment of a hidden fine. We have witnessed this phenomenon in recent times in certain unnamed countries.

The motives of the collector are various. Usually it is a hobby, sometimes it is an intellectual pursuit, and in some cases it is the challenge of becoming an expert in a new field. It can sometimes be seen in private equity, where an investor goes about collecting businesses of a similar kind. Sometimes there is a form of reverse investment, where collectors with proven business acumen end up buying the company that helped them foster their collection in the first place. Bringing their business skills to this area often gives the company a new direction and leads to significant expansion. This, in turn, helps realize the individual's investment.

Conclusion

This chapter has addressed the interplay between investment and collecting issues. We have discussed in some detail the roles of managers and experts in facilitating the joint process of investment and collecting. We have also touched briefly on the use of investment tools such as psychological questionnaires and portfolio construction products. Later chapters look at specific investment themes, and further work could well build portfolios based on traditional financial assets and collecting indices.

2 The Neuropsychology of the Collector

Shirley Maloney Mueller

Introduction

In a magazine article written years ago, the author suggested that collectors are individuals who sublimate their libidos by acquiring objects. The author based this concept on Sigmund Freud's essays in which he described collecting as a "redirection of surplus libido onto an inanimate object" (Ehrenfeld, 1993). Though Freud's theory sounds intriguing, even titillating, it probably has little if anything to do with the real reason that collectors collect. Though earlier theories, like Freud's, conjecture that there are multiple psychological motivations that cause people to seek out and gather almost everything imaginable, the search is rooted in our very neurobiology. This is where the modern story of why collectors collect begins.

The first section in this chapter introduces the contemporary approach to decision making and how it affects collecting decisions. To facilitate this discussion, terms that might be unfamiliar, such as *nucleus accumbens, amygdala, anterior insula,* and *prefrontal cortex,* are introduced. Though initially foreign to the reader, these words become manageable when appreciated in terms of their role in decision making. The *nucleus accumbens* is the pleasure seeker that drives the collecting process. If it is left unfettered, the goal—in this case, the collectible—would be acquired with abandon. But normally there are modulating influences. One is the *amygdala*, which attenuates desire because of fear or caution, the equivalent of throwing water on a flame. Another is the *anterior insula,* which reacts negatively to excessive pricing. Sadness and disgust, also emanating from the anterior insula, can further dampen desire. It is the *prefrontal cortex* that modulates these disparate influences to finally blossom forth with a decision suitable for the particular collector who is selecting the collectible.

Collectible Investments for the High Net Worth Investor

The second section in this chapter covers more familiar territory: the psychological motivators that thrust collectors toward collecting. Included is pride, bragging rights, a sense of history, creating a legacy, intellectual stimulation, social rewards, or even crafting a sense of order with an object display. These factors are called *secondary reinforcers*. They are person specific; for example, one individual might be stimulated more than another by pride. Each influences the nucleus accumbens positively.

However, the vast neurological network that contributes to collecting can occasionally go awry. Then collecting as a healthy outlet is derailed. This issue is covered in the third section of this chapter. One important cause of derailing is neurochemical abnormalities of the brain. Other origins are considered as well.

Two special situations that relate to collecting gone awry are covered in the fourth section. The first involves abnormalities that can occur during normal aging and how they could relate to poor collecting decisions. The second looks at a recent study examining collecting behavior in patients with brain lesions.

Finally, the neuropsychology of the high net worth individual (HNWI) is covered. This is important because the HNWI's reinforcers are not necessarily the same as a collector in the traditional sense. It is acquisition of money that can be her primary driver rather than pride, bragging rights, or a sense of history. This means that her acquisition pattern is different from that of the traditional collector, as is the method in which she chooses to collect.

The neuroscience of collecting is an emerging field. Though prospective work is just beginning, it is progressing rapidly. Future findings can benefit those collectors who pay attention. That knowledge can put them on the cutting edge of decision making when executing a collecting judgment.

The Modern Story: Neuroeconomics Meets Neurophysiology

Since the pursuit of reward is the stimulus that drives human activities, it too is what inspires us to collect. For some people, what better reward could there be than the expectation of collecting a rare object, or maybe even not such a rare object? Two Stanford University researchers (Kuhnen and Knutsen, 2005) confirmed the concept that expectation is a stimulus to our pleasure center using functional magnetic resonance imaging (MRI), which measures changes in blood flow and oxygenation due to activity in the brain. This relatively new technique has revolutionized our understanding of the neurofunction behind decision making and is the basis of the majority of the studies cited in this section.

Kuhnen and Knutsen (2005) found that their human subjects' nucleus accumbens, the pleasure center, was stimulated when they anticipated a monetary reward. The participants hadn't yet received the recompense. Still, their nucleus accumbens lit up as though it was on fire, the same as it does when food, sex, or addicting drugs were the pleasures that provided the incentive. The nucleus accumbens is located deep in the primitive brain in an area called the basal ganglion.

However, it isn't just the pleasure center that determines whether or not we collect. Other factors are at work too. Though the nucleus accumbens is the energizer for activities that we consider enjoyable, our amygdala acts as a depressor (Berntson et al., 2007). It also lies deep in the brain, in the temporal lobe (roughly inside the external ear area). The amygdala looks at a collector's inclination to buy (or sell) an item from a different point of view than the nucleus accumbens. It adds caution or even fear. For example, I conjecture that it could be asking these questions, among others:

- Is the piece what the dealer says it is?
- Did the auction house attribute this object to an earlier date than its actual production?

This warning effect could be advantageous if it drives the collector away from a decision that would result in buying an item that is not what it is represented to be. Alternately, an exaggerated amygdala response that leads to unwarranted alarm could be counterproductive. It would mean not buying an object that is correctly attributed, because the collector feels uncomfortable that he has never seen that particular shape or design before. Instead of going with his "gut," he intellectually talks himself out of the piece. When he goes home, he is still thinking about it. He might reflect on it in the days or weeks or months or even years to come, second guessing his best judgment at the time of the decision.

Whether we are born with a strong amygdala response or environmental circumstances cause or exaggerate an underlying propensity, the result is the same: Caution or fear are stirred when we make a collecting decision, sometimes to our advantage, at other times to our detriment.

Incidental emotions influence buying and selling decisions, too. Researchers at Carnegie Mellon University (Lerner et al., 2004) showed that sadness and disgust drive people to sell at a discount. One third of the researcher's subjects watched *The Champ,* a movie that elicited gloom, while a second set watched a disgust-evoking scene from *Trainspotting*. The third group, the controls, watched a neutral documentary.

The subjects were then asked to price highlighter pen sets that they would sell to one another. The neutral subjects asked $4.58 for the highlighters; the participants exposed to the disgusting scene asked $2.74. Those who observed the sad film asked $3.06. Clearly, the neutral set valued their pens more than

A Story That Demonstrates the Point

In June 1996, I was at one of the major antique fairs in the world—Olympia, in London, England. A dealer from Harrogate (in the north of England, near York) had a vessel he simply called an Arita coffee urn, circa 1700. There was no further description, nor did he offer one. His booth was crowded with all sorts of pottery and porcelain, with only an occasional Asian piece. There was no reason for me to think he was an expert in Asian porcelain. I had never seen a vessel like this before. It was thickly potted compared to other Asian porcelain and had an outer body with open fretwork. It was also rather densely painted compared to the more delicate decorative applications I had been accustomed to seeing.

Deciding whether to buy this piece presented a conundrum for me. First, I knew I wanted the object if it was what he said—an Arita coffee urn, circa 1700. This was because I was collecting early Asian coffeepots, thinking that eventually I might write an article about them. My nucleus accumbens was at work here; this little-known object would be a wonderful addition to the early coffeepots I already owned. In addition, I could use it as an illustration in my projected paper.

But caution intervened. If I had never seen one of these before, how did I know it was what the dealer claimed? Further, it didn't appear that he was an expert this area. That was my amygdala kicking in.

As I weighed these factors, it was impossible for me to decide. I went back to the dealer's stand several times. Finally, I asked the price. It was reasonable in pounds, and the dollar really was worth something in 1996. Therefore, the pot was affordable. Further, the price I would pay was not so enormous that I couldn't afford to lose it if my bet was wrong. I bought the piece.

Later, while perusing the book *Interaction in Ceramics Oriental Porcelain and Delftware* (Jorg, 1984), I found the pot, the only time I've ever seen it anywhere. The author called it rare, and I would agree, as I know of only two in the world—the one in the Groninger Museum in Groningen, Holland, illustrated in the book, and the one I own.

So I lucked out. In telling this story, I don't want to give the impression that I am always so fortunate. The point here is that my judgment about buying the Arita coffee urn involved nucleus accumbens and amygdala activity. In this case, they were dueling. In the end a piece of information, the price, was the tie breaker. This is where the prefrontal cortex and the anterior insula (both discussed in a moment) kicked in. The risk/reward of spending 600 pounds (translated into a reasonable dollar amount) on an Arita urn that wasn't an Arita urn was less to me than not having the urn at all.

individuals who were sad or disgusted. The latter devalued the items by more than one third.

The researchers concluded that sadness prompted participants to try to change their situation, which translated into a greater willingness to sell their possessions. Though the localization of this emotion in the brain has been studied, the results have been variable. Eugène et al. (2003) suggests that individual differences might be responsible for the inconsistencies.

The same highlighter pen study also suggests that disgust causes people to want to rid themselves of property, meaning that the disgusted individuals were more inclined to sell at a cut-rate price. The portion of the brain activated by disgust is the anterior insula (Krolak-Salomon et al., 2003), also deep in the brain, like the nucleus accumbens and amygdala.

The anterior insula is also influenced by price. If the cost is excessive, the anterior insula is activated (Knutson et al., 2006). At the same time, the prefrontal cortex (discussed in a moment) is deactivated. This suggests cause and effect—that the activity of the anterior insula acts as an inhibitor of prefrontal cortex activity under these circumstances.

All of this means that the brain weighs potential expenditures against rewards before a final buying or selling decision is made. Appreciation of these complex mechanisms can help collectors make better collecting decisions. For example, disgust, unrelated to the sale of an object, can make a person want to rid herself of property and thereby sell at a discount. Additionally, an unrelated feeling of sadness could prompt a seller to try to change her situation, which could translate into a greater willingness to sell at a lower price than otherwise.

On a very practical note, often when estate sales occur, one spouse has died. The remaining partner, consumed by grief, is much more likely to sell collectibles and other objects at a discounted price than he would have prior to or substantially after the event that produced the melancholy.

All these factors pulling and tugging in the brain when a collecting decision is in process do have a modulator. It is the *prefrontal cortex* (Anderson et al., 2005; Denburg et al., 2007). This well-organized region is at the front of the brain, over the eyes, a position in accord with its importance and a more recent evolutionary development compared to primitive brain areas (the nucleus accumbens, amygdala, and anterior insula).

Some call the prefrontal cortex the modern brain. It orchestrates thoughts and actions in accordance with our goals. The prefrontal cortex is the steering wheel that guides our collecting decisions. It is the executive that navigates between conflicting emotions to work toward a defined goal. It filters among incoming messages from the energizer, the nucleus accumbens, and the depressors, the amygdala plus the anterior insula, to process information and finally make a decision. There are other contributing areas of the brain as well (Hare et al., 2008), about which less is known. Therefore, I will not include them in this discussion.

A Brain Conversation: "Should I buy this?"

Nucleus accumbens (energizer): "Yes, I want it."
Amygdala (caution/fear, depressors): "Spending the money makes me fearful. We need to seriously think about saving for Susie's education. I have to be careful how I spend money."
Anterior insula (price sensitivity or external factors such as disgust or sadness depressors): "Don't do this. The object is priced at four times one at auction two years ago."

If the individual is sad or disgusted about another concern, the anterior insula input could be further amplified.

Prefrontal cortex (modulator): "The piece fits into my collection; it fills a gap. Nevertheless, this object has been coming around at auction every two to five years at a lesser price. My need is not urgent. I'll wait; the money could be better used for Susie's education."

Before Neuroeconomics: Psychological Reinforcers

Collectors are not seeking pleasure in a diffuse way when they collect. They are pursuing it in a very specific manner—by gathering collectible objects. This is because there are psychological reinforcers that feed into their nucleus accumbens and spark their desire for collectibles. In fact, the possibilities of what these reinforcers are is so vast that only the most common can be covered here (Akin, 1996; Belk, 1995; Blom, 2003; Formanek, R. 1994; W. D. McIntosh and B. Schmeichel, 2004; W. Muensterberger, 1994; Pearce, 1994).

One contributing factor is *pride* in acquiring exquisite objects. This can be further heightened by the pleasure of gathering objects together as a group for the first time. During the search, excitement can be sharpened by finding a rare piece, which sets that collector apart from all others in his peer group. This can provide peer recognition and admiration by associates.

Other collectors, aside from the rareness of the piece, want to acquire it at a modest price. That is their joy and gives them pride in being so astute. It's the object's possession for comparatively little money that excites them and qualifies them for *bragging rights*.

Different from bragging rights is the *thrill of the chase*. Here it is finding the most desirable object that is the goal, not the favorable price of the piece. In *The Cone Sisters of Baltimore: Collecting at Full Tilt* (Hirschland and Ramage, 2008), the authors talk about a pair of siblings striving to outwit not only each other but also dealers in their effort to find the best Rembrandt or Raphael.

Some authors would suggest that these sisters were atypical in that the "chase" trait is more male than female (Buck, 2004). This is because competi-

Bragging Rights

A friend of mine of modest means seems to be able to collect objects at almost a third to half the price of anyone else. Then he talks relentless about his find. His pleasure is to not only the chase in acquiring the discounted piece but also discussing his good fortune. The item itself is of less consequence.

He obtained one object after taking photos of a ceramic piece at a small antiques store. George (not his real name) suspected that the dealer had an object of quality that he didn't recognize. To verify this further, George read some reference books. This confirmed his suspicion. Then, gaining confidence that was fueled by his original "gut feeling," George sent photos of the object to specialists at Christie's and Sotheby's. He was delighted with the answer, "Yes, it is 18th century and in the price range of \$2000–3500." George purchased the lovely little porcelain pot for \$700 and it now sits in his living room. It is the conversation piece that is sure to start a story that is lovingly elaborated by my friend.

tive pursuit is considered more a manly than womanly characteristic. Our phylogenetic history supports this concept. Hundreds of thousands of years ago it was the males who had to hunt and kill animals to provide their families with food. This was because of their greater muscle mass. They were better equipped for the job, so to speak. Thereby, pursuit was a male necessity, rather than a choice.

Women, on the other hand, because of their smaller muscle mass, were left to the home area to gather nuts and berries and care for the children. They did not have to be so aggressive to survive. Their continued existence depended more on negotiation with the other women of their group and their ability to perceive their communal place correctly and work into and around it.

At auction, the *bidder's curse*—the potential for overbidding at auction—supports the chase mentality of some collectors. Lee and Malmendier (2007) found that 42% of online auctioneer eBay's final auction price ended above the fixed price of an identical object also offered elsewhere on the same site. The authors attributed this phenomenon to limited attention on the part of bidders and their willingness to spend money to obtain the object, which was enhanced in the competitive auction (utility of winning).

Other collectors feel a *sense of history* when they assemble objects. By owning antiques, they feel closer to antiquity or perhaps even their own dead ancestors or important people or circumstances of long ago. The reverse of feeling a sense of history is looking into the future. The creator might hope to build a larger *legacy* for herself by passing on special objects to future generations.

Others collect because it is an intellectual process and provides *intellectual satisfaction*. The gathering of pieces in a specific area requires discipline, knowledge, and an eye for the unusual or particularly beautiful. This might have been the impetus for Stephen W. Bushnell, M.D., who was physician to Her Majesty's legation in Peking (now Beijing) at the end of the 19th century. He was a medical doctor in an outpost remote from other colleagues. Collecting Chinese porcelain, readily available in Peking but a novelty in his home country of Britain, offered him intellectual stimulation. He put this to good use. Bushnell produced a number of books about his hobby, really an avocation. In many ways, it must have been his passion. His books were not only popular in his day; they're still read today. These pursuits turned out to be beneficial to Bushnell's nation in terms of introducing serious Chinese scholarship through the eyes of a contemporary Englishman. They were also, no doubt, advantageous to Bushnell, who was able to benefit initially from intellectual stimulation and later the social recognition that was generated when his works were published.

It has also been said that some collectors gather objects to enhance their *social lives*. My guess is that their love of objects came first. Then, somewhere along the way, they realized that there are organizations for collectors like themselves. Friendships forged through these groups no doubt expanded their social lives. Additionally, the "wow" factor of a friend or neighbor who visits a collector's home and admires the cherished pieces is worth a great deal to almost anyone.

Others enjoy *arranging and rearranging* a collection. Though this can serve as a means of feeling in control, it could simply be the demonstration of organizational skills applied to collecting as taste and knowledge accumulates. It is also a pleasure that could wane with age because diminishing mental and physical ability could set limitations not only on collecting acquisitiveness but on the ability to organize and rearrange pieces.

Last, but certainly not least, is that all these reinforcers to collect involve *anticipation*. In its nascent stage, as yet unactuated, the collector's desire allows her or him to imagine anything he wants to about the desired returns the object will bring. It is in this hopeful phase that the pleasure center burns most brightly. When magnetic resonance imaging is performed, the nucleus accumbens erupts with activity when a reward is anticipated (Kuhnen and Knutson, 2005). Once the prize is actually obtained, the nucleus accumbens shows less activity. The anticipation of the reward is more exciting to our pleasure center than the reality of obtaining it. This might explain, in part, why collecting often transcends a mere pastime and becomes a passion. It gives sufficient pleasure during anticipation of acquiring that special collectible that the participant wants to continue it more and more vigorously.

Collecting Gone Awry

Sometimes, though, all these complex normal and healthy reasons to collect go awry. The modulator, the prefrontal cortex in the front of the brain, is no longer able to navigate between conflicting primitive emotions arising from deep in the brain. It cannot draw a suitable conclusion. This is because either the prefrontal cortex itself is damaged or the conflicting emotions are too strong and overpower the judgment of the prefrontal cortex. Then poor collecting decisions are made and a whole new set of emotions erupts. These new feelings may or may not be on the part of the collector, because his deficits might not allow him to understand his situation. They almost always involve family, friends, and advisers.

An initially benign form of collecting gone awry is 'too much, too often," the process whereby initially healthy collecting becomes overly consuming and other areas of life are neglected. An example is the Reeves couple that ultimately gave their Chinese porcelain collection to Washington and Lee University in Lexington, Virginia, in 1967. Mrs. Reeves, originally Louise Herreshoff, married a man 28 years younger than herself. The glue that bound them together was likely not romantic but instead a passion for collecting. This passion resulted in the Reeves buying a second house next to the one in which they lived, specifically for their gathered objects. Ultimately there was no living space in either house; both were filled to capacity with furniture and stacks of porcelain. This quote from Elinor Gordon, a well-known Chinese export porcelain dealer, cited in James W. Whitehead's book (Whitehead, 2003), gives an idea of the ferocity with which Louise Herreshoff Reeves collected:

> *It was 1951 and I was participating in my first New York antiques show. The large punch bowl was placed in the most prominent position in my booth as a "show stopper."*
>
> *It was an extremely rare item dating to the 1785 to 1810 period. The decoration, with flags flying, depicted the warehouses or "hongs" where foreign nations dealt with the Chinese. The hongs were located in Canton along the Pearl River, not far from Whampoa, served merchant ships from England, Bourbon France, Spain, Holland, Sweden and, after 1784, the United States of America.*
>
> *Mrs. Reeves, dressed in black with a long knitted coat, spotted the bowl and inquired of the price. I politely replied, "The bowl is not for sale. It belongs to my husband, Horace." She in rapid order stated in a cultured, soft-spoken manner, "Mrs. Gordon, any item on display in this show is for sale. How much is the bowl?" Nervously I explained I would attempt to contact my husband who was in a business meeting in Philadelphia. Eventually reaching Horace I explained the dilemma.*
>
> *He gave me what I thought to be excellent advice: "This is your first major show, and it is important to establish an excellent reputation. Fix the price so outrageously high that she will not pursue the matter."*
>
> *Running to the booth and screwing up all the courage at my command, I informed Mrs. Reeves that Mr. Gordon would sell the bowl and the price was $1,500. Seemingly undaunted, she opened her black pigskin bag, retrieved a small change purse and handed me 15 one-hundred-dollar bills. The bowl was hers and became a valued part of the collection. I understand that she and Mr. Reeves left immediately by taxi for Grand Central Station and Mrs. Reeves held the bowl on her lap the entire train trip to Providence.*

As you can see from the quote, there were few, if any, cautionary modulators functioning when Mrs. Reeves found something she wanted. Only her nucleus accumbens, the pleasure center, seemed to be at work.

The need to acquire an object with little if any inhibition is considered by Black and his colleagues (Black et al., 1998) to be an impulse control disorder. It is classified as one of the symptoms of a broader psychiatric abnormality—obsessive compulsive disorder. Compulsive shoppers fit in this category, and collectors who are unable to resist buying objects could be some variety thereof. Table 2.1 lists some characteristics that differentiate compulsive shoppers from recreational shoppers.

A compulsive collector could have her own unique value system, compared to the norm. She assigns an importance to the desired object that causes it to exceed its real worth. Therefore, the craving for that object is heightened. This is not to say that Mrs. Reeves was a compulsive shopper. Though she might have been fulfilling an emotional need by buying special objects, she did have the money to pay for them.

Another type of collector acquires objects of little value or significance to anyone except himself. These collectors do not possess the kind of prefrontal cortex modulation routinely used by others in normal life. Still, they are not necessarily considered pathological unless the pursuit is accompanied by extreme clutter. Then the objects collected in the chase have nowhere to be placed because the collector cannot get rid of one object to make room for another. These collectors *hoard*. This results in overcrowding and disorder in their homes and often leads to distress on the part of family members. For example, this collector's children might not invite friends over because they are ashamed that their house is so crowded. In extreme cases, there might be only a path in which to walk through rooms. The most terrible consequence of all this is that normal living ceases. There is so much "stuff," often considered by the collector

Table 2.1 How Recreational Shoppers are Different from Compulsive Shoppers

Recreational Shoppers	Compulsive Shoppers
1. May buy to show success and express themselves but do so within their budgets. Spending money is an acceptable way to enhance feelings of security and even attract positive attention, if done tastefully and according to a financial plan.	1. Use money to fulfill an emotional need without understanding what is happening. This leads to a downhill spiral in which the individual is driven to fulfill his own desires beyond what his wallet supports.
2. Spend money with care by: • Paying off accumulated bills • Purchasing within a budget • Setting aside appropriate money for upcoming needs	2. Spend money with abandon by: • Incurring outstanding debt • Buying first and thinking about consequences later • Little or no planning for future needs

as precious objects (but not necessarily considered so precious by others), that rooms can't be used for their intended purposes.

Using positron emission tomography, Saxena and his associates (2004) showed that compulsive hoarders are different from other obsessive/compulsive patients and their group of normal comparison subjects in their pattern of glucose metabolism. The hoarders showed lower glucose metabolism in specific areas of the brain compared to nonhoarding obsessive/compulsive patients and comparison subjects. This finding suggested to the authors that individuals who are obsessive/compulsive and also hoard might be a distinct subgroup or variant of obsessive/compulsive disorder, one that is notoriously difficult to treat.

In another study that did not involve examination of glucose metabolism but simply clinical categorization of hoarders, the results were somewhat different. Twenty percent of hoarders examined in Hong Kong revealed no apparent mental illness (Chiu et al., 2003). Of the remaining subjects, almost half were schizophrenic; 10% suffered dementia. The others had assorted emotional problems, including depression, mild mental retardation, unstable personality, and a delusional disorder. The study included about half males and half females, mainly from among the lower socioeconomic class. Therefore, the results might not apply to higher socioeconomic levels. Furthermore, hoarders in Hong Kong might have little to do with American hoarders, who are different culturally. Nevertheless, the study begins to shed light on the complex origin of hoarding.

One might think at first consideration that the Reeves were hoarders. They were both comfortable with collecting to excess and had trouble disposing of their precious objects. For example, after James W. Whitehead from Washington and Lee University visited the Reeves because they were thinking of giving their collection to that institution, he described his visit in this way:

> *Quickly glancing around the room, it became obvious that Mr. Reeves had carefully guided me along a three-foot aisle to my chair. Not only were the surfaces of furniture covered with ceramics, items were stored under the bed, on and under the piano, atop and below the chairs. The drawers of the chest, the secretary bookcase, and the desk were also overflowing with pieces of porcelain. (Whitehead, 2003, pp. 122–123)*

Yet the Reeves were not hoarders according to definition—those who fill their home with worthless objects—junk. On the contrary, the Reeves collected valuable objects. It is also important to note that Chiu et al. (2003) found that even hoarders, according to the classical definition, can be normal, that is, without any apparent mental illness.

Special Situations

Aging

Recent evidence suggests that about a third of elderly individuals are particularly prone to poor investing decisions. By extrapolation, this would apply to collecting decisions as well. Natalie Denburg, Ph.D., from the University of Iowa, is a leader in this field. She and her colleagues (Denburg et al., 2005) studied healthy adults divided into two groups, younger (26–55 years) and older (56–85 years). Their study used the Iowa gambling test (IGT), which is designed to provide a parallel to real life by figuring in reward, punishment, and unpredictability.

It works like this: The participants choose cards from four decks, each of which has a different payoff. Then the subjects receive feedback so that they know how much money they lost or gained. Because of the feedback, normal subjects learn to avoid card decks that give high immediate gains but larger future losses over time.

But one group in the study was different. Denburg found that a subset of the older individuals exhibited a decision-making impairment on the gambling test, even though they had otherwise intact cognitive functioning. They persisted in choosing the card decks that gave high immediate gains but larger future losses over time, just the reverse of their age-comparable colleagues and the younger group. Since the prefrontal cortex is critical to decision making, the authors postulated that this subset of the older group might have alterations in this location that their age-matched coparticipants and younger controls did not. Denburg (2008) summarized her work as follows:

> *Those studies support the notion that some older individuals, approximately 35%, have significant difficulty with reasoning and decision-making, as indexed by the IGT. This impairment occurred in the absence of frank neurological or psychiatric disease, and there was no evidence that it could be explained by premorbid factors, overall health status, or cognitive weaknesses. This finding raises the possibility of disproportionate aging of the ventromedial prefrontal cortex in these individuals.*

This aging deficit in some seniors could have important implications as to why some older people so often fall victim to fraud. It also could contribute to other poor financial choices such as buying and selling objects.

The Abnormal Brain

Anderson et al. (2005) studied 86 subjects with brain lesions. Thirteen exhibited abnormal collecting behavior that was severe and associated with troublesome accumulative of useless objects. In the study, the collecting set of subjects exhibited this behavior only after the onset of their lesions, not before. A close relative, usually a spouse, was the source of this information. To qualify as a collecting subject, the individual had to accumulate objects of little value to excess in such a way that the collecting interfered with daily function. Here is an example:

> *A 70-year-old, right-handed, retired bank clerk with 13 years of education underwent resection of an orbitofrontal meningioma. Her husband noted that*

> *all of her life she had been reluctant to throw away items with potential value, but that this characteristic was not so prominent as to cause any problems. However, following surgery, she began to collect large quantities of a wide array of items, to the extent that serious space problems arose in their home. She began ordering large quantities of unneeded items, particularly clothes, from mail-order catalogues, most of which her husband would intercept and return. (Anderson, 2005, Patient 8, pp. 201–212)*

When the collecting set was compared to the noncollecting set, they did not differ in age or standardized neuropsychological tests designed to determine intellectual abilities. Additionally, the two groups were alike when examined for executive function skills and anterograde memory. *The difference between the two sets of subjects was that the collecting group all had damage to a specific part of the frontal lobe called the* mesial frontal region. *The noncollecting group did not.*

The authors interpreted the presence of this specific lesion in the collecting group to mean that a normal overriding inhibitory system was disrupted by the frontal mesial lesion. Without its influence, the drive to collect objects is free to operate without its usual restraints. Then disinhibition occurs, which results in collecting behavior gone awry. It is important to note that the objects collected in the study were of little or no value, and therefore the results do not directly apply to those who gather valuable objects. Nevertheless, the authors drew some inferences from their study that apply to all collectors. They postulated that in people without brain damage, deep brain structures initiate the drive to collect. It then is modulated by a prefrontal neural system including mesial sectors. Without the tempering influence from the frontal mesial area, collecting behavior goes unbridled.

Though these findings have clinical implications when objects of little or no worth are indiscriminately collected, they could also have relevance for individuals who buy valuable pieces. These collectors rely on good decision making to select pieces that they not only like but that have some chance of appreciation. If the inhibitory pathway for this process is weak, the collector will be less able to reject pieces that are not suitable or are of questionable value. Then he could buy the wrong piece or choose too many identical items or another variation on the inability to control a collecting impulse.

The High Net Worth Individual

Motivation: Reinforcers

To invest in art because the reinforcer for the motivation is pride, intellectual satisfaction, or a connection to history is one thing. To invest in it purely because money is the reinforcer is another.

Yet this may be the only reinforcer for selected HNWIs—those with $25 million or more. There are roughly some 47,000 HNWIs in the United States (people with $20 million or more, according to IRS Statistics of Income Division data, 2004). What causes the nucleus accumbens of some of them to burn brightly is the potential profit that art or other high-end luxury goods can bring rather than personally selecting and possessing the objects.

This is not to say that all HNWIs collect art only for money. There are those who are collectors in every sense of the word. They buy specially selected art or luxury items themselves or with the aid of an art advisor. This pursuit is motivated by the reasons other collectors collect, with little if any thought of making money on their purchases.

These HNWIs who are also collectors might consider their ability to assemble high-end pieces, the cost of which is above the budget of most collectors, as a perk of their wealth—a privilege that few can achieve. An example of a HNWI who was also a collector in the traditional sense is Ben Edwards of A. G. Edwards and Company (W. Moonan, 2002). He collected over 5000 pieces of Chinese export porcelain, which he eventually sold at auction.

Money as a reinforcer for other HNWIs is based on the fact that it is the universal currency that can buy so many comforts in our modern society. It is equivalent to food that was the primary motivator hundreds of thousands of years ago. In fact, today it is even better than food because not only does it allow people to acquire their food, they can purchase other things with it as well.

Delgado et al. (2006) explain it this way:

> *[Money is an] example of a secondary reinforcer. It acquires its reinforcing properties through its association with primary reinforcers (i.e., money can be used to acquire food). Due to societal and cultural factors, money has evolved to become a powerful incentive in driving human behavior, perhaps equally as important as primary reinforcers.*

The psychological reinforcers mentioned earlier in this chapter would also be considered secondary. However, our need to seek them—for example, pride, a legacy, or "bragging rights"—is something we desire but not essential to our survival. Satisfaction of these less essential secondary motivators could enrich our lives, but they aren't required for our continued existence the way money, the most essential secondary reinforcer, is.

This means that there is a difference between the secondary reinforcer, money, and the others (also secondary) mentioned earlier. The desire for money is universal because it is essential for survival. Pride, intellectual satisfaction, or a connection to history are also present in each of us, but they're not required for survival. Therefore, they can be "shed" if necessary to ensure survival. Intrinsically, the degree of pride, intellectual satisfaction, or a connection to history and so on in every individual is more person specific and elastic than the need for money. (See Table 2.2.)

Table 2.2 Comparison: HNWIs and Collectors

Differences	Specific HNWIs	Collectors, Including Some HNWIs
Monetary resources	$25 million or more	Less, except for some HNWIs
Reinforcer behind motivation to collect	Universal: Money	Person-specific: Multiple
Involvement in collecting	Indirect	Direct
Nature of collection	Asset class that includes multiple categories of art/luxury items	Single category of art (fine or decorative) or small number of categories
Vehicle	Investment portfolio	Possession of objects

The Process: The How

Why do specific HNWIs invest in art or luxury items to make money rather than any of the other secondary motivators mentioned, when that goal is not recommended for the individual collector (S. M. Mueller, 2003, 2005)? In a nutshell, it is because they have the resources and their advisors recommend it.

Ultra-affluent individuals naturally want to make as much money with the money they have, just as all of us do. To accomplish this, they try to invest more like endowments rather than individual investors since the returns of the former have been better. For example, at fiscal year end, June 30, 2007, Harvard's Management Co. Inc., in Cambridge, Massachusetts, earned a 23% return (*Harvard Gazette* online, 2007). This was three percentage points over that of the S&P (20%) for the same period. The manager achieved this feat using more than the traditional three- or four-asset classes (stocks, bonds, cash, and real estate) normally included in a conventional portfolio. *Asset allocation* refers to the process of dividing investments across various kinds of assets, such as stocks, bonds, cash, real estate, commodities, hedge funds, private equity, and even art. The idea is to optimize return and minimize risk. This is because when one asset class goes up in value, another goes down, so they balance each other, providing stability in a portfolio. Studies by Israelsen (2007) and others have shown that a wider array of asset classes perform better with less risk. Harry M. Markowitz, along with Merton H. Miller and William F. Sharpe, won the Nobel Prize in Economics for this concept in 1990. This division across a wider group of asset classes is the technique that Harvard's investment manager used.

Most of the time, it is an investment advisor who chooses the asset classes for the HNWI who is not really interested in the objects per se but in the potential return they might bring. That means that these HNWIs' involvement

The "Brown" Story

In 1992 I bought some lovely George II centennial chairs from Sotheby's in New York that looked period and fit in with my 18th-century décor. Though they were meant primarily to be functional, I certainly appreciated the fact that they gave a sense of elegance. Since they were antique and purchased from a major auction house, I hoped that when I sold them they would bring at least the sum I paid for them. With inflation, I still would have lost money, but that would have been okay. They were useful and beautiful.

In reality, when I sold the chairs 16 years after I bought them, this particular antique furniture was out of style. It was selling for quarters on the dollar. "Brown" was out.

This was a powerful lesson: Investing in just one category of the art market can lead to monetary loss if the timing of the sale of the objects is not tailored to the peak of its cyclical value.

in art is indirect rather than direct, as it is for collectors themselves. In addition, when the advisor invests in art or luxury goods for his client, he is choosing not just one category, but multiple ones, so that the correlation within the asset class is not associated. This has the effect of smoothing out the overall return within the ups and downs of specific categories in the art/luxury markets. The story below details a basic example of the necessity of investing in more than one category of art/luxury item.

The HNWI who collects for profit rather than the other reinforcing factors covered earlier in this chapter would be chagrined at losing money on her investment. That's why this individual hires a financial advisor, who in turn hires a specialist group to collect art or luxury items if they are to be part of the client's portfolio. These art or luxury item consultants, knowledgeable in many areas of collecting, put together a diversified portfolio that is meant to weather the ups and downs of the various collectibles in its asset class. In that way, their values average out and provide balance as another asset class for the HNWI's total investment portfolio. This is because a basket of luxury collectibles that contains different categories such as art, wine, books, and violins can be added to other classes of assets such as equities, bonds, cash commodities, and real estate, to diversify them further.

Whether adding art as another asset class is beneficial to return is currently a matter of conjecture (L. Johnson, 2008; A. De Knecht, 2008; S. M. Mueller, 2008). The British Rail Fund (BRF) used art in its portfolio for 25 years and made an annualized return of 11.3%, which is perfectly respectable but not as high as the rest of the BRF portfolio (D. Blake, 1995). Today the BRF does not invest in art as an asset class. Its concerns could have included the cost of storage and insurance for the art or luxury item. In addition, this category has no dividends or income, as stocks and bonds do. Moreover, they cannot be disposed of rapidly. They are only worth what someone will pay for them, and the market can be very thinly traded. Therefore, valuing art and luxury items can be speculation more than a solid determination.

Still, there are other art funds—for example, the London-based Fine Art Fund, which consists of Old Masters, Impressionists, and modern plus contemporary art. Its return is not open to the general public, so the benefit, if any, is not known.

A recent research paper (R.A.J. Campbell, 2008), however, suggests that art is worth considering as an asset class in an HNWI's investment portfolio. Campbell entitled her paper, *Art as a Financial Investment.* She looked at art as yet another alternative asset class and treated it like real estate, commodity futures, private equity, and hedge funds. Each of these can be used to broaden diversification within an investment portfolio. She focused on bear markets because it is there that the benefit of diversification is most needed. The author used data from both the Art Market Research and Mei Moses All Art Index, which compare repeat sales prices of particular items at auction. She found that using a hypothetical fund (dates 1985–2006) consisting of 30% Old Masters, 15% European Impressionists, 15% modern, and 40% contemporary art would return an average of 7.05%, with an average annual standard deviation of 6.93. She also found low correlation with other asset classes. This lack of correlation between art and other asset classes offers attractive diversification for the HNWI. Campbell concludes: "Optimal portfolio allocations using historical returns make a case for investors to consider art as an attractive, albeit small addition to their investment strategy."

This concept is expanded in a working paper (De Roon et al., working paper) currently titled *Emotional Assets,* in which not only art is examined as an alternative asset class. The authors also include wine, stamps, watches, and atlases. These items were chosen because they make up more than 50% of the HNWI investment in the luxury sector. The authors found that a diverse portfolio, which they term *emotional assets*, could provide the investor with a positive and highly significant increase in the Sharpe ratio. The *Sharpe ratio* measures the risk/return profile of an investment portfolio. Emotional investments might be an inapt term in this context because the HNWI uses a luxury portfolio not because of feeling for the items in it but only to make money. The authors conclude, "Before advocating any investment into the emotional asset class arena we would suggest that a comprehensive study of the size of the market is undertaken for each alternative emotional asset class." They also indicate that this is likely to be of interest to HNWIs for only a small allocation of their portfolio.

Campbell's (2008) and DeRoon's (DeRoon et. al., working paper) information is just what the HNWIs and their advisers are looking for because a substantial proportion of their portfolios is in unconventional investments. For example, a recent survey by the New York-based Institute of Private Investors (IPI) indicated that in 2005 its HNWI members had 40% in alternative investments versus 36% in long-only equity (Welch, 2008). This large proportion of alternatives indicates the value that affluent families and their advisers put on this category. Collectibles are one such alternative. They are specifically mentioned as part of an effective diversifying strategy by Welch in his 2008 paper, *Consulting to the Ultra Affluent*. In fact, he includes art advisory as one of the essential services that financial advisers must provide to their ultra-wealthy clients.

In summary, the HNWI might not be like the typical collector. If her reinforcer is one of the multiple factors that drive collectors, she is a collector in the traditional sense. On the other hand, if the reinforcer is money, that HNWI is acting like an investor rather than a collector. This means that her involvement in collecting (indirect versus direct) and the process in which she collects (asset class in investment portfolio versus acquiring objects) differs as well.

Who Is in Control?

Nucleus accumbens: Seeks pleasure—energizer
Amygdala: Caution/fear—depressors
Anterior insula: Excessive price (directly relevant to the object in question) and/or disgust and sadness (due to another source, not directly related to the object)—depressors
Prefrontal cortex: Navigates between conflicting emotions—modulator

Conclusion

Although early books and papers on collecting were largely based on psychological and psychoanalytic concepts (proven or not), our new world embraces a fresh approach, one that combines economic and neuroscience studies. The two disciplines together reach beyond what was previously possible. They are beginning to lay down the basic brain mechanisms underlying decision making that are applicable to the process of collecting.

For example, a collector can imagine the energizer, the nucleus accumbens, grabbing his brain power in an effort to mobilize action toward a desired object. Then, he can visualize other parts of the brain sidetracking the initial fire of desire. Fear and/or caution from the amygdala may leap forward and attenuate the enthusiasm. Sadness or disgust, present independently, may further dampen enthusiasm as the anterior insula responds. Alternatively, an excessive price could stimulate the anterior insula into action and further diminish any positive response. These attenuating factors act through the prefrontal cortex, located in the modern part of the brain. It weighs positives and negatives to ultimately come forth with a conclusion consistent with an individual's previous experience and present needs. This ideal situation, though, could be altered when pathology is present.

Then collecting can become an albatross rather than a pleasure. For example, about one third of the aging population develops prefrontal lobe abnormalities that relate to poor decision making. Likewise, brain lesions, such as tumors, that shape important brain pathways can adversely influence collecting decisions. Psychiatric disorders, too, due to abnormal brain chemistry, can also contribute to collecting decisions that go awry.

The HNWI is in a category by herself. Although she might collect art or luxury items just as other collectors do, there is another avenue open to her because of her wealth. Her indirect possession of art and luxury items as an asset class in her investment portfolio could increase her net worth. Her reinforcer is pursuit of money. Passion for an object because it increases pride, intellectual stimulation, or a connection to history might not be a reinforcer for her. Her decision to include art/luxury items in her investment portfolio is purely a monetary decision, often based on the recommendation of her financial adviser.

The exciting news here is that we know so much more about the science behind collecting than we did as few as 10 years ago. This new knowledge and future findings (Preston et al., submitted; Preston et al., in press) can further expand our understanding of collecting decisions. Savvy collectors can use this information to catapult themselves forward to better collecting decisions, and thereby better collections.

References

Anderson, S. W., Damasio, H., and Damasio, A. R. (2005) A Neural Basis for Collecting Behaviour in Humans, *Brain* 128:201–212.

Akin, M. (1996) Passionate Possession: The Formation of Private Collections, in David Kingery (ed.), *Learning from Things: Essays on Material Culture Studies*, Chapter 9, pp. 102–128, Smithsonian Institution Press.

Berntson, G. G., Bechara, A., Damasio, H., Tranel, D., and Cacioppo, J. T. (2007) Amygdala Contribution to Selective Dimensions of Emotion, *Social Cognition Affect Neuroscience* 2:123–129.

Belk, R. W. (1995) *Collecting in a Consumer Society*, Routledge.

Black, D. W., Repertinger, S., Gafney, Gary R., and Gabel, J. (1998) Family History and Psychiatric Comorbidity in Persons with Compulsive Buying: Preliminary Findings, *American Journal of Psychiatry* 155:960–963.

Blake, D. (1995) *Pension schemes and pension funds in the United Kingdom*, pp. 346–347, Oxford University Press.

Blom, P. (2003) *To Have and to Hold: An Intimate History of Collectors and Collecting*, Overlook Press.

Buck, L. (2004) *Market Matters: The Dynamics of the Contemporary Art Market*, Arts Council, England.

Campbell, R. A. J. (2008) Art as a Financial Investment, *The Journal of Alternative Investments*, Spring:64–81.

Chiu, S. N., Chong, H. C., and Lau S.P.F. (2003) Exploratory Study of Hoarding Behavior in Hong Kong, *Hong Kong Journal of Psychiatry* 12(3):23–30.

De Knecht, A. (2008). The Aft Market Is Not Like Shares or Commodities, *Financial Times*, September 5, p. 8.

Delgado, M. R., Labouliere, C. D., and Phelps, E. A. (2006) Fear of Losing Money? Aversive Conditioning with Secondary Reinforcers, *Social Cognitive and Affective Neuroscience* 1(3):250–259.

Denburg, N. L., Tranel, D., and Bechara, A. (2005) The Ability to Decide Advantageously Declines Prematurely in Some Normal Older Persons, *Neuropsychologia*, 43(7):1099–1106.

Denburg, N. L., Cole, C. A., Hernandez, M., Yamada, T., H., Tranel, D., Bechara, A., and Wallace, R. B. (2007) The Orbitofrontal Cortex, Real-World Decision Making, and Normal Aging, *Annals New York Academy of Science* 1121:480–498.

Denburg, N. L. (2008) Email correspondence, June 4.

De Roon, F. A., Koedjik, C. G., and Campbell, R. A. J., Emotional Assets (working paper). Available at SSRN: *http://ssrn.com/abstract=1102652*.

Ehrenfeld, Temma (1993) Why Executives Collect, *Fortune*, January 11.

Eugène, F., Lévesque, J., Mensour, B., Leroux, J. M., Beaudoin, G., Bourgouin, P., and Beauregard, M. (2003) The Impact of Individual Differences on the Neural Circuitry Underlying Sadness, *NeuroImage* 19(2):354–364.

Formanek, R. Why They Collect: Collectors Reveal Their Motivations, in Susan M. Pearce (ed.), *Interpreting Objects and Collections*, Chapter 38, pp. 327–335, Routledge, 1994.

Hare, T. A., O'Doherty, J., Camerer, C. F., Schultz, W., and Rangle, A. (2008) Dissociating the Role of the Orbitofrontal Cortex and the Striatum in the Computation of Goal Values and Prediction Errors, *The Journal of Neuroscience* 28(22): 5623–5630.

Harvard Gazette Online (2007) El-Erian to Step Down as Head of Harvard Management Company, September 11.

Hirschland, E. B., and Ramage, N. H. (2008) *The Cone Sisters of Baltimore: Collecting at Full Tilt*, Northwestern University Press.

Israelsen, G. L. (2007) The Benefits of Low Correlation, *Journal of Indexes* 10(6): 18–26.

Johnson, L. (2008) Artful Practitioners of a Confidence Trick, *Financial Times*, September 3, p. 12.

Jorg, C.J.A. (1984) *Interaction in Ceramics Oriental (Porcelain & Delftware)*, # 82, pp. 128–129, Hong Kong Museum of Art.

Kuhnen, C., and Knutson, B. (2005) The Neural Basis of Financial Risk-Taking, *Neuron* 47(5):763–770.

Knutson, B., Rick, S., Wimmer, G., Prelec, D. and Loewenstein, G. (2006) Neural Predictors of Purchases, *Neuron* 53:147–156.

Krolak-Salomon, P., Henaff, M., Isnard, J., Tallon-Baudry, C., Guenot, M., Vighetto, A., Bertrand, O., and Mauguiere, F. (2003) An Attention Modulated Response to Disgust in Human Ventral Anterior Insula, *Annals of Neurology* 53(4):446–453.

Lee, Y. H., and Malmendier, U. (2007) The Bidders' Curse, NBER Working Paper No. W13699. Available at SSRN: *http://ssrn.com/abstract=1080202*.

Lerner, J. S., Small, D. A., and Loewenstein, G. (2004) Heart Strings and Purse Strings: Carry-Over Effects of Emotions on Economic Transactions, *Psychological Science* 15(5):337–341.

McIntosh, W. D., and Schmeichel, B. (2004) Collectors and Collecting: A Social Psychological Perspective, *Leisure Sciences* 26:85–97.

Moonan, W. (2002) Antiques: Just Crazy About Imari, and Picky, *New York Times*, January 4.

Mueller, S. M. (2003) Consider Investing in Antique Furniture, *Physician s Money Digest*, May.

Mueller, S. M. (2005) Add a Splash of Color to Your Portfolio, *Physician s Money Digest,* March 31.

Mueller, S. M. (2008) Part of the Game of Making Money, *Financial Times,* September 11.

Muensterberger, W. (1994) *Collecting: An Unruly Passion—Psychological Perspectives*, Princeton University Press.

Pearce, S. M. (ed.) (1994) *Interpreting Objects and Collections*, Routledge.

Preston, S. D., Anderson, S. W., Stansfield, R. B., and Bechara, A. (2009) *Shopping Decisions* (submitted).

Preston, S. D., Muroff, J. R., and Wengrovitz, S. M. (in press) Decisions About Objects, *Depression and Anxiety*.

Saxena, S., Brody, A. L., Maidment, K. M., Smith, E. C., Zohrabi, N., Katz, E., Baker, S. K., and Baxter, L. R. (2004) Cerebral Glucose Metabolism in Obsessive-Compulsive Hoarding, *American Journal of Psychiatry* 161:1038–1048.

Welch, S. D. (2008) Consulting to the Ultra Affluent, *CFA Institute Conference Proceedings Quarterly* 25(1:)47–56.

Whitehead, J. W. (2003) *A Fragile Union: The Story of Louise Herreshoff*, Colonial Printing.

3 Collecting and Behavioral Finance

David Johnstone

-University of Sydney

Introduction

"You collect because you love the object, not for investment." How many times have you heard that said? I well remember my last time: I was driving across the Sydney Harbor Bridge and a spokesman from an antiques publishing house was conducting a radio talk show on the wonders of collecting. I remember thinking that some parts of the antiques trade have such an ingrained tradition of taking their own clients for fools. By telling the buyer that it's all for love, the dealer auditions for the role of matchmaker rather than his actual role as a market maker (that is, as a trader who both buys and sells, profiting on each "round trip"). The implicit message to the buyer is that the price is high but that someone of such good taste will naturally expect that and will not let money stand between him and his emotional well-being.

Not all buyers are deluded by such emotive button pushing. Some are amused more than insulted—and go ahead and buy anyway. This might be their own psychological counterploy, since part of a buyer's game can be to persuade the dealer that she is indeed so gullible. That might come in handy later on, when the dealer has something in his inventory that she really wants. The point of all this is to show that collecting is a psychological game, just as much as it is a contest of appreciating what is worth buying and what isn't. And there is also much to laugh about. How farcical, for example, is the "buy for love, not money" incantation. Apart from its implication that you should accept that you are donating to a worthy charity, it is recited by dealers whose profession it is to buy at auction on Wednesday and retail by the weekend at double the price, or more. At that rate of financial return, it is the dealer, at least as much as the client, who has reason to love the object.

It would be wrong, of course, to tar all collectibles dealers with the same brush. There is a highly evolved pecking order among dealers in collectibles markets, and those few at the top of the pyramid (sometimes known within the trade as "the food chain") are generally much less likely to resort to transparent appeals to the buyer's psyche. Such high-end dealers often have the advantage

Collectible Investments for the High Net Worth Investor

of greater knowledge, appreciation, and financial reserves with which to elicit better-quality items. They also have the backing of some discerning and enduring clients who know that certain prices simply have to be paid because there are items that are too good to miss. This is where the investment aspect of collecting is most at stake. Items of such distinct quality will almost certainly appreciate strongly over time, to the point at which the dealer himself must sometimes wonder whether his taking a short-term profit is really a sound financial decision.

So, getting back to the point, this chapter discusses the economic psychology of collectors and collecting. The best place to start such a topic, I suggest, is to identify the two most important rules or guiding principles by which a rational economic decision maker should approach the task of collecting. By *collecting* I mean the process of building a worthwhile and valuable (highly saleable) collection. First, whatever the psychological forces at play, collecting is necessarily also investing, for the same reason that a share trader will not accumulate a diverse and valuable share portfolio by losing on each transaction and buying "for love." Second, investment decisions should be made with the psychology of others and the marketplace in mind, but they should not be driven by one's own inbuilt psychological biases or failings, not at least without these being noted and taken into account (perhaps even exploited, as we see later in the chapter).

The first of these requirements means that as sensible collectors we must adopt all of the theoretical principles of rational investment and financial decision making. These principles are the basis of neoclassical microeconomics and statistical decision theory and involve logical reasoning in terms of subjective probabilities, predicted future market values (selling and buying prices), and the "opportunity costs" associated with each asset purchased, retained (rather than sold) or indeed never purchased. (All experienced collectors can name the exact items that they most regret not buying.)

The second point is about psychological maturity. Although it is possible to learn the principles of rational economic decision making, it is not always easy to put these rules into effect. We each have our own emotional predispositions working against us and often encouraging conclusions or (in)actions that are not at all in our own best interests financially. This psychological slippery slope has been thoroughly exposed academically since at least the 1970s, when the now famous Nobel Laureate economic-psychologist Daniel Kahneman observed and explained theoretically all manner of biases in his subjects' economic decision processes. That was essentially the start of the new and now highly influential field of behavioral finance (see the many references that follow).

It is not only the economic logic or reasoning by which we make our decisions that is at issue. It is also the subjective inputs required to implement that logic. For example, suppose that we understand logically that if the attractive bookcase we are looking at in the auction room is as genuine as it seems, we would be right to buy it (at some not unreasonable price) and offload the one we have at home. That would be a good decision, since we would not only have a rarely fine bookcase to enjoy (a noneconomic benefit), we would also have a more productive long-term investment. Before coming to this commitment, however, we need to judge whether the bookcase at auction (or in a dealer's stock) is indeed genuine and not, for example, a demonstrable or likely "marriage," as some people are saying of it. That will require an intuitive probability assessment, made perhaps on the basis of professional advice or by assimilating different opinions and pieces of evidence.

The assessment of relevant probabilities is one of the more crucial subjective tasks in a rational decision process. We might have a clear and economically logical way of thinking in mind, but success hinges ultimately on our assessment of the evidence and commensurate probabilities. Statisticians call this inference process *belief revision.* There is a vast and in part very complicated academic literature in mathematics and related fields on how to make such inferences rationally (in keeping with the laws of probability). The matching literature in psychology and behavioral economics describes some of the ways in real life that inferences are not made so cleverly (by psychologically flawed individuals such as us).

This brief depiction of a rational or not-so-rational collector's mind at work might seem ridiculously technical, and of course we don't really expect people to do any formal probability calculations. We must, however, come to an instinctive assessment or belief about the bookcase or other potential investment piece on which to either act or sit tight. If our psychological makeup is such that we get such assessments wrong too often, we will soon enough fail as collectors and probably give up trying. But if we have the psychological maturity and sophistication to make good probability assessments and to act on them logically, we have a decisive competitive edge as collectors—an advantage that will, by the laws of probability, manifest itself over the long run in terms of the sum of what we buy and what we sell.

The same applies to professional traders or dealers. If they don't possess such innate abilities, their continued existence in a highly competitive marketplace is unlikely, to say the least. Conversely, even if they have all the necessary insights at both a rational and psychological level, they must still be prepared for some setbacks. Good dealers will often make assessments of the value of some item, such as a "sleeper" at auction, that are starkly at odds with the common or consensus view. Often a highly expert dealer will be right, and those who watched her buy some item at auction, or discover later that someone else bought it for her, will grow to admire or envy her appreciation and "eye." Yet among such audacious purchases there will necessarily be some mistakes. It is this acceptance, for one thing, that marks a dealer or collector as having the psychological mettle to succeed and lead the way. And it is what she does next that matters too, since the most common financial predilection of all, and the one that has probably brought about the demise of more collections and professional dealers than any other, is to refuse to sell something for less than was paid for it. Kahneman named this the *disposition effect.* It is just one of the many common psychological hang-ups of investors (and collectors) everywhere. Such human biases and other propensities are the subject of the field of behavioral finance, to which this chapter owes its existence.

A Brief Overview of Behavioral Finance

Finance in the normative tradition of neoclassical economics is concerned with the theory and consequences of rational financial decision making. *Rational behavior* is interpreted as the process of preference formation and decision (choice of action) satisfying the axioms of expected utility theory. Although the decision tools of finance and statistics rarely make use of utility theory explicitly, their underlying rationale is expected utility maximization. In most financial decision contexts, the cognitive processes required to formally maximize expected utility, such as Bayesian probability revision, are onerous and have been revealed by experimental and field studies in psychology to be largely beyond human (actual) decision makers. Beginning notably with the published work of Kahneman and Tversky (1979, 1981, 1984), *economic psychology* offers a description of individual decision making under uncertainty that contrasts with the normative neoclassical theory and seems in general to capture more of the characteristic "human" decision process than is countenanced under the rational model.

In recent years, economists—including, notably, Thaler (1980, 1985, 2000), and Shiller (1981, 1990)—have applied and extended the psychological theory of human (ir-rational or a-rational) decision making and, partly in collaboration with psychologists (e.g., Kahneman et al., 1990, 1991), have developed a theory of behavioral finance concerning the decisions of real-life investors. According to this theory, people are rational only within human limitations (Thaler's "quasi-rationality"). They have bounds on how much information they can, or want to, assimilate, they use convenient rules of thumb (heuristics) rather than strictly logical formal analyses, and they are affected by personal psychological biases, reference points, and cognitive illusions (Goldstein and Hogarth, 1997; Gilovich et al., 2003). More appealingly from the perspective of research, individual decision makers are observed to be systematically (predictably) irrational in scientifically testable ways.

Like traditional positivist financial economics, the theory of behavioral finance yields empirical hypotheses concerning human economic behavior. There is now a very large research literature documenting known and apparent departures from rationality observed in laboratory and other studies of individual financial decision making. Summaries of this literature include DeBondt and Thaler (1985), Statman (1985, 1999), Hogarth and Reder (1987), Thaler (1991, 1992, 1999), Goldstein and Hogarth (1997), Schwartz 1998, Kahneman and Riepe (1998), Tvede (1999), Kahneman and Tversky (2000), Shefrin (2000), Shiller (2000), Shleifer (2000), and Barberis and Thaler (2005). A daunting aspect of behavioral finance is the seemingly unending diversity of ways in which individual decision makers can be "irrational" (that is, depart from the rational decision model).

Unlike economic rationality, for which there is, in principle, a single unified theory, an exhaustive understanding of all aspects of individual irrationality is out of the question. Nonetheless, from what is already known, certain pervasive and empirically replicable human biases and other "mistakes" are known to effect even the most consequential real-world financial decisions. In the following section, a good number of these quirks of human nature are described, first in general terms and then in ways that apply or have been observed within the behavior of collectors and collectibles markets.

Known Behavioral Biases and Effects

The object here is to describe in brief some of the important psychological biases or instinctive departures from economic rationality. Such illogical and yet predictable patterns of behavior can be considered "laws of irrational decision making," since they are evident to the point of being nearly "compulsory" in many individuals' decision-making processes much of the time.

The sunk-cost effect, disposition effect, or loss aversion

The inclination to ignore and even add to previous mistakes (to "ride losses") rather than accept them and rationally alter direction (Arkes and Blumer, 1985; Shefrin and Statman, 1985; Thaler and Johnson, 1990; Odean, 1998a).

Example: A collector (or dealer) holds onto an item of little intrinsic merit rather than selling at a loss (possibly even a large loss in percentage terms, given the very high sales commissions in collectibles markets) and then using the proceeds to help buy a worthwhile replacement. This mistake is all the worse when the collector has gained the requisite knowledge since making the original purchase to now make a much more discerning acquisition, yet is prevented from doing so by his psychological inability to "take a loss." Rationally, that loss has already been taken, like it or not, and is only getting larger over time as money remains tied up in an item that is not increasing in realizable market value. (An investor's effective wealth is just his cash plus the realizable sale value of his assets.)

Dealers know that clients can't easily come to terms with their losses. The flip side is that the same individuals are sometimes prepared to sell, provided they "get their money back." A common dealer gambit, based on this psychological characterization of most clientele, is to ask a potential seller the seemingly inoffensive question, "What does the item owe you?" The owner's mental reaction to this query, particularly if current values have moved on from when he bought the item, should be that it is not what he has spent historically that matters; instead it is what the item is worth today. And if prices have fallen, his thinking must rationally be the same, in that he should erase from his mind what was spent and do the best thing now for the long term (whether that be sell or hold).

One day I was standing next to a dealer who bought a pair of painted cedar colonial timber fire surrounds for what seemed like a very good price. I complemented him on his sharp eye and readiness to strike, and he confessed that there was unfortunately no reason for celebration, since the surrounds were indeed his own and that he had been forced to buy them back (and pay both vendor and buyer commissions) because the auction price was just too low. His explanation was that it was commercially sensible to treat the commissions as just an extra cost and take the surrounds back to his shop, where in time he would get a much higher price. This showed a very well-developed business psyche, where the dealer's only considerations were what economists call the "marginal" costs and revenues of his action. He believed that the marginal (extra) revenue from retaining the items rather than letting them sell to the under-bidder would exceed the marginal costs of that action (namely the buyer's premium, since he would have paid the vendor's premium anyway).

Gambling with the house money

Reduced risk aversion when investing recent gains from the same or closely related ventures (Battalio et al., 1990; Thaler and Johnson, 1990; Arkes et al., 1994; Keasey and Moon, 1996).

Example: A collector (or dealer) who has recently had some windfall gain or perhaps sold an item for a very handsome price feels right in the mood to buy something and is less discerning as a result. Rationally, if the quality is not available, the collector should exercise his option to wait rather than act as though the windfall proceeds are burning a hole in his pocket.

Endowment effect

The unwillingness to sell something in possession at a price higher than would be offered by the same person to buy it (were it not already owned). (Thaler, 1980; Knetsch and Sinden, 1984; Knetsch, 1989; Kahneman et al., 1990)

Example: Collectors, more so than dealers, tend to overvalue things in their own collections or inventories. This precludes them from selling and upgrading, since they will not accept the prices that others feel items in their personal collections are worth. For example, my friend has a very early and beautiful piano that has been valued at a large sum, say, $50,000. He is also a mathematician and an avid student and patron of the betting markets, so has a good feel for real-world human decision making. His comment on seeing this valuation was that he treasured the piano and would not sell it for $50,000; however, if someone else owned it, he would certainly not be willing to pay the same amount to buy it. Economists sometimes refer to two different measures, WTA and WTP (*willing to accept* and *willing to pay*) and observe that these are often materially different amounts for one individual and object.

Break-even effect

The disposition to "bet on long shots" where success would mean full loss recovery and failure would cause only immaterial added loss (Thaler and Johnson, 1990). Similarly, "doubling-up" (Brown and Steenbeek, 2001)—the willingness to bet larger and larger sums, attempting to recover all previous losses.

Example: A collector (or dealer) attempts to recover from a run of poor acquisitions by spending more heavily and less discriminately, hoping for a gem or "sleeper" to surface among the new acquisitions. This is somewhat akin to "spending good money chasing bad," as occurs under the sunk-cost effect.

Precommitment to arbitrary investment limits

To counter the sunk-cost effect, commitment to a project or investment is terminated mechanistically at an arbitrary preset limit (e.g., "sell if price drops 10%" or "give it three months"), regardless of circumstances remaining or arising in favor of rational persistence (Thaler, 1980, 1981; Heath, 1995).

Example: Even successful dealers often set themselves quite arbitrary bidding limits at auction. Although this is understandable as a way of self-control, a bit like sitting on one's hands, it is strictly irrational in that it does not allow for "learning" or rational reaction to the strength of bidding from other parties. In finance, it is known that a big part of the "price discovery" process is the assimilation of information signalled by one trader to another through his bidding actions. That is why expert dealers often like to bid anonymously or through a proxy, thereby not giving away free information on which other bidders will raise their bidding limits. A related ploy is for the expert to bid flamboyantly up to some point and then pull out with a shake of the head, thus signalling that the price is now "too high," when in fact his bidding goes on through his proxy.

Avoidance of regret

Outcomes are measured not by their realized or realizable market values but in relation to what "could have been" (Bell, 1981; Loomes and Sugden, 1982). A monetary gain comes with a sense of loss if it would have been higher under another action. Expected money value (or utility) is foregone so as to avoid regret (e.g., selection of action that minimizes maximum regret rather than maximizes expected utility).

Example: Collectors often get a second chance to buy something they really want. For example, a dealer buys an item at auction, perhaps outsmarting the collector in some worldly way, and then offers the same item at a fair for a much larger price. The collector would pay this higher price but for one thing—namely, her feeling that she is losing the difference between that amount and the price she could have paid to obtain the item at auction. Rationally, the past is history (or "sunk"), and if the new price is still reasonable relative to the innate quality and rarity of the item, it should be paid with no rational feeling of regret. In fact, this might still be the best investment the collector ever made. Furthermore, it has the side benefit that it teaches her to be sharper and more ready to back her own beliefs the next time such an item appears at auction.

Choosing not to choose

A fear of making things worse outweighs the attraction of possible gains, causing inertia and preventing change from the status quo. Decision outcomes are forecast not in absolute terms but relative to what would occur under existing arrangements, and actions that could cause regret (when results are compared with what would occur if no action taken) are foregone, regardless of their possible upside (Thaler, 1980).

Example: Sometimes at auction an item appears that could be really something (if only we had the appreciation, inspection time, details of provenance, or whatever else would confirm its story). In the lead up to sale, doubts exist and there is much talk—there are always armchair experts and those with axes to grind and possibly bitter already that they will not be the buyer. Sometimes the only cause for doubt that makes much sense is that buyers can't remember a similar or even closely related item ever appearing. That is a given, of course, when indeed the item is unique, so it is hardly conclusive. Bidding for such an unusual and fascinating item often attracts much anticipation, yet is not always enough to attract a really high price.

The most common cause of such an anticlimax is that people are torn between two competing emotions, one saying "buy this, it's your chance" and the other saying something like "it's not what its seems," it's "much later" than claimed, it's "made-up," it looks "wrong for the period," "that artist never painted children," or whatever else is the going bit of sophistry on the day. The fear of being wrong, particularly in full public view, often translates into indecision, and the chance to bid goes by before many potential buyers get over their state of fright and mental paralysis. The actual buyer is then approached within minutes by several others all wanting to "give him a quick profit," usually just confirming to him that he was right and that this item is one to be examined in all aspects and savored before ever (if ever) being sold again.

Overconfidence and overtrading

Overconfidence, meaning subjective probability estimates overly close to 1 or 0 (certainty) relative to the available evidence (Stäel von Halstein, 1972), breeds excessive optimism and induces overtrading by indicating profit opportunities that don't actually exist (DeBondt and Thaler, 1987; Daniel et al., 1998; Odean, 1998b, 1999; Barber and Odean, 1999).

Example: Overdoing it is common in auctions where the buyer is prompted to bid more just because someone else is bidding more. In the worst cases, two bidders take the bidding from some given price to a multiple of five times that amount or even much higher, leaving all other bidders, including expert dealers, out of the running and lost for words. The resulting price is then far more than the same item could be sold for later or at another sale and can be said to be just too "bullish" by far. Game theorists know this as the winner's curse, in that by definition the buyer who outbids all others, including another individual who sets out simply to do the same thing, must inevitably pay (far) too much from any rational investment perspective. Sometimes when this happens, another vendor is moved by the high price to put an identical or equivalent item up for sale at the very next sale, and the underbidder from the first sale is the successful buyer at a fraction of the price achieved at the previous sale. Otherwise, the original buyer must push him up again, so as to "protect his investment" of the week before, which only encourages a third vendor to come forward. This process can't continue indefinitely.

Myopic loss aversion

Investors who feel losses more heavily than gains (of the same magnitude) ignore good long-term investments because of their frequent short-term price falls (a possible explanation of the equity premium puzzle). The more frequently an investment's price is evaluated or posted, the lower must be its price volatility (relative to its mean return) to appeal to the investor (Benartzi and Thaler, 1995).

Example: The general equivalent of the stock market is possibly the art market, where there are frequent sales of certain well-known artists' work and much volatility in realized prices, over both long-term bull and bear markets and occasionally drastic short-term downturns. A collector who is conscious of the possibility of buying just before the market goes into sudden decline will sometimes be too preoccupied with this possibility to take an objective long-run view based on the "fundamentals" of the picture in question. Great works coming up for sale when there is a market fixation on the short term are often sold at prices that turn out to be very low in the long term. This was seen clearly at the end of the 1980s and early 1990s, when there were many public and private examples of newly wealthy investors and major corporations taking large short-term losses on major works of art.

Mental accounting

Investors partition their finances into separate "mental accounts," like coins kept in different jam jars, and then think of these differently, as though money in one is different from money in the other (Thaler, 1980, 1985). Sometimes they "package" two accounts together or alternatively segregate them mentally so as to make themselves feel better (this is called *hedonic editing*). Losses on one account are often "bundled up" psychologically with gains on another so as to cancel out any mental construction of loss. *Prospect theory* (Kahneman and Tversky, 1979, 1981, 1984) holds that losses carry greater emotional weight than gains of the same size, meaning that losses will always be mentally aggregated with gains. Second, losses and gains both have diminishing marginal psychological impetus per dollar, implying that gains will be segregated into separate mental accounts but losses will be aggregated into a single account.

Example: Both buyers and sellers interpret their auction results on any given day in the way that feels best. If someone bought two items, both at very good prices, she will think of these transactions separately. If one item was really too expensive, the buyer will tend to aggregate the two transactions in her mind so as to avoid any feeling of loss on the one overly costly item. Similarly, when someone is selling several or more items and some go very cheaply, that individual will aggregate the day's trade into a single mental parcel. Most people in the trade understand these mental processes instinctively. I once sold several items in one auction sale, and the last was sold well below reserve. The auctioneer said to me afterward that he knew I would not mind too much as I had some "overs" on the earlier items. He was right enough and I did not complain in the least.

Mental accounting is one of the most important psychological factors at work in a collector's behavior. The same goes for dealers. It is very common, for example, for a dealer to have some really desirable item in his own collection and refuse to sell it—not for any rational reason but because it cost him hardly anything. The businesslike outlook is to sell at a very good price (relative to what he would get at auction now or in the future or what he would pay to buy a similar item), with no reference at all to what the item cost. This is the principle of *sunk cost*, which basically says that we should be looking forward, not backward, and that all inventory should be sold if the price is right, regardless of whether that price exceeds historic cost (and whether the item is at home or in the shop).

The irrational view so often explained by dealers is quite the opposite—namely, that there will be no sale at any price, because the item cost so little in the first place! This is a pattern of behavior that was apparently "invented" in collectibles markets and probably says something about the emotional rather than financial benefits that accrue to the owner of a very desirable or sought-after object. All experienced dealers feel the ongoing regret of having sold certain very special items, even when the price achieved at the time was very high (even outrageous). Such lasting emotion makes the dealer doubly hard to budge on the prized item that was bought cheaply and is still in his private collection. Put simply, his mind works differently when it comes to items on show in the shop and those at home in his drawing room. This is mental accounting in such an original and untainted form that behavioral finance theorists will, I suggest, add it to their collection.

Examples of such economic idiosyncrasy in collectibles markets are endless. Another I have seen repeatedly is that of the collector or dealer who at auction would consider buying a certain item except that it belongs to some rival or adversary who the defiant party opts "not to support." The loser here is any potential buyer who could otherwise add usefully to her collection or to the profits of her business by simply contributing one more bid (perhaps as little as $50) to the sale price already on its way to the adversary (and that's before the 20% commission or more that does not go to the vendor). So, in effect, a dealer opts not to buy a rival's stock, even when she has the right clientele for that item, forgoes a profit of, say, $500 to take $50 from her rival (add zeros to either number as required). This can be understood as an instance of mental accounting in that competing dealers often carry a running "mental ledger" of how much money they have put in a rival's bank account versus how much he has put in theirs. There is no rational explanation for this quite insidious way of thinking, since the value or worth of buying an item, once that item has been properly inspected, rarely depends on who is selling it. Put another way, if it's a good buy, it does not matter that it once belonged to someone else!

A similar absence of rationale applies to buyers who cannot bring themselves to bid when the auctioneer is or is assumed to be "running them up" (that is, adding fictitious bids). This is often the practice when there is a reserve price and the auctioneer wants a sale (both for his vendor and for himself, and for the long-term viability of the auction house, which cannot exist if items don't sell). The buyer must look at the price on offer and decide whether the object is worth it or not, and if he decides that it is, it should make no difference to him rationally that he is being run up. In fact, a sophisticated buyer might choose to buy at an auction house where this age-old practice occurs, since it puts off genuine competition. If the buyer has the emotional fiber to base his decision on nothing but the price and not on how that price is being contrived, he will buy items that other collectors want at prices that they would readily pay under other circumstances. To understand more about such apparently perverse incentives in markets, see the textbooks on financial market microstructure by Harris (2003) and Hasbrouck (2007).

A Personal Confession

The following tale convinced me of my own psychological fallibility. I was trying to buy a painting at auction and the bidding was at about $700. I did not want to pay much more and was close to the point of bidding no higher. The auctioneer was calling for another bid, and I was unsure whether it was me who was the current highest bidder or the lady standing directly in front of me, in the same line of sight as the auctioneer. There was no further bidding and I was feeling tempted to put my hand up, yet naturally disinclined to be seen to bid against myself, if indeed I was the highest bidder. Before I had gotten my thoughts in order, the hammer came down and the auctioneer looked up to me for my bidder's number. I felt a wave of remorse as I realized that I was indeed the buyer and had paid "too much" for something that I did not really want that much. But just as I was about to put my hand up, the lady in front waved her paddle and the auctioneer recorded her number as the buyer of the lot. Instantaneously I felt a surge of regret, certain now that I wanted this painting and annoyed that I had not been aware enough to bid one more time.

These directly opposing mental reactions occurred in the space of a few seconds and were driven not by the price but by the simple fact that in the first case I thought I was the buyer and did not want the item at that price, whereas in the second I was not the buyer and most definitely wanted the item, even at a higher price. There is little that can be said to rationalize such contrary "chemical transactions" in the brain. From a strict rational economics point of view, my only excuse would be that I knew now that there was another buyer at the price on offer and that I was not the only one who held the view that this price was justified. This is a reasonable theoretical interpretation in cases where the buyer is known to be astute and buying on his own account, but I did not know this of the lady in question. So really, there is nothing much to it other than the feeling that we tend to want something when it's not ours but not when it is ours, all at the same price.

I have seen a related phenomenon in dealer behavior whereby an item sits in a shop and attracts great interest but has no price ticket. Each time someone asks for a price or expresses interest, the dealer puts up the price in his own mind and says that the item is not for sale. That someone wants to buy it, even when there is no stated price, reassures him in all sorts of ways, and makes him want to keep the item even more, which of itself is a curious action when in fact he is in business expressly to sell that very kind of object. There is, of course, much psychology to this situation, including the fact that a keen but unsuccessful buyer might console himself or perhaps attempt to woo the dealer by buying something else in the shop or by offering to buy two or more things, including the unpriced item, all as a package.

A Wonderful Book (by Philip Mould)

My favorite book on trading collectibles and the intellectual challenges that this activity can present is the paperback by London-based art dealer Philip Mould (1997), first published in 1995 under the title *Sleepers: In Search of Lost Old Masters*. This book provides the most sophisticated and intimate account of life as a high-end art dealer hunting for precious but unrecognized artworks and trying to buy them without attracting the interest of competitors and others (such as auctioneers and wealthy collectors) who might thwart their acquisition. The book recreates the intense excitement and satisfaction gained by those select art dealers who combine a deep intellectual understanding of art and art history with highly developed aesthetic appreciation and the finely honed judgment and cunning required to identify underpriced art and to successfully buy and sell it. To my knowledge, there is no other account that offers the same cocktail of rational and emotional dealer insights.

To illustrate the substance and spice of the many tales and detective stories contained in the book and their lessons for someone trying to appreciate the psychology and rational motivations that underpin the behavior of an expert and successful dealer, I quote and discuss three typical passages from the book:

> *I went to the auction the following week, giving myself a limit of £20,000, which although perhaps a fifth of the value of an original work of this type, reflected a lingering degree of doubt. My sincere hope was that beneath all the over-painting I would not only find a genuine picture, but one in salvageable condition. But I could not count on either with certainty. I knew it was a gamble, and although the risks had been lessened by research, I had to remain sensible to the fact that the chance of restoration revealing a picture in fine condition was far from sure.* (Mould, 1997, p. 58)

This passage reveals all the rational elements of a dealer's decision making, along with a great self-awareness and introspective sense of skating on thin ice. The somewhat arbitrary self-imposed £20,000 limit is strictly irrational (see the preceding section), but Mould knows this and is merely trying to contain his own enthusiasm within reasonable limits when there is relatively little that he is likely to learn from the bidding of others. (They can't know the underpainting's condition any better than he can, even if they know as much as he does.) Furthermore, if bidding is strong and the bidders are known experts or their agents, there is little doubt that Mould would bid beyond his preconceived limit, at least by a few thousand.

As an aside, note that collectibles dealers sometimes refer to figures like the quoted £20,000 as a "nonprice," since they represent the value of neither of the "possible truths" (these being a genuine painting in salvageable condition or something else of not much value at all). Rationally, however, such a price makes utter sense when there is no clear evidence either way, for the same reason that shares in a promising but unproven gold mine might trade for, say, $2.50 rather than $0 or $20 each.

> *The overwhelming trend, however, as I have witnessed it over 15 years of dealing, has been for dealers to conquer a containable area, accumulating a group of loyal clients, a specific store of knowledge, and a skill and expertise with which the auction rooms, and other dealers, are not always able to compete on equal terms. For those who take their specialization seriously, discoveries arise naturally, and provide essential compensation for the narrowness of the field.* (Mould, 1997, p. 105)

This short passage reveals how elite dealers need to evolve in expertise and customer focus, but it also demonstrates an instinctive understanding of the functioning and role of information in markets. It is acknowledged that certain specialist market sectors, a subclass of highly specialist dealers, have the statistical edge in any transaction and are likely to get the better of vendors, despite the general expertise and overview available to the auction house. This state of affairs is not seen as unnatural or unsustainable but rather as merely just compensation to those dealers who so limit their focus that they miss out on the more readily available returns that come to others with more generalist expertise. Again, this understanding of the marketplace is quite rational and insightful. Vendors, especially once-ever vendors, can't become overnight experts so as to avoid selling to a better informed dealer, and the auction house needs only a workable balance between overall turnover and the cost of in-house expertise rather than to achieve a specialist High Street gallery-like hammer price on each item sold. The only factor that might bring to an end such "unfair" trades is the diminishing supply of unrecognized or lost Old Masters.

> *Richard is a consummate dealer, and when presented with a discovery [of a "sleeper" or lost masterpiece] of his own making, his commercial facilities work in tandem with his emotions. His reaction was typically pragmatic. "In that one glance, in the split second I was able to see it, I knew it was to be bought. I could see it was by Van Dyck and that its condition—though superficially offputting—was extremely fine. But," he added, and here he was emphatic, "there is of course a limit to what such a thing is worth. To buy a discovery, whatever the price, just because you have discovered it, is a form of vanity which can quickly lead to bankruptcy."* (Mould, 1997, p. 21)

It is common for collectors and sometimes dealers to bid strongly on an item to which their intellectual pride is somehow attached, as when they have been the first (at least in their minds) to have noticed it. A variation of this lapse in objectivity occurs when a collector finds some desirable and previously unseen item in a country sale or in an out-of-the-way secondhand shop. The thrill of the catch and the thought that unless the item is taken home there will be no trophy for their being first or smartest seems often to fuel a greater than usual willingness to pay. As before, this can easily result in a "winner's curse" whereby the item is acquired at a price that those who come later regard as too high. In objective financial terms, such an acquisition might never live up to its promise, since the buyer invests an overly large sum in his "find"—an expenditure that cannot be recovered by immediate sale and that would come to be worth more if simply left in the bank earning interest. That foregone interest, or profit from the best alternative use of the money, is what economists call *opportunity cost.*

Conclusion

In this essay I have described some of the most important of the many psychological biases or instinctive departures from microeconomic rationality that have been observed (repeatedly) in human financial decision making. This list presents only a glimpse of the literature in behavioral finance. Behavioral finance is not merely a collection of "anomalies" contradicting notions of decision makers as rational but a coherent body of theory, mostly originating in psychology, explaining and predicting the systematic patterns of irrational economic behavior in virtually all human decision making.

It is no coincidence, I suggest, that the considered and astute economic decision making depicted by Philip Mould applies to very high-end art dealers, where the prices paid and asked are potentially ruinous and there is little room for error in either a dealer's substantive judgments about the paintings in question or the economic logic that underpins his trading behavior. In a series of papers on the workings of those markets in which some traders are more accurately informed than others, Blume and Easley (1992, 2002, 2006) demonstrated that even small biases in a trader's probability assessments or in the decision rule by which those assessments are transcribed into actions (e.g., the proportion of one's bank or working capital wagered on a painting with a 60% chance of being "right") can almost guarantee a decline into bankruptcy. This is particularly so of collectibles markets, where objects can be very illiquid (hard to sell even at a "fair" price) and where brokerage rates are exorbitant by comparison with stocks and other financial markets.

An aspect of the psychology of collecting that has been alluded to here but not properly explained is the potential exploitation of one's own behavioral biases and predispositions so as to aid in the building of a collection. A good example is discussed in Johnstone (2002), where I introduce the *reverse sunk-cost effect*. This effect is apparent when the decision maker loses patience with something that was bought previously and gains enough sophistication to know that there are better examples to buy and that it is best for the long term to face his mistake and sell out. In selling, he might sometimes need to take a very low price (net of commission) relative to what was paid, but if the emotions run high enough and the collector is optimistic enough to feel that there is a much better buy waiting for him, he will have no difficulty accepting what can be an irrationally low price.

For example, if the item was bought some time ago for $500 and is going to yield only a $250 hammer price and, say, $125 after all costs, including carriage to the auction house, it might be rational to forego that $125 (what help is $125, anyway?) and buy the new item out of money from one's bank account. An emotional response, however, that can assist the longer-term assembly of a really worthy collection is to take the $125—not because it's much help financially but because the item is gone and the collector can look forward with a positive and more informed outlook, free of the daily distraction of an earlier false step sitting in the hallway.

Sometimes people overcome their (apparent) mistakes by hiding them from sight until they can be reevaluated objectively. Mould (1997) gives an example of an important picture that was left for many years in a cupboard. The crucial thing is to take a forward-looking perspective and not be influenced in current decisions by any or all of those mistakes made previously. Their only importance is to give the collector greater substantive appreciation for her objects and to become more astute psychologically for the next time a decision is to be made.

As is often said, the painful experience of taking a financial loss is a very good teacher. I doubt that there is any experienced and successful high-end dealer (in anything) who would think otherwise. In fact, there is a common story that the mistakes made early in a dealer's career are ultimately his making. This underlines the pivotal difference between those dealers and collectors who can accept their mistakes and learn and those who can't and are bound in the end (possibly in the very short term) to give up in a state of either penury or denial. A very worldly art dealer told me once that when she was far less experienced, she stood beside a wily old dealer and asked for a hint on the qualities of a picture they were both staring at. The other dealer turned to her and said, "Young woman, I would love to tell you, but what I know cost me too much."

This is not to say that buying collectibles is only about the contest and is devoid of any collegiality or camaraderie. At a weekly auction a few years ago, I overheard a witty conversation between two committed, albeit far from affluent, secondhand dealers, one of whom had been the owner of the lot just sold. The other recognized the lot as one that his friend had bought excitedly at the same sale just a week or two earlier, for much the same price. He turned to the seller and exclaimed, "Why did you sell?" The other replied just as succinctly, "So that I can buy," and they both laughed knowingly, amused with each other's grasp of what might seem to others quite irrational behavior. From their seasoned perspective, simple economic rationality is only part of the challenge and satisfaction of being a dealer or collector and is not always essential or even admired when deeper emotional forces and desires take hold.

Perhaps the most sophisticated of all personal attitudes to either dealing or collecting is to be cognizant at all times of the competing rational and psychological motivations at work, and to compare and decide between them or to weigh them up and adopt some compromise between them. That might be rational human behavior of the highest order.

References

Arkes, H. R., and Blumer, C. (1985) The Psychology of Sunk Cost, *Organizational Behavior and Human Decision Processes* 35:124–140.

Arkes, H. R., Joiner, C. A., and Pezzo, M. V. (1994) The Psychology of Windfall Gains, *Organizational Behavior and Human Decision Processes* 59:331–347.

Barber, B. M., and Odean, T. (1999) Trading Is Hazardous to Your Wealth: The Common Stock Investment Performance of Individual Investors, *Journal of Finance* 55:773–806.

Barberis, N., and Thaler, R. H. (2005) A Survey of Behavioral Finance. In R. H. Thaler (ed.), *Advances in Behavioral Finance*, Vol. II, pp. 1–78, Princeton University Press.

Battalio, R. C., Kagel, J. H., and Komain, J. (1990) Testing Between Alternative Models of Choice Under Uncertainty: Some Initial Results, *Journal of Risk and Uncertainty* 3:25–50.

Bell, D. E. (1981) Regret in Decision Making Under Uncertainty, *Operations Research* 30:961–981.

Benartzi, S., and Thaler, R. H. (1995) Myopic Loss-Aversion and the Equity Premium Puzzle, *The Quarterly Journal of Economics* 110:73–92.

Blume, L., and Easley, D. (1992) Evolution and Market Behavior, *Journal of Economic Theory* 58:9–40.

—— (2002) Optimality and Natural Selection in Markets, *Journal of Economic Theory* 107:95–135.

—— (2006) If You're So Smart, Why Aren't You Rich? Belief Selection in Complete and Incomplete Markets, *Econometrica* 74:929–966.

Brown, S. J., and Steenbeek, O. W. (2001) Doubling Up: Nick Leesons's Trading Strategy, *Pacific-Basin Finance Journal* 9:83–99.

Daniel, K., Hershleifer, D., and Subrahnanyam, A. (1998) Investor Psychology and Security Market Under- and Overreactions, *Journal of Finance* 53:1839–1886.

DeBondt, W. F. M., and Thaler, R. H. (1985) Does the Stock Market Overreact? *Journal of Finance* 40:793–805.

—— (1987) Further Evidence on Investor Overreaction and Stock Market Seasonality, *Journal of Finance* 42:557–581.

Gilovich, T., Griffin, D., and Kahneman, D. (eds.) (2003) *Heuristics and Biases: The Psychology of Intuitive Judgment*, Cambridge University Press.

Goldstein, M., and Hogarth, R. M. (1997) *Research on Judgment and Decision Making: Currents, Connections and Controversies*, Cambridge University Press.

Harris, L. (2003) *Trading and Exchanges*, Oxford University Press.

Hasbrouck, J. (2007) *Empirical Market Microstructure*, Oxford University Press.

Heath, C. (1995) Escalation and *De*-escalation of Commitment in Response to Sunk Costs: The Role of Budgeting in Mental Accounting, *Organizational Behavior and Human Decision Processes* 62:38–54.

Hogarth, R. M., and Reder, M. W. (1987) *Rational Choice: The Contrast Between Economics and Psychology*, University of Chicago Press.

Johnstone, D. J. (2002) Behavioral and Prescriptive Explanations of a Reverse Sunk Cost Effect, *Theory and Decision* 53:209–242.

Kahneman, D., Knetsch, J. L., and Thaler, R. H. (1990) Experimental Tests of the Endowment Effect and the Coase Theorem, *Journal of Political Economy* 98:1325–1348.

Kahneman, D., Knetsch, J. L., and Thaler, R. H. (1991) The Endowment Effect, Loss Aversion, and Status Quo Bias, *Journal of Economic Perspectives* 5:193–206.

Kahneman, D., and Riepe, M. W. (1998) Aspects of Investor Psychology: Beliefs, Preferences and Biases Investment Advisors Should Know About, *Journal of Portfolio Management* 24:661–687.

Kahneman, D., and Tversky, A. (1979) Prospect Theory: An Analysis of Decision Under Risk, *Econometrica* 47:263–291.

—— (1981) The Framing of Decisions and the Psychology of Choice, *Science* 211:453–458.
—— (1984) Choices, Values and Frames, *American Psychologist* 39(April):341–350.
—— (eds.) (2000) *Choices, Values and Frames*, Cambridge University Press.
Keasey, K., and Moon, P. (1996) Gambling with the House Money in Capital Expenditure Decisions: An Experimental Analysis, *Economics Letters* 50:105–110.
Knetsch, J. L. (1989) The Endowment Effect and Evidence of Non-reversible Indifference Curves, *American Economic Review* 79:1277–1288.
Knetsch, J. L., and Sinden, J. A. (1984) Willingness to Pay and Compensation Demanded: Experimental Evidence of an Unexpected Disparity, *Quarterly Journal of Economics* 99:507–521.
Loomes, G., and Sugden, R. (1982) Regret Theory: An Alternative Theory of Rational Choice Under Uncertainty, *The Economic Journal* 92:805–824.
Mould, P. (1997) *The Trail of Lot 163: In Search of Lost Art Treasures*, Fourth Estate.
Odeon, T. (1998a) Are Investors Reluctant to Realize Their Losses? *Journal of Finance* 53:1775–1798.
—— (1998b) Volume, Volatility, Price and Profit When All Traders Are Above Average, *Journal of Finance* 53:1887–1934.
—— (1999) Do Investors Trade Too Much? *American Economic Review* 5:1279–1298.
Schwartz, H. (1998) *Rationality Gone Awry? Decision Making Inconsistent with Economic and Financial Theory*, Praeger.
Shefrin, M. (2000) *Beyond Greed and Fear: Understanding Behavioral Finance and the Psychology of Investing*, Harvard Business School Press.
Shefrin, M., and Statman, M. (1985) The Disposition to Sell Winners Too Early and Ride Losses Too Long: Theory and Evidence, *Journal of Finance* 40:777–790; reprinted in Thaler, R. H. (ed.), *Advances in Behavioral Finance*, 1993, pp. 507–525, Russell Sage.
Shiller, R. J. (1981) Do Stock Prices Move Too Much to Be Justified by Subsequent Changes in Dividends, *American Economic Review* 71:421–436.
—— (1990) Market Volatility and Investment Behavior, *American Economic Review* 80:58–62.
—— (2000) *Irrational Exuberance*, Princeton University Press.
Shleifer, A. (2000) *Inefficient Markets: An Introduction to Behavioral Finance*, Oxford University Press.
Stäel von Holstein, C. A. S. (1972) Probabilistic Forecasting: An Experiment Related to the Stock Market, *Organizational Behavior and Human Performance* 8:139–158.
Statman, M. (1985) Behavioral Finance Versus Standard Finance, In S. S. Wood (ed.), *Behavioral Finance and Decision Theory in Investment Management*, AIMR.
—— (1999) Behavioral Finance: Past Battles and Future Engagements, *Financial Analysts Journal* November:18–27.
Thaler, R. H. (1980) Towards a Theory of Consumer Choice, *Journal of Economic Behavior and Organization* 1:39–60.
—— (1981) An Economic Theory of Self Control, *Journal of Political Economy* 89:392–406.
—— (1985) Mental Accounting and Consumer Choice, *Marketing Science* 4:199–214.

—— (1991) *Quasi-Rational Economics*, Russell Sage Foundation.
—— (1992) *The Winner's Curse: Paradoxes and Anomalies of Economic Life*, Princeton University Press.
—— (1999) The End of Behavioral Finance, *Financial Analysts Journal* 55:12–17.
—— (2000) From Homo Economicus to Homo Sapiens, *Journal of Economic Literature* 14:133–141.
Thaler, R., and Johnson, E. J. (1990) Gambling with the House Money and Trying to Break Even: The Effects of Prior Outcomes on Risky Choice, *Management Science* 36:643–660.
Tvede, L. (1999) *The Psychology of Finance*, 2nd ed., Wiley.

4 Collecting as Luxury Consumption: Effects on Individuals and Households

Russell W. Belk

-University of Utah

Introduction

In a recent short story about an American couple's collecting activity (Boyle, 1994), a partial inventory of their collected possessions includes Marsha's 212 antique oarlocks, 600 doilies, 120 potholders, and her Thimbles of the World set, Julian's 1000 astronomy books and his science fiction collection, and their joint collections of 309 bookends, 47 rocking chairs, and over 2000 plates, cups, and saucers. The recognition that their various collections might be a problem comes when Marsha's latest acquisition—a mahogany highboy with carved likenesses of Jefferson, Washington, and Adams as drawer pulls—literally will not fit in their overflowing suburban house, porch, garage, or storage shed. In desperation they hire a professional organizer to get their life in order. The organizer, a Ms. Susan Certaine, begins by diagnosing the problem: they are "filthy with things" (with Freudian anal retentiveness intended) and critically in need of her promised liberating and cleansing organizational services. After making a payment and signing a contract they leave the house while their possessions are inventoried. Marsha is enrolled in a therapy center for acquisitive disorders and Julian in a codependent hostel. When they return in a week, they find their house totally devoid of possessions. Marsha and Julian learn that the contract they signed gives them a 60-day grace period during which they may reclaim up to one item per day from the warehouse where their possessions have been taken. After that the contents will be auctioned off and the proceeds given to charity. Ms. Certaine assures them that many couples feel freed from the burden of their things and never reclaim anything. But she adds with some malice, "This is what it's all about, this—cutting people down to size, squashing them" (p. 62). And Julian concludes as he surveys the noncontents of their

Collectible Investments for the High Net Worth Investor

house, "It is cold out there, inhospitable, alien. There's nothing there, nothing contained in nothing. Nothing at all" (p. 63).

Like Goldilocks visiting the three bears, we are given two extremes here—too much and too little—with the suggestion that there is a golden mean of moderation that lies somewhere in the middle. Yet the story also implies that collecting may become addictive and require all-or-nothing solutions like those of Alcoholics Anonymous and similar programs. Marsha and Julian are co-dependents supporting each other's habits. Furthermore, the description of their collections suggests that there may be something a little ludicrous and shameful in all collecting activity. In my investigations I have run across some collectors and collecting families almost as extreme as Marsha and Julian. But I have also encountered more subtle problems and benefits among the estimated one-third of individuals (O'Brien, 1981) and nearly two-thirds of American households with one or more collectors (Schiffer et al., 1981). In this chapter I discuss both positive and negative aspects of collecting that have emerged in qualitative interviews with collectors and offer an assessment of its personal, interpersonal, and cultural effects.

The data are from observations and in-depth interviews with more than 200 collectors. Most are from the United States and Canada, but 10 are from Europe or Australia. These collectors are a nonrepresentative sample recruited from special collector shows, conventions, and exhibits, from fortuitous encounters, and snowball sampling based upon nominations by other collectors. Thus my findings focus more on detailing the nature of collecting and its impact on collectors and their families than on measuring the prevalence of these effects. Interviews generally lasted one to two hours, typically in the informant's home, and were tape recorded. The analysis was emergent and employed constant comparative method (Glaser and Strauss, 1967). A more complete interpretation of collecting based on these interviews is presented in Belk (1995). While a variety of collectors ranging from children just beginning inexpensive collections to adult collectors of art worth several million dollars were sampled, passionate collectors are probably overrepresented.

The Nature of Collecting

Collecting, defined as "the process of actively, selectively, and passionately acquiring and possessing things removed from ordinary use and perceived as part of a set of nonidentical objects or experiences" (Belk, 1995, p. 67), is an acquisitive, possessive, and materialistic pursuit. It differs from most other types of consumption in the concern for a set of objects, the passion invested in obtaining and maintaining these objects, and the lack of ordinary uses to which these collected objects are put. Thus Marsha's 212 antique oarlocks are not likely to ever again see service in their original functional capacities. This, coupled with the nonidentical uniqueness of objects in a collection, differentiates collecting from hoarding and accumulating. Similarly, the passionate possessiveness of collecting differentiates it from ordinary consumption and from consumer acquisitions where investment is the primary motivation (in which case the objects of investment matter little). Because it involves hunting, searching, or shopping for unique useless objects, collecting is a form of materialistic luxury consumption *par excellence*. It commits the collector to a continuing quest for inessential consumer goods that are removed from any functional capacity they may once have had.

In Clifford's view, collecting is an organized acquisitive obsession: "an excessive, sometimes even rapacious need to *have* [transformed] into rule-governed meaningful desire" (Clifford, 1985, p. 238). In analyzing collector motivations Muensterberger (1994) concludes that collectors seek psychological security due to deep feelings of insecurity from childhood. Based on questionnaire responses, Formanek (1991) finds collecting to be the result of multiple motivations including self expression, sociability, and the search for a sense of personal continuity through a focus on the sorts of objects Pearce (1991) calls souvenirs. And Belk et al. (1991) find that collecting is a form of acquisitiveness legitimized as art or science that provides the collector with an expanded sense of self. To be as pervasive as it is, collecting is likely to serve multiple motives and it is not likely that we can categorically dismiss it as something that is uniformly good or bad. In the next two sections I consider first the problems that collecting may create and then the benefits. In a final section I pull together both sets of concerns in order to offer a net assessment of collecting.

Problems of Collecting

Problems for the Individual

Collectors often refer to themselves, only half in jest, as suffering from a mania, a madness, an addiction, a compulsion, or an obsession. Because collecting is generally a socially approved activity, no one is likely to treat such a confession as stigmatizing in the way that it would be for an alcoholic, a heroin addict, a compulsive gambler, or someone truly believed to be mentally ill. Claiming such an addiction humorously frees collectors of responsibility for their behavior. The majority of collectors who offer such a self-reference are not out of self-control to the point that they cannot help or stop themselves from purchasing ever more objects for their collection. But like much humor there is an uneasy fear behind these self-admissions, for some collectors really are out of control. The most vivid example I have encountered is a dealer and collector of Disney cartoon character replicas who is described in Belk et al. (1988):

> *A recovering polydrug abuser, he described his current collecting behavior as an addiction. He has accumulated a large collection of Mickey Mouse memorabilia, and often obtained his "Mickey fix" (an emic term) in lieu of paying rent or meeting other financial obligations. The thrill of collecting and displaying these objects eventually threatened his well-being, so he stopped collecting "cold turkey" (again an emic term). (p. 549)*

Similarly, Eisenberg (1987) describes a New York area record collector who inherited his parents' 14-room house and a sum of money and spent it all on records, which, as with Julian and Marsha, completely filled the house, including the stove and refrigerator. He exhausted his inheritance and was even without heat in the house, but remained dedicated to his records above all else. But while such fanatical and obsessed collectors do exist and are also the subject of a number of fictional portraits of collectors (e.g., de Balzac, 1968; Chatwin, 1989; Connell, 1974), they are clearly outliers on the scale of collecting passion. For such people collecting is a real problem, as Goldberg and Lewis (1978) explain:

> *Obsessed collectors ... are driven. The acquiring of a certain oil painting or a rare jade carving becomes a matter of life and death. Their obsession overrules every other aspect of their lives and they devote every waking minute to thinking and planning how to obtain the next object for their collection or how to display it. Objects ultimately become more (in this case a narrow range of important than people, and fanatic collectors progressively alienate themselves from friends and family, occasionally even becoming suspicious that others will take away their prized possessions. They tend to withdraw from interpersonal relationships and often do not concern themselves with everyday problems like paying bills or getting the car serviced.* (pp. 94–95)

If there is guilt and a little fear of ludicrousness in all collecting, it seems to be because collectors can see themselves potentially headed in this direction as they become more involved in their collecting. In Ellen's synthesis of the psychoanalytic, anthropological, and Marxian uses of the term, such collections have become a fetish and it is no longer clear whether the collector controls the objects or the objects control the collector (Ellen, 1988).

A more common collecting problem at the individual level is that the collector narrows sources of perceived enjoyment opportunities to those involving the collection. This belief that happiness lies in possessions possession) has been labeled *materialism* (Belk, 1985). This trait has been found to be moderately but significantly correlated with unhappiness (Belk, 1985; Richins and Dawson, 1992) and is defined as:

> *The importance a consumer attaches to worldly possessions. At the highest levels of materialism, such possessions assume a central place in a person's life and are believed to provide the greatest sources of satisfaction and dissatisfaction.* (Belk, 1984, p. 291)

Nevertheless, presumably because a the collector is absorbed with only a narrowly defined range of objects, the collectors to whom I have administered materialism scales have not consistently scored above general population levels of materialism as broadly construed.

Problems for the Household

Even though collections are overwhelmingly individual possessions rather than household possessions, they nevertheless have implications for other household members. For all but the most affluent, the presence of a collector in the household means that money that might otherwise be spent on joint or individual consumption by other family members is spent on the collector and collection. Even if the objects collected are found, there are normally expenses of traveling to obtain specimens, maintaining, storing, and displaying them, acquiring supporting literature and equipment, and participating in activities with other collectors. Nevertheless, the majority of collectors' families "supported their habit" in the codependent sense of Julian in Boyle's (1994) story by understanding the collectors' expenditures, buying them gifts related to the collection, traveling with them, and helping them locate objects for the collection. In cases where both spouses in a household collect (usually different things), they may be abetting one another's addictions in the same way that two alcoholics might. This appeared to be the case with one couple in their sixties whose collections included stamps, Franklin Mint coins, salt cellars, beaded purses, blue plates, deer replicas, Cupid pictures, opera glasses, James Whitcomb Riley leather-bound books, perfume bottles, silver spoons, and figurines of women (Belk et al., 1991).

When collecting acquisitions become undeniably excessive, expenditures on the collection are secreted and became a guilty pleasure. The notion by Mick and DeMoss (1990) of self-gifts applies here, and collections are an important category of such gifts, except that such excessive self-gifts are not acknowledged openly to other family members. One 48-year-old man in fact acquired a double garage full of toy metal vehicles while his wife had only a vague appreciation that he had some little toys in the garage. Danet and Katriel (1986) interviewed a woman who feels guilty because she spends money on a pipe collection that she feels should have been spent on family and household needs. Some collectors keep their collection at their offices in order to hide it from their families. The shame, guilt, and hiding is not much different from that found with pornography collections, at least in earlier times (Kendrick, 1987). Such secrecy and guilt has also been found by O'Guinn and Faber (1989) to characterize compulsive shoppers. Even where the collecting is not done in secret or with shame, it may supplant love of people. For instance, Muensterberger (1994) describes the 19th-century British book collector Sir Thomas Phillips, who solicited his friends in order to find a wife with wealth enough to support his collecting avarice.

While many household expenditures can be anticipated and budgeted, the collector's uncertainty about when a treasured and desired object might be encountered and the fear that if a unique object is not acquired immediately it will be gone forever make budgeting for collections problematic. Some collectors try to always have a reserve of cash "just in case." Because collecting is a competitive activity linked to prestige and feelings of competence, there is always something just out of reach that seems infinitely desirable to the collector. Such a psychology is especially evident at the auctions where many collectibles are sold (Smith, 1989). This creates a tendency to devise ways to buy the unaffordable by cutting back in some other area. While the typical portrait of the hedonistic, materialistic consumer is one of lavish conspicuous consumption, because the collector focuses on a single area of expenditure, lifestyle outside of this consumption area is likely to be disproportionately austere. Thus I have interviewed collectors of automobiles worth several times their annual salary, gun collectors who have sold their vehicles to be able to afford an expensive rifle, and art collectors with paintings worth more than their homes. The reason for these seeming incongruities in lifestyle are found in that portion of the definition of collecting emphasizing that it is a passionate form of consumption. Sometimes this passion becomes all consuming and overrules any rational calculation. At the extreme the collection becomes the highest priority and expenditures within the household are made as if nothing else and no one else mattered.

Another interpersonal problem apart from concerns of money is that the collector necessarily devotes time and affection to the collection that might otherwise be used with family members. It seemed baffling at first that although many collectors had parents who were collectors, they seldom collected the same thing and were often highly reluctant to take over the collection of an elderly or deceased parent. Heirship strategies involving skipping a generation and trying to interest grandchildren rather than children in taking over the collection were sometimes employed by collectors (see Wallendorf and Belk, 1987). It eventually became clear that many children and spouses of collectors viewed the collections as rivals. The last thing they wanted to do was take over the care of these rivals for their loved one's affections. In several literary examples, like *Utz* by Chatwin (1989), *Hunters and Gatherers* by Nicholson (1994), and *The Crying of Lot 49* by Pynchon (1966), the collection stands between two lovers in a modified version of the eternal triangle. And Gelber (1992) also finds cases of collectors whose families resent the love that is spent on the collection rather than the family. Goldberg and Lewis (1978) and Olmsted (1988) report a number of divorces precipitated by collections.

Problems for Society

Although the rise of consumer culture democratized collecting, there is still a dominance by the more economically upscale and by males in most areas of adult collecting. Nearly all Western children collect something and boys and girls are equally likely to collect (although not the same things) until adolescence (e.g., Danet and Katriel, 1989; Katriel, 1988/1989; McGreevy, 1990; Newson and Newson, 1968). Families, schools, and youth organizations all promote collecting as an activity that nourishes desirable habits in children, including selectivity, categorization, acquisition of knowledge, competition, specialization, and focused goal-directed activity. The male dominance that begins in adolescence in many collecting areas may be because men continue to control more financial resources (Rigby and Rigby, 1944), because it allows men to exercise creative potential that women can express more broadly, including via childbirth (Baekeland, 1981), or because it is an aggressive and competitive activity that corresponds more closely with male gender role socialization (Belk and Wallendorf, 1997). The resources explanation also helps explain why collecting continues to be dominated by those with higher incomes. Nevertheless, with the proliferation of collecting into categories ranging from inexpensive seashells, comic books, and beer cans to expensive art, automobiles, and antiquities, there is a wide opportunity to collect something. The sex and class biases found in collecting (not only in who collects, but also in what is collected and the status accorded such collectors) may be seen to recapitulate the biases found in society more generally. In my nonrepresentative sample of collectors, men are much more likely than women to collect automobiles, guns, stamps, antiques, books, beer cans, wines, and sports-related objects, while women are much more likely than men to collect jewelry, housewares such as dishes and silver, and animal replicas. These patterns are supported by other studies of collectors in various specialty areas (e.g., Crispell, 1988; Dannefer, 1980; Gelber, 1992; Olmsted, 1988; Soroka, 1988; Stenross, 1994). In one husband and wife couple studied he collected fire engines, African hunting trophies, and Western American artwork, while she collected mouse replicas. These collections may be thought of as encoding the following dichotomies with the male collection characteristics listed first: gigantic/tiny, strong/weak, world/home, machine/nature, extinguishing/nurturing, science/art, seriousness/playfulness, functional/decorative, conspicuous/inconspicuous, inanimate/animate (after Belk et al., 1991). In addition, the male-dominated collecting areas generally have more to do with active production and the female-dominated collecting areas have more to do with passive consumption. There are exceptions to these generalizations, but gender stereotypes tend to reinforce and be reinforced by collections.

Most areas of popular collecting are dominated by middle income categories, including stamps (Bryant, 1989), baseball cards (Rogoli, 1991), model airplanes (Butsch, 1984), beer cans (Soroka, 1988), and "instant collectibles" such as limited edition plates (Roberts, 1990). But more than 40 percent of both stamp and coin collectors are white collar, managers, or professionals (Crispell, 1988) and fine art collecting is restricted to higher social classes (Marquis, 1991; Moulin, 1987). Bourdieu (1984) attributes this bias not only to income but to "taste cultures" and the possession of "cultural capital" by the dominant social classes, who in turn assure that their children are more likely to possess such knowledge and taste (see also Halle, 1993). Again there are exceptions, but just as other consumer luxury goods act as "marker goods" announcing social class (Douglas and Isherwood, 1979), so do collections. Both because of such bias and the elitist tendency of cultural institutions such as museums and galleries to preserve only the "best," the cultural legacy of collecting is to present a very distorted sample of earlier material cultures, concentrating on only the finest of its luxuries. The democratization of collecting has reduced but hardly eliminated this bias.

The Benefits of Collecting

Although collectors of even such humble objects as beer cans, elephant replicas, and nutcrackers can envision their collections in a museum with a thankful public paying homage to the collector's memory, few private collections enter museums today. This is not to say that collectors do not benefit from believing that they are acting as noble saviors of treasures that would otherwise disappear. Ironically, given that collecting is the quintessence of selfish acquisitiveness and possessiveness, for many collectors collecting is experienced as a self-transcendent passion in which the collected objects become more important than their health, wealth, or inner being. Collecting, in other words, becomes a religion for such collectors, and they envision themselves playing the role of savior of society by preserving all that is noble and good for future generations. A collector of elephant replicas who had opened an "elephant museum" described his expectation that future generations would one day "stand in awe" at what he had been able to accomplish in assembling these replicas.

Most commonly, however, the major benefits accrue to the collector rather than future generations of culture as a whole. In this age of convenience, it is no small miracle that collecting becomes such a labor of love. Purcell and Gould (1992, p. 12) observe that "In an age of passivity, where Walkman and television bring so much to us and demand so little in return, we must grasp the engaging passion of these collectors." For some, collecting provides a sense of purpose and meaning in life (Smith and Apter, 1977). Collecting also may provide a sense of mastery, expertise, and accomplishment that is lacking in the workplace (Belk et al., 1991). Like blue-collar workers' heavy recreational expenditures (Chinoy, 1955), I suspect that many collections are pursued to compensate for a lack of career success and recognition. Collecting adds excitement to life through the thrill of the hunt and the eager anticipation that a coveted acquisition may lie around the next corner. Success in competition with others may provide prestige and status within the world of collecting (Storr, 1983). Collections may literally make us larger people through an extended sense of self (Belk, 1988). And, as Walter Benjamin (1968) illustrated in reflecting on his book collection, collected objects may be cues that recall past collecting activities and contribute to our identities through this sense of past.

Collecting may provide a support system of friends encountered in pursuing the collection (Christ, 1965; Dannefer, 1980; DiMaggio, 1987). One Swedish beer can collector who traveled to annual beer can collecting "canventions" reflected that those he saw once a year at these gatherings were his best friends in the world. Like fellow believers in a religion, fellow collectors share a faith that what they are doing is important. Collecting also does things for us that ordinary consumption cannot. Although collecting provides only the illusion or excuse of investment opportunity for most collectors, other contemporary consumption activity does not even provide that. And by focusing on collecting rather than the fads and fashions of the general consumer marketplace, the collector is opting out of the broader commodity and fashion rat race and instead finding meaning, knowledge, and self through the pursuit of collecting.

Conclusions

As an essentially materialistic activity, collecting is a lens for viewing all luxury consumption more clearly. At the extreme in which collecting becomes an addictive or compulsive activity that the collector hides out of shame, clearly both the collector and his or her family are harmed financially as well as psychologically. Still, society generally regards collecting as less self-indulgent and frivolous than many other forms of consumption. Given that money might be spent on individual travel, clothing, recreation, dining and drinking, or collecting—all luxury expenditures—collecting would generally be judged to be the most serious and least selfish allocation of funds (although not of time).

Collecting is also vaguely believed to be something done in the service of science or art. It enriches the life of the collector and sometimes others as well. The collector is a knowledgeable person with an expertise, no matter how narrow and esoteric. Being able to offer a nomenclature of matchbooks or judge the quality of antique clocks or know the year and circulation of a comic book may be highly specialized skills, but there is no denying that they are skills. Moreover, successful collecting involves a connoisseurship, preservationism, scholarship, daring, perseverance, and judgment that rehearses or parallels traits we generally value in careers and in Western culture generally. And if collecting tends toward a principle of having too many things that have too little use or importance, consider the poverty of "… nothing contained in nothing. Nothing at all" and the possessionless feeling of coldness, alienation, and being squashed found in Boyle's story of Marsha and Julian. Collecting reiterates and exemplifies the values we hold dear as a consumer culture. It is a never-ending search, acquisition, accumulation, and possession of useless things. This fundamental consumerism may well be a deeper reason that we are loath to criticize collecting activity.

However, other than articulating socially valued traits and consumption values, there is little difference between spending money on a collection and spending it on gambling or drugs. Each may be pursued with equal diligence and produce comparable emotional highs. Each may hurt significant others when selfishly pursued with money, time, and attention that might otherwise be lavished upon people rather than things. Such is the dialectical balance that collectors hang in due to the simultaneous potential benefits and problems of collecting. The fact that some collectors find the extent of their collecting embarrassing and capable of producing guilt or shame suggests that we recognize the dark side of our collecting proclivities. Erich Fromm (1976, p. 96) once asked, "If I am what I have and if what I have is lost, who then am I?" Having dealt with several dedicated collectors who have been devastated by the loss of their collections to natural or financial disasters, the answer was clearly, as Julian suggested: nothing at all.

References

Baekeland, F., 1981. Psychological aspects of art collecting, *Psychiatry* 44:45–59.

Belk, R. W., 1984. Three scales to measure materialism: Reliability, validity, and relationships to measures of happiness. In: T. Kinnear (ed.), *Advances in Consumer Research*, pp. 753–760, Association for Consumer Research.

Belk, R. W., 1985. Materialism: Trait aspects of living in the material world, *Journal of Consumer Research* 12:265–280.

Belk, R. W., 1988. Possessions and the extended self, *Journal of Consumer Research* 15:139–168.

Belk, R. W., 1995. *Collecting in a Consumer Society*, Routledge.

Belk, R. W., and M. Wallendorf, 1997. Of mice and men: Gender identity and collecting. In: K. Ames and K. Martinez (eds.), *The Material Culture of Gender; The Gender of Material Culture*, University Press of New England.

Belk, R. W., M. Wallendorf, J. F. Sherry, Jr., and M. B. Holbrook, 1991. Collecting in consumer culture. In: R. Belk (ed.), *Highways and Buyways: Naturalistic Research from the Consumer Behavior Odyssey*, pp. 178–215, Association for Consumer Research.

Belk, R. W., M. Wallendorf, J. F. Sherry, Jr., M. B. Holbrook, and S. Roberts, 1988. Collectors and collections. In: M. Houston (ed.), *Advances in Consumer Research*, pp. 548–553, Association for Consumer Research.

Benjamin, W., 1968. Unpacking my library: A talk about book collecting. In: H. Arendt (ed.), *Illuminations* (H. Zohn, trans.), pp. 59–67, Harcourt, Brace and World (original 1955).

Bourdieu, P., 1984. *Distinction: A Social Critique of the Judgment of Taste* (R. Nice, trans.), Harvard University Press (original 1979, La Distinction: Critique Sociale du Jugement, Paris: Les Editions de Minuit).

Boyle, C. T., 1994. Filthy with things. In: *Without a Hero: Stories* (pp. 41–63), Viking.

Bryant, J., 1989. Stamp and coin collecting. In: T. Inge (ed.), *Handbook of American Popular Culture*, 2nd ed., Vol. 3, pp. 1329–1365, Greenwood Press.

Butsch, R., 1984. The commodification of leisure: The case of the model airplane hobby and industry, *Qualitative Sociology* 7:217–235.

Chatwin, B., 1989. *Utz*, Viking.

Chinoy, E., 1955. *Automobile Workers and the American Dream*, Beacon Press.

Christ, E. A., 1965. The "retired" stamp collector: Economic and other functions of a systematized leisure activity. In: A. M. Rose and W. A. Peterson (eds.), *Older People and Their Social World: The Subculture of Aging*, pp. 93–112, F. A. Davis Company.

Clifford, J., 1985. Objects and selves—An afterword. In: G. W. Stocking, Jr. (ed.), *Objects and Others: Essays on Museums and Material Culture*, pp. 236–246, University of Wisconsin Press.
Connell, E. S., Jr., 1974. *The Connoisseur*, Knopf.
Crispell, D., 1988. Collecting memories, *American Demographics* 60:38–41.
Danet, B., and T. Katriel, 1986. Books, butterflies, and Botticellis: A life-span perspective on collecting, paper presented at the Sixth International Conference on Culture and Communication, Philadelphia, October.
Danet, B. and T. Katriel, 1989. No two alike: The aesthetics of collecting, *Play and Culture* 2:253–277.
Dannefer, D., 1980. Rationality and passion in private experience: Modern consciousness and the social world of old-car collectors, *Social Problems* 27, 392–412.
de Balzac, H., 1968. *Cousin Pons* (H. J. Hunt, trans.), Penguin (original 1848).
DiMaggio, P., 1987. Classification in art, *American Sociological Review* 52:440–455.
Douglas, M., and B. Isherwood, 1979. *The World of Goods: Towards an Anthropology of Consumption*, W. W. Norton.
Eisenberg, E., 1987. *The Recording Angel: Explorations in Phonography*, McGraw-Hill.
Ellen, R., 1988. Fetishism, *Man* 23:213–235.
Formanek, R., 1991. Why they collect: Collectors reveal their motivations. In: F. W. Rudmin (ed.), *To Have Possessions: A Handbook on Ownership and Property*, special issue of *Journal of Social Behavior and Personality* 6:275–286.
Fromm, E., 1976. *To Have or To Be?* Harper & Row.
Gelber, S. M., 1992. Free market metaphor: The historical dynamics of stamp collecting, *Comparative Studies in Society and History* 34:742–769.
Glaser, B. G., and A. L. Strauss, 1967. *The Discovery of Grounded Theory: Strategies for Qualitative Research*, Aldine.
Goldberg, H., and R. T. Lewis, 1978. *Money Madness: The Psychology of Saving, Spending, Loving, and Hating Money*, William Morrow.
Halle, D., 1993. *Inside Culture: Art and Class in the American Home*, University of Chicago Press.
Katriel, T., 1988/1989. *Haxlàfot:* Rules and strategies in children's swapping exchanges, *Research on Language and Social Interaction* 22:157–178.
Kendrick, W., 1987. *The Private Museum: Pornography in Modern Culture*, Viking.
Marquis, A. G., 1991. *The Art Biz: The Covert World of Collectors, Dealers, Auction Houses, Museums, and Critics*, Contemporary Books.
McGreevy, A., 1990. Treasures of children: Collections then and now, or treasures of children revisited, *Early Child Development and Care* 63:33–36.
Mick, D. G. and M. DeMoss, 1990. Self-gifts: Phenomenological insights from four contexts, *Journal of Consumer Research* 17:322–332.
Moulin, R., 1987. *The French Art Market: A Sociological View* (A. Goldhammer, trans.), Rutgers University Press (original 1967, Le Marché de le Peinture en France. Paris: Editions de Minuit).
Muensterberger, W., 1994. *Collecting, An Unruly Passion: Psychological Perspectives*, Princeton University Press.
Newson, J., and E. Newson, 1968. *Four Year Old in an Urban Community*, Aldine.
Nicholson, G., 1994. *Hunters and Gatherers*, Overlook Press.

O'Brien, G., 1981. Living with Collections, *New York Times Magazine*, April 26, Part 2, 25–42.

O'Guinn, T. C., and R. J. Faber, 1989. Compulsive buying: A phenomenological exploration, *Journal of Consumer Research* 16:147–157.

Olmsted, A. D., 1988. Morally controversial leisure: The social world of gun collectors, *Symbolic Interaction* 11:277–287.

Pearce, S., 1991. Collecting reconsidered, In: G. Kavanagh (ed.), *Museum Languages* (pp. 135–153), Leicester University Press.

Purcell, R. W., and S. J. Gould, 1992. *Finders, Keepers: Eight Collectors*, W. W. Norton.

Pynchon, T., 1966. *The Crying of Lot 49*, Jonathon Cape.

Richins, M. L., and S. Dawson, 1992. A consumer values orientation for materialism and its measurement: Scale development and validation, *Journal of Consumer Research* 19:303–316.

Rigby, D., and E. Rigby, 1944. *Lock, Stock and Barrel: The Story of Collecting*, J. B. Lippincott.

Roberts, G., 1990. "A thing of beauty and a source of wonderment": Ornaments for the home as cultural status markers. In: G. Day (ed.), *Readings in Popular Culture: Trivial Pursuits?* pp. 39–47, St. Martin's Press.

Rogoli, B., 1991. Racism in baseball card collecting: Fact or fiction?, *Human Relations* 44, 255–264.

Schiffer, M. B., T. E. Downing, and M. McCarthy, 1981. Waste not, want not: Anethnoarchaeological study of refuse in Tucson, Arizona. In: M. Gould and M. B. Schiffer (eds.), *Modern Material Culture: The Archaeology of Us*, pp. 67–86, Academic Press.

Smith, C. W., 1989. *Auctions: The Social Construction of Value*, Harvester Wheatsheaf.

Smith, K. C. P., and M. J. Apter, 1977. Collecting antiques: A psychological interpretation, *The Antique Collector* 48:64–66.

Soroka, M. P., 1988. In heaven there is no beer, that's why we collect it here. Paper presented at Eighteenth Annual Meeting of the Popular Culture Association, New Orleans.

Stenross, B., 1994. Aesthetics in the marketplace: Collectors in the gun business, *Qualitative Sociology* 17, 29–42.

Storr, A., 1983. The psychology of collecting, *Connoisseur* 213:35–38.

Wallendorf, M., and R. W. Belk, 1987. *Deep Meaning in Possessions: Qualitative Research from the Consumer Behavior Odyssey*, video, Marketing Science Institute.

Part Two

Major Collectibles Related to Investing

5 An Overview of the Art Market

Jeffrey E. Horvitz

-Moreland Management Company

Introduction

Although there certainly is a market for art, there is no homogenous art market similar to the public securities markets—that is, a broad-based, consistent trading market. Public market securities are bought and sold for the sole purpose of making a profit, whereas the art market is a fluid mix of buyers and sellers, most of whom probably do not have profit as a motivation. Investing in art, meaning to hold it solely for future appreciation rather than dealing in art (buying at wholesale and selling at retail), is a minor part of the overall market. The art market is highly fragmented into specialty areas, each of which has its own value criteria and its own community of interested buyers and sellers.

If you are new to a specialty area, you are unlikely to be able to quickly learn all the nuances of what is desirable and what sets value. The intermediary costs can be daunting; they include exceedingly high commissions plus marketing, insurance, shipping and storage, preservation and restoration, taxes, and the associated travel costs of finding works of art to buy and clients to whom to sell. There is no way to buy a low-cost passive index of the "market," as one can with stocks and bonds, and it is very hard to diversify. To the extent that some works of art can qualify as investments, the investor needs to be fully aware of the hurdles to making a profit.

Despite all the high-profile stories in the press about astronomical prices being paid for a few select works of art, many of these were not good investments, and they are out of range for the vast majority of private investors. Art is such a specialty financial activity that it is impractical for those who might have enough money but do not have enough understanding or expertise. The insiders have a definite advantage because price information is highly asymmetrical, although this has been improved with Web-based auction result databases, particularly those with images.

To explain why the art world is difficult investment terrain, this chapter attempts an overview of the scope, structure, and mechanisms in the art market

Collectible Investments for the High Net Worth Investor

and summarizes the barriers to profitable investing. For those still undeterred, the end of the chapter summarizes some possible investment strategies.

How Are Works of Art Different from Stocks, Bonds, and Commodities?

Stocks represent an ownership interest in the profits and value of an enterprise, whereas bonds represent a claim on an ascertainable amount secured by all or some of its assets. Publicly traded stocks and bonds have very broad markets with many buyers for every security with significant market capitalization, and they are highly liquid, with prices that are public and well understood. For any particular issue, buyers and sellers can deal with fungible quantities. Publicly traded securities can be traded in minutes or seconds.

Art is completely different. A work of art generates no further change in its own value and in that way is like most commodities, that is, its value is solely a function of supply and demand. But unlike commodities that have broad markets because the commodities are generally fungible, most works of art, being unique, have a very small number of interested buyers at any point in time. It is not unusual at auction for a work of art to have no bids at any price or just a single buyer bidding against the *reserve*, the minimum price acceptable to the seller. By law, as with New York auctions, or by industry practice, the reserve price does not exceed the low estimate. Typically, the reserve will be set about 20% below the low estimate, but not necessarily, and some lots will have no reserve.

Many record prices are achieved simply by a bidding war between two, and only two, buyers at stratospheric prices. Though there is some degree of substitution in the art world—for example, similar works by a given artist might be of interest to the same group of buyers—it is impossible to replicate the characteristics of the fungible commodity markets. Art can remain for sale for years before a buyer is found. Even selling at public auction requires a lead time of months for a place in a scheduled sale because appropriate topical or specialty sales generally occur only a few times a year. It would seem impossible to create derivatives for works of art, although it might be possible to create derivatives for indices of works of art.

Because the art market is dominated by museums and private collectors, not investors and speculators, the market value might not reflect any net present value of a particular piece, whereas in the public securities markets there are no buyers who purchase solely for the pleasure of owning the asset. Artwork, being unique, cannot be divided, and most of the artwork suitable for investment is high priced; this rules out a broad-based market of small transactions. Each specialty field has factors and weightings of factors that establish value, but these are usually highly specific to the specialty. A novice will not have the experience or expertise to understand why two pieces, seemingly similar, can command wildly different prices. Often the important differences are very subtle to the untrained. In economic terms, art has high model uncertainty in that the relevant participants do not have a clear shared model as to how to value a particular work of art and do not always assess the factors the same way, so valuation can be very subjective. Contrast this with the pricing of bonds, where if one knows only the credit quality, the maturity, and the slope of the yield curve, one knows precisely the value of the bond.

For art, the asking price itself functionally carries information about the subjective value, but it is an unreliable indicator. Auction house estimates can have an effect on the perception of value and can be used as a marketing device. McAndrew (2007) found that auction estimates were generally unbiased, although not necessarily accurate for any particular work, but part of this could be the influence of the estimate on the final price, although estimates that are too high can discourage any bidding at all. A dealer's asking price can say as much about the dealer's overhead, operating margin, and clientele as about the current market value of the work of art itself. Because works are essentially unique and often not easily comparable to other works, pricing can be very subjective and inefficient. Two dealers with essentially similar works can ask wildly different prices. It is not unusual to see a piece in thc hands of a swank dealer at double the price that was being asked by a small dealer who had the piece but was unable to sell it.

Because dealers often sell to each other, the same work of art can escalate in price simply moving between art galleries. Some dealers might have the clientele and reputation that allow them to ask, and receive, substantially more than could be obtained by another dealer. For example, Dutch Old Master paintings in the hands of the top dealers in that field would typically sell for much more than the same painting in the hands of a dealer in modern art or even a dealer in Italian Old Master paintings. Many buyers would be shocked to find that these interdealer pricing differences or anomalies can routinely reach magnitudes of double or even triple from one seller to another.

What Is the Size of the Art Economy?

Accurate estimates of worldwide art sales are necessarily difficult to obtain, particularly for sales outside public auctions, but most sources that hazard an estimate seem to put the size in the range of $40 billion to $70 billion, placing it larger than the revenues of all but the top 40 or even top 25 of publicly traded U.S. corporations. The size of the art market has roughly doubled in the past seven years. McAndrew (2007) estimates 2006 sales at 50 billion, split approximately 50/50 between dealers and auctions, although she estimates decorative art sales split between dealers and auctions at 70/30. She puts Sotheby's and Christie's, which dominate the auction market, at 46% of the auction total, or approximately 23% of worldwide sales, split fairly equally between them. Of fine arts sales, Sotheby's and Christie's reported combined 2007 sales of about $12 billion, of which about 80% and 69%, respectively, were fine art sales (Kinsella, 2008). Because dealer sales are largely unreported, it is possible that the total market and the dealer share are larger than most estimates.

Auction revenues are dominated by 20th- and 21st-century art, which generally commands the highest prices. The U.S. market dominates geographically, with most observers estimating year-to-year fluctuations, depending on economic conditions and currency exchange rates, of a 40–50% global market share. Europe follows as the next most important market, although it is hard to be precise as to which country is at the top, because the country where a purchase is made might not match the country of the purchaser.

What is truly astonishing is the number of buyers worldwide who are able and willing to spend significant amounts of money to buy art. It is now common, particularly for auction sales of modern and contemporary art, European Old Master paintings, and Chinese art, to see many pieces sell in the seven- and even eight-figure range, with dozens of pieces selling in the six-figure range per auction. Over the course of a year of auction sales, there must be thousands of buyers willing to spend more money on a single piece of art than is earned by upper middle-class professionals in a year.

Several factors seem to be driving this phenomenon. Global wealth has expanded and spread across many countries, including many of the developing market economies. Similar to the globalization of luxury goods, information about the art market has become widely available through the media, and taste has become more international. It is common for the financial press to carry frequent articles about the art market, particularly auction sales, even though the art market is a miniscule portion of the global economy. It is a subject that appeals to the readership of the financial press and is of general interest, much like celebrity gossip.

The nature of wealth has also changed, with relatively high mobility (economic and geographic) and much higher amounts of personal liquidity. Whereas in earlier times the ultra-wealthy often owned capital-intensive businesses or land, many of today's ultra-wealthy, such as hedge fund managers, earn fantastic sums using other people's money, so they have extremely high levels of personal liquidity with which to indulge themselves.

It is no longer newsworthy for a painting of modest quality by a big-name artist to sell for more than $1 million. The buyer base is more diverse and less subject to economic shock and dislocation than probably at any other time in the history of the art market, and there is little reason to think this trend will abate any time soon.

What Constitutes a Work of Art?

A longstanding philosophical question is, what makes something "art"? This is a vexing problem that resides as much in the eye of the beholder as it does in the object itself. Some examples will give a feel for the question.

Almost all the major museums that have general collections have displays of African art, but there is little evidence that most of these objects we revere today were conceived as works of art in their own right. Pieces used in most rituals were discarded when they had lost their magical power and simply rotted away. In other words, pieces that were neither conceived nor intended as works of art nor viewed as such in their original context are now considered art. The production of Vietnamese ceramics of the 14th and 15th centuries, emulating Chinese porcelain styles, was a large-scale industry, with cargo shipments numbering in the hundreds of thousands of pieces per vessel sent as far away as Japan and the Middle East. Not much has survived of what must have been annual production of millions of units. Yet museums with Asian collections display these ceramics as works of art. American folk art such as quilts, weather vanes, shop signs, and cigar store Indians that originally had utilitarian and commercial functions are now bought and sold as works of art, transcending the classification of antiques. One of the most famous works of art in the 20th century is Marcel Duchamp's urinal, titled *Fountain*, signed "R. Mutt" and exhibited on its back. In a BBC survey of 500 art experts it was judged the most influential work of art of the 20th century. Two of the most striking and popular objects in the Museum of Modern Art in New York City are a 1963 Jaguar XKE roadster and a 1945 Bell-47D1 helicopter.

All these examples constitute "works of art" by a type of consensus, at least among experts and connoisseurs of art, yet they involve objects that were commercial, utilitarian, sometimes mass produced, and not necessarily beautiful or even attractive. Analogous to the struggle to define pornography in the famous 1964 quote of U.S. Supreme Court Justice Potter Stewart—"But I know it when I see it ..."—art is not always immediately recognizable as such, and its value depends on some sort of consensus among the relevant observers as to what is and what is not art. Remarkably, within any specialty field or category, that consensus exists. This consensus involves a type of community standard, but one in which the "community" is the community of interest for particular classes of objects that are grouped by the affinity of the interested buyers as much as by the intrinsic characteristics of the objects.

Museums do much to inform us as to what art is, and most museum curators are very open to an expansive definition, albeit one that involves some emphasis on the uniqueness of the artistic image as made by the artist. The opinions of curators and scholars in the museum world provide valuable guidance as to what is and what is not art. Yet, prior to the 20th century it was not unusual for Western museums to use copies—for example, plaster casts of Roman sculpture—as perfectly acceptable substitutes for the real thing, the original object. The Cast Courts at the Victoria and Albert Museum still have many copies on display.

A working definition of what constitutes art is any object that is judged to have substantial artistic merit by the community of interest that participates in the study, display, and collecting of objects of the same category. Note that this definition does not involve considerations of function (or lack of function), beauty, value, or intention as to its creation.

What Constitutes "Investible Art"?

A definition of *investible art* builds on this general definition of art. Investible art must have certain characteristics that allow pieces to be transacted. The object must be readily identifiable to the buyers and sellers for whom it is a relevant transaction and have characteristics that can be valued by reference to basic characteristics. For example, two pieces of Chinese jade that are essentially similar in size, jade quality, and subject, but one is Ming and one is Qing period, will have different market values. Unlike financial instruments, real estate, or businesses, works of art are market valued based on comparable objects rather than on discounted cash flow or replacement value.

Market participants practically define which works are investible. The two global auction houses, Sotheby's and Christie's, dominate the art market as a duopoly. Table 5.1 lists all Sotheby's and Christie's sales categories that prima-

Table 5.1 Major Auction House Sales Categories

Sotheby's	Christie's
Ancient and Ethnographic Arts	
Aboriginal Art	African and Oceanic Art
African and Oceanic Art	Ancient Art (Antiquities)
American Indian Art	American Indian Art
Antiquities	Australian Art
Islamic Art	Islamic Art
Pre-Columbian Art	Oceanic Art
	South African Art (Modern and Contemporary)
Asian Art	
Chinese Ceramics and Works of Art	Asian Contemporary and Chinese 20th-century Art
Chinese Classical and Modern Paintings	Chinese Art (20th century)
Chinese Contemporary Art	Chinese Ceramics and Works of Art
Indian and Southeast Asian Art	Chinese Classical & Modern Paintings
Japanese Art	Indian and Southeast Asian Art
Korean Art	Indian Art (Modern and Contemporary)
Southeast Asian Paintings	Japanese Art
	Korean Art
	Southeast Asian (and Indian Art)
	Southeast Asian Modern and Contemporary Art

Table 5.1 (*Continued*)

Sotheby's	Christie's
Books	
Medieval Illuminated Manuscripts	Books and manuscripts
	Manuscripts
Ceramics and Glass	
Ceramics and Glass	Ceramics and Glass (European)
	Glass
	Porcelain
Decorative Arts	
19th-century Furniture, Sculpture, and Decorative Works of Art	American Folk Art, Antique Decoys
20th-century Decorative Arts and Design	Furniture, Decorative Objects, and Early Sculpture (European)
American Furniture, Decorative Works of Art, and Folk Art	Furniture, Sculpture, and Works of Art (19th century)
European Furniture	Sculpture (Early European)
European Sculpture and Works of Art	Sculpture (19th century)
French and Continental Furniture, Decorations, and Tapestries	
Judaica	
Paintings, Drawings, and Sculpture	
19th-century European and British Paintings	American Art
20th-century British Art	Arab and Iranian Art (Modern and Contemporary)
American Paintings, Drawings, and Sculpture	Austrian Art
Australian Art	British and Irish Art
British Drawings, Watercolors, and Portrait Miniatures	British Art (20th century)
British Paintings 1500–1850	British Art on Paper
Canadian Art	Contemporary Art
Contemporary Art	Decorative Art and Design (20th century)
Fine Arts	European Art (19th century)
German and Austrian Art	German and Austrian Art
Greek Paintings and Sculpture	Greek Art
Impressionist and Modern Art	Impressionist and Modern Art
Irish Art	Iranian and Arab Art (Modern and Contemporary)
Israeli and International Art	Irish Art
Latin American Art	Latin American Art

Table 5.1 Major Auction House Sales Categories (*Continued*)

Sotheby's	Christie's
Marine Paintings and Nautical Works of Art	Maritime Pictures
Old Master Drawings	19th-Century European Art
Old Master Paintings	Nordic Art and Design
Orientalist Paintings	Old Master Drawings
Scandinavian Paintings	Old Master Paintings
Scottish Art	Orientalist Art
Spanish Paintings	Portrait Miniatures
Sporting Art	Post-War and Contemporary Art
Swiss Art	Scottish Art
Victorian and Edwardian Art	Spanish Art
	Sporting Art
	Swiss Art
	Travel Art
	20th-Century British Art
	Victorian and Traditionalist Pictures
Photographs	
Photographs	Photographs
Prints	
Old Master, Modern, and Contemporary Prints	Posters
Prints	
Silver, Russian and Vertu	
American Silver	Fabergé
English and European Silver and Vertu	Icons
Russian Paintings, Works of Art, Fabergé, and Icons	Russian Pictures, Works of Art, and Fabergé
Silver	

rily sell works of art. The clustering of works in each category is done by functional groups where the demand is sufficiently high to allow targeted sales and where there is sufficient supply to populate a sales catalogue with objects desirable to the marketplace. Unlike the stock market, not all the buyers and sellers in the art world are investors; in fact, investors are probably a minority, even if one includes dealers in the count. Both auction houses hold specialty sales of items that are not necessarily works of art—books and manuscripts, ceramics and glass, collectibles and memorabilia, furniture and decorative arts, fashion, jewelry, musical instruments, stamps, coins and medals, watches and clocks, and wine—but in many of these nonart collectible categories there *are* works of art, often very expensive ones. For example, ceramics and glass auctions might group together antiques such as Wedgwood with art pottery such as pieces by Lucy Rie or Hamada Shoji. Books and manuscripts might include books illustrated by artists such as Matisse or medieval illuminated manuscripts. Jewelry sales can include pieces now considered works of art—for example, Art Nouveau designs by René Lalique. There are "art" categories that can include objects that have limited artistic merit and would not be of interest to most museums, yet that have a strong following, such as sporting art or marine paintings and nautical works. Generally, the auction houses have arranged their categories along various criteria, such as medium (silver, paintings, drawings, ceramics, etc.), subject matter (sporting art, maritime), and national or regional origins (Scandinavian art, aboriginal art, African and Oceanic art), period or epoch (antiquities), or even religious affiliation (Judaica, Islamic art). To an outsider this world might look chaotic and without a logically consistent taxonomy, but in fact the art market organizes itself very much according to supply-and-demand relationships that are manifest through types of affinities of interest as self-defined by the market participants.

No definition of "investible art" can be absolutely precise, and it is as likely to fail at the margins by both what it includes and what it excludes. However, some practical components might be:

- It must by recognizable by typical buyers and sellers in its category.
- It must be of the type and quality sold by the leading auction houses.
- It must of a quality level suitable for at least a small or university museum.
- It must be of a type routinely handled by more than a trivial number of dealers.
- The transaction, transportation, and storage costs must be reasonable relative to the value of the object.

What Are the Components of Value?

Art certainly has similarities with luxury goods in that it confers status and provides pleasure in sheer ownership. However, there are clear distinctions, including those articulated by U.S. Federal tax court cases, such as the distinction between gold bullion and numismatic coins, the former of which was valued and traded as a commodity and the latter valued for their rarity, artistic interest, and collectability. In other words, the purpose for which the thing is transacted and the criteria by which it is valued make art different from general luxury goods.

The main components of value that contribute to price are described in the following subsections.

Scarcity

Generally, rare objects are more desirable than plentiful objects. This is a straightforward reflection of the law of supply and demand; however, the market value of scarcity in many cases seems to be more than just supply and demand, including a type of implied premium whereby the scarcity is valued for its own sake as a quality. *Uniqueness* is related to scarcity, although things that are too unique, that is, atypical, might actually have relatively less value. The Guennol Lioness, a stone carving only a few inches high from an obscure ancient culture, sold at Sotheby's for $57 million in 2007; it was unique and of sublime quality. It was obviously scarce, but by itself that does not explain the extraordinary price. The works of a number of important artists whose drawings are scarce, such as Nicolas Plattemontagne (French), Corrado Giaquinto (Italian), and Bartolome Esteban Murillo (Spanish), sell for relatively modest prices. Picasso, an extraordinarily prolific artist, is hardly scarce, yet even his abundant late works, even those of questionable quality, fetch significant prices. Scarcity, per se, is not a driver of value. Scarcity probably has an enhancing effect on value, mostly when there is either the perception that the work is a masterpiece or where there is significant demand from a highly knowledgeable market of buyers.

Subject and Color

Attractive subjects are more highly valued than unattractive subjects, although in modern and contemporary art that principle can be turned upside down. Generally, nude women are more salable than nude men, but in 18th-century portraits men are often more valuable than women, and the same is usually true of Ingres's portrait drawings (the main reason is that until the 20th century, men were depicted with more character than women, who were more idealized, and this psychological aspect appeals more to our current taste). Flowers are more salable than dead animals. Religious subject matter is generally less desirable than secular subject matter, and New Testament subjects generally will be less valuable than Old Testament subjects. Certain colors are more desirable than others—for example, red and blue will generally dominate yellow and green. An extreme example of this was the commoditized market for Joseph Albers paintings of colored squares within squares in the late 1970s, when these paintings were used to circumvent currency export restrictions in Italy. Paintings were selling for prices based solely on size (proportionate to the dimension of one side) and colors. There were premiums of approximately 20% for all-red or all-blue paintings, with lesser premiums for all-green and all-yellow; but mixed colors of the squares, such as brown, orange, and green, sold at a discount.

Recognizability

To the extent that art is purchased for prestige and social status, it is important that it be recognizable to one's peers. An Andy Warhol, Roy Lichtenstein, Willem de Kooning, or Jackson Pollack is easily recognizable to the general art public, whereas identifying the artist for an Old Master painting might be difficult even for experts. Recognizability also relates to liquidity in that the more recognizable an object is, the broader the market. As Picasso did many times, an artist can change styles but remain recognizable. This feature of immediate identification by others is an important feature in the high value of modern and contemporary works of art; consequently, buyers tend to want iconic works.

Status

Certain types of objects have higher prestige than others, and the degree of the prestige might be related to the social circumstances of the owner. As the sociologist/economist Thorstein Veblen recognized in *Theory of the Leisure Class* (1994), expensive art can be a way of displaying wealth, social status, power, and prestige. At the end of the 19th century and into the early 20th century, America's wealthiest industrialists were keen to display their wealth, power, and culture. British portraits were very fashionable because they implied a linkage to an aristocratic lineage and sense of culture. Many then-fashionable paintings, such as Barbizon landscapes, later became unfashionable, and some might still not have recovered their peak value in real terms. In today's art world the highest prestige comes from iconic works by key Impressionist and 20th-century artists such as Monet, Renoir, Picasso, Matisse, Pollack, de Kooning, and Warhol. All these artists' works are easily recognizable and convey prestige by association, showing the owner to be a person of wealth and culture. The current contemporary art market is similar except that instead of prestige being conveyed by association with an illustrious and aristocratic ancestry, the key criterion is to be seen as *avant garde*, cool, trendy, in the know, and ahead of the curve.

Liquidity

A vibrant market requires buyers and sellers—the more activity, the more liquidity. Generally, this enhances the value of works of art. The works of Picasso, who was a prolific artist, are also among the most expensive. His works have a high degree of liquidity because there are many buyers and many sellers who provide constant opportunities for transactions. On the other hand, Khmer bronzes or Burgundian Gothic sculptures, which are relatively scarce, do not generally command stratospheric prices. Here the number of buyers is limited, as are the number of pieces on the market at any one time. In the case of Picasso, there are scores of dealers who transact his works; in the case of Khmer bronzes or Burgundian Gothic sculptures, very few dealers have the knowledge or interest.

Provenance

Provenance is the history of ownership. Years ago this was not an important factor in valuation, but today for many objects the legal status of prior ownership affects its value. Art that might have been transacted under duress during the Holocaust or looted from the temples around Angkor Wat is tainted in the marketplace. Various international and domestic laws specifically affect other works of art, including those of Native American objects, Khmer stone sculpture, Egyptian works of art, and particularly all other antiquities that do not have clear legal title and export permits. The issue of provenance are beyond the scope of this chapter, but it is a growing issue in the art market. Types of artwork, particularly antiquities, where legal title is affected by national or international patrimony laws transact for much higher prices when good provenance and clear legal title are clearly established. Countries such as Egypt and Italy, which are very aggressive in making claims on works thought to have been removed illegally, have caused the market for otherwise similar objects to become two-tiered in value, where objects with good provenance command substantial premiums.

An illustrious provenance can also confer prestige to the object and the new owner, which also enhances the relative value. Art that has been owned by celebrities, famous historical personages, or important collectors can command extraordinary premiums. Examples include the sale of David Rockefeller's Rothko for almost $73 million and the jewelry given by Edward VIII of England to Wallis Simpson; these were sold at auction for prices far in excess of what similar pieces without the illustrious history would have realized.

Related to provenance is freshness to the market, the opposite of which is a "burned" picture. Auction experts generally believe that for a work to get a premium for being fresh to the market, it should not have been for sale for at least the last 10 years and preferably much longer. A painting that has been offered at auction or widely offered privately but has not sold is much harder to sell than a nearly identical work fresh to the market. This is partly the folklore of the market, but it also is related to pricing model uncertainty discussed elsewhere in this chapter.

Publication

Works of art that have been published are generally more valuable than those that have not. Publication helps establish authenticity and provides an imprimatur of quality, whether or not it's deserved. Works of art, where there is a lot of published material of similar pieces, also benefit from this availability of information because it helps to validate the quality. One of the strengths of the 20th- and 21st-century markets is the wide availability of published information, including extensive descriptions, photographs, indisputable provenance, and clear authenticity.

Works of an artist with a *catalogue raisonée* (a listing of the all known works by the artist) are much more easily transacted than works of art without similar documentation; however, some *catalogues raisonée* might not be accurate or are even intentionally wrong by including misattributed pieces as though to financially benefit the owner. Pieces that have been published in museum catalogues are also more valuable because such publication confirms authenticity and carries scholarly approval implied by the publication. Works illustrated on the cover of a book or auction catalog get a premium value.

Size (transportability, storage, display)

In general, larger works are more valuable than smaller works, but this relationship is not exact and not without many exceptions. Paintings are two dimensional, but any size-to-value relationship is more likely to be based on the lineal dimensions rather than proportional to the surface area. Often artists will execute their most important work on a relatively larger scale, so size can be a surrogate for quality or importance. Rubens had a pricing system of various factors, one of which was size.

Works of art that are too big to be displayed in a home setting generally will have less value than other works, but below that threshold larger works generally are more valuable than smaller ones. Museums often prefer larger works because of the way their visitors view them, but not too large so that they become a problem to hang or to store. Works of art that are extremely large, as is the case for many contemporary works, have only a limited market. A very large outdoor sculpture that requires heavy equipment to move and install means a limited market, and in some cases sculpture does not sell in the secondary market for very much more than the fabrication and installation costs. Size, weight, and bulk can also affect shipping costs, which often means that markets dealing in things like antique furniture require larger margins than works such as drawings or prints on paper, which are generally lightweight, small, and easily stored.

Affinity (nationalism and ethnic preferences)

Much of the art world pricing is driven by feelings of nationalism or its equivalent along ethnic lines. An example is the American 19th-century art market, where American Impressionist painters whose quality is often inferior to the best French Impressionist painters still command staggering prices because American buyers are very wealthy and numerous, relative to the supply. Although American 19th-century paintings are extremely expensive, there is almost no demand for them outside the United States, meaning that with a finite supply all the change in demand is homegrown.

As some of the emerging economies, such as China, Russia, and India, have become much more prosperous and have developed a class of extremely wealthy potential buyers, prices have been soaring for works of art that reflect their national heritage and even more for the leading contemporary artists that reflect cultural competitiveness. When an economy is emerging with a rapidly developing ultra-high net worth class, it is a good bet that the price of the art that reflects the nationalism of that country will rise along with it. In recent years the Latin American and Asian modern art markets have reflected the ups and downs of the macroeconomic conditions in those regions.

Currency

Because so much of the demand for art is among end users such as collectors and museums, the currency exchange relative to the buyer and the seller can make a substantial difference in how attractive the price is in the home currency of the buyer. For art that has demand across multiple currencies, this can be a very important factor, because works in near-universal demand, such as Picassos, can become more or less expensive, in home currency terms, solely based on changes in the currency exchange rates. To an extent, art will become priced to the strongest currency. However, because the United States represents such a large percentage of the art market, the relative value of the dollar will be paramount for most submarkets. Dealers will often take currency into consideration when purchasing for inventory, because they have to anticipate into which market the particular work will likely be sold and how the price will appear in the buyer's home currency.

Quality

The affirmation of experts, including critics, curators, and scholars, is very important to value. Works similar or related to works in museums are easier to sell and of relatively higher value. Reviews by critics can make or break a show of a contemporary artist. Even theory can affect value. The critic Clement Greenberg became enamored of the Washington color field painters, such as Morris Louis, Kenneth Noland, and Jules Olitski, and helped make them highly salable and very valuable. After his death, as his influence waned, their market values plummeted. Interestingly, "quality"—although seemingly subjective and ineffable—seems to have a high degree of agreement among the *cognoscenti* of the art world. In social science terms, there seems to be a high level of interobserver reliability in that a group of experts will generally share a common assessment of the "quality" of any particular work of art. Art historical importance can be a part of quality but might have comparatively more relevance to museums than collectors.

Condition

Many buyers of art are inadequately attentive to the physical condition of the pieces. For modern and contemporary pieces, current condition is relatively obvious, although there could be long-term issues with novel media and how they will hold up. In areas such as Old Master paintings, condition cannot be assessed simply by looking at the surface. Some paintings that look to be in poor condition are simply in need of new varnish, whereas other paintings that look pristine have undergone massive restoration that is only visible under ultraviolet light. Many three-dimensional objects have restoration that is hard to detect by the untrained eye and can even fool experts. However, physical condition can be a very important aspect of value and is not readily discerned from photographs or the online database services such as ArtNet, making it difficult to understand price differentials when comparing images only.

Authenticity and attribution

Outright fakes are a concern outside of modern and contemporary art, although there are fakes even in these areas. Some of the most treacherous types of art in this regard are Pre-Columbian, Chinese jade, tribal art (particularly African), and Chinese tomb terracotta. Some dealers believe that there are cottage industries creating fake objects of these types and that possibly 80–90% of what is coming onto the market is fake, although very hard to detect.

Related to fakes is *misattribution*, whether intentional or inadvertent. *Attribution* refers to the identification of the artist or the period of a work of art. Even scholars and other experts in a field might make an attribution (or reject an attribution) only to later have a change of opinion. Dealers and auction houses have a financial incentive to go with the most favorable attribution. For example, a piece of Chinese cloisonné that might be Ming or Qing period would likely be presented as just the earlier and more valuable Ming.

Old Master paintings and drawings that could be by an important artist and his studio are simply given to the artist without acknowledging studio participation. Some experts are overly accepting of works that plausibly, but not definitively, can be attributed to a valuable artist. The more sure the attribution and the more definite the authenticity, the more relatively valuable will be the work of art.

How Does the Principle of Supply and Demand Operate in the Art Market?

With only a few important exceptions, supply is fixed at any point in time and generally declines over time. The reason for the decline is that works of art can be damaged, lost, destroyed, or purchased by museums, never to come on the market again. The important exceptions to this type of supply constraint are new discoveries and contemporary art. In the case of new discoveries, there are occasions when a cache of works of art hitherto unknown or unrecognized shows up on the market. When this happens there is often an increase in demand due to the excitement or interest generated by new material, but this excitement can be offset if the supply is too large to be quickly absorbed by the interested buyers. Supply can be added or removed by reattribution, as was the case with Matisse drawings discovered to be by the notable forger Elmyr de Hory. Supply in the antiquities market can be increased by looting of archeological sites, but the marketable supply has been reduced by enforcement of national patrimony laws.

Changes in demand are driven mostly by changes in taste and perception, which include the active reprioritization of interest among museums and collectors. It is not unusual to see a type of social contagion of interest among museums in certain selected artists and types of works of art; for example, drawings by the French artist Jean-Baptiste Greuze quickly ended up on the priority wish list of one U.S. museum after another with no particular change in scholarship for this artist as curators watched what other curators were doing. In the past decade, European Neoclassical paintings, drawings, and sculpture also became of high interest among many museums for no apparent reason except a type of social contagion within the museum world. This spurred additional interest among collectors, making Neoclassical works of art much more expensive as demand shifted against a limited supply. Similar contagion effects have occurred with 19th-century Scandinavian paintings and *en plein air* European paintings from the second decade of the 19th century. As would be expected, the new demand increased prices, and new supply started appearing more frequently on the market, albeit at higher prices.

Where prices have become very high for very limited supply—of, for example, French Impressionist paintings or key 19th-century American paintings—the market will reach down toward lesser artists and works of the same type, creating both a new taste and a new demand, which raises prices for what were formerly considered midrange works. School of Paris and minor Impressionist artists that were rarely seen at major auctions because Impressionist and Post-Impressionist paintings of high quality were available are now bringing six-figure prices. Similarly, some American 19th-century artists who were virtually unknown to the auction markets, and even to art history books, command substantial prices as fine works because the luminaries of that period are nearly unavailable or priced out of the reach of most collectors and even most museums. In other words, as these goods become scarce, consumers find substitutions, and that new demand drives up the price of the substitute goods. When prices rise high enough, owners take notice and a new supply comes into the market; this can have the effect of broadening the interest base (aggregate demand), which eventually runs up against relatively finite absolute supply.

The field of contemporary art is different in that the energetic and booming market for works of the present time and high prices for very young and often untested artists has created an industry that virtually eclipses the entire Old Masters market. There are scores of dealers just in the Chelsea section of New York City who are devoted to newly produced art, while the number of Old Masters dealers in all of New York is probably fewer than two dozen. Because the supply of contemporary art is somewhat elastic, high prices and high levels of market activity induce artists to produce quantities to meet this demand. One can expect both supply and demand for contemporary art to grow significantly in emerging economies that transition toward developed economies.

Who Are the Buyers, Sellers, and Intermediaries?

There are several categories of buyers and sellers, including collectors, museums, investors, dealers, and auction houses. There are also buyers who will purchase works of art, sometimes at astonishing prices, who are not collectors per se but who are buying works of art as decoration without the intention of further purchases, often on the advice of interior decorators; this is likely an underestimated category.

Collectors

Collectors tend to be very focused on particular works of art that represent their taste and to some extent are public reflections of their selves. In many cases, a collector will be willing to buy a particular work of art but might not accept a substitute simply because it is nearly as good, approximately similar, or at a lower price. Collectors are often passionate about their purchases and often will pay more than what a purely rational buyer would pay for fair market value. There are numerous instances of collectors in the heat of bidding at auction far exceeding their maximum price, and many private buyers simply have no clear maximum price in mind when they enter the auction room.

There are also many collectors who feel uncomfortable negotiating with dealers and who either pay what is asked or simply walk away empty handed. Collectors are mostly reluctant sellers, particularly because they can feel strong attachments to the pieces in their collections. Motivations for selling include creating liquidity to trade up to a better piece, trimming an overly large number of pieces to a more manageable level, or perceiving a selling opportunity that is too good to pass up. At the upper end of the market, some collectors employ the services of art advisors who help them locate, select, and negotiate their purchases; this is a growing part of the business and is of interest to private banking establishments that cater to the very wealthy.

Museums

Museums are usually focused buyers, yet it is not unusual to see very idiosyncratic purchases due to the importance of the individual curator's tastes in selecting specific purchases. For museums the process of getting approval is often slow and multilayered, requiring curatorial approval, the approval of the director, and, often, additional approvals by a collection committee and the board of trustees; consequently they are not as able to take advantage of a "good deal" as private buyers might and will usually pay a premium price for works that they want. Although museums do not like to overpay, the decision process as to how much to pay can represent the amount of funding available more than a specific concern about fair value. It is not unusual for a museum to purchase a work from a dealer just after an auction but at a substantial markup, even if the museum knew of the auction in advance. In large part this is due to the cumbersome purchase approval process involving many sign-offs.

Most museums today can no longer seriously compete for pieces at the top end of the market simply because they do not have the ability to pay the millions or tens of millions of dollars now required for the most expensive works. To add these works to their collections, museums must rely on donors for specific pieces. What this means is that museums generally play an important direct financial role—not at the top of the art market for the finest and most expensive pieces but in the next tier below, but this adds to the liquidity and stability of the upper-middle range.

Museums are generally reluctant to sell works (a process called *deaccessioning*), but it does happen. Usually only lesser works or items that were received as parts of bulk donations or works that do not fit the mandate of the museum get sold, although there have been some high-profile exceptions where important pieces have been sold, particularly to further upgrade or diversify the collections by buying works deemed more desirable. The Guggenheim Museum sold major works by 20th-century artists that would have been the envy of other museums yet were inferior to pieces that were retained by the Guggenheim. Most European museums, being public and state sponsored, do not sell their works at all.

Casual Buyers

Seriously underestimated by observers of the art market is the sales volume accounted for by occasional buyers who are not collectors *per se*. This diverse group is made up of purchasers who spend at every price level but approach their purchases on a one-off basis. For some, often on the advice of decorators, the purchases are made to enhance the décor of their homes. In addition, crossover buying is common, with collectors in one field buying the occasional work from an entirely different field, such as contemporary collectors purchasing Roman sculpture.

Aside from the few corporate collections, many of which have been sold off under pressure from shareholders, there are corporate buyers, often working with art consultants, who decorate their offices with expensive works of art. It is now *de rigueur* for major office buildings to decorate their lobbies with large-scale, expensive works of contemporary art.

Anecdotal reports from dealers indicate that for some, particularly those showing at art fairs where impulse buying can be seen even at the multimillion-dollar level, sales to these one-off buyers can be as much as a third of their turnover. Very eclectic buyers can be either collectors or consumers; it is often a distinction without a real difference.

Dealers

Dealers play a critical role in the art market as both buyers and sellers and as a key distribution channel. Dealers typically have public galleries where their clients can view works for sale simply by walking in, but other dealers operate privately, by appointment only, seeing clients in their homes or in private offices. Unlike public auctions, dealers are less likely to quickly "burn" a work from over exposure, because they can control to whom they show it. A work that has been "bought in"—in auction parlance, unsold—can be seen as undesirable, even tainted. In the field of contemporary art, many galleries represent the works of living artists (known as the *primary market*), but most also deal in the resale of works (known as the *secondary market*). Dealers provide essential liquidity to the market as both active buyers and distribution channels in the sale of art. It is common for dealers to own pieces together in partnership or as a syndicate, which diversifies the risks and the capital required and broadens the number of clients to whom the work can be offered. Dealers will also exchange unsold inventory with each other when their own client base is exhausted.

Art Fairs

An innovation in the past few decades is the art fair in which dealers, both public and private, rent temporary display booths together in one larger facility. The art fair provides a convenient setting for buyers to peruse offerings from many dealers—a kind of one-stop shopping. It also provides the dealers an important venue for meeting new customers.

Art fairs are now an essential distribution channel for all categories of works of art and all price points. Some of the leading fairs are Art Basel and Art Basel-Miami for modern and contemporary art, TEFAF–Maastricht for Old Masters, antiquities, and *object d'art,* and the International Fine Arts Fair in New York for a wide range of mostly European and American paintings, drawings, and sculpture. There are now art fairs in almost every major and not-so-major city, covering every type of artwork imaginable. There are both generalist fairs and specialist fairs. Fairs are now so numerous that some dealers do almost all their business in these settings, traveling almost monthly from one to another. The costs of rental, installation, advertising, shipping, and insurance are substantial and must be added to the cost of goods sold for the dealers to make an adequate profit.

Many buyers, including museum curators with limited funds or time to travel, prefer the art fairs because of the speed and relative anonymity they can have browsing. What is lost is the in-depth client relationship and the transfer of dealer knowledge to the clients, which require time. Art fairs as a distribution channel would appear to make for a broader but less stable art market.

Many larger art fairs have vetting committees that review each of the works of art that dealers propose to offer at the fair. The committees are often composed of other dealers, curators, and scholars who try to determine whether the work is, in fact, as represented—that is genuine per its description. The vetting process is an important aspect of the marketing efforts and is intended to give buyers comfort that the piece they are buying is genuine, not overly restored, and correctly attributed as to artist and period. This is important in a setting where transactions are often done quickly on the spot. Unfortunately, this vetting process is not always reliable due to the difficulty of correctly and accurately identifying many kinds of objects and the sheer volume of pieces to be considered in a short period of time under less than optimal conditions. As with the auction houses, there is an important element of *caveat emptor*.

Auction Houses

Auction houses are critical to the art market because they provide the closest approximation to a trading exchange. Although it is more common than in the past for auction houses to take an equity or creditor interest in works they are selling (primarily for the most desirable and expensive lots), for most pieces they act as agent. For very important consignments, the main auction houses are now in the habit of providing guarantees to the consignor of a minimum price, usually in exchange for a larger share of the upside if the work sells above the guaranteed amount.

The auction world is dominated by the duopoly of Sotheby's and Christie's, but there is, in aggregate, significant volume controlled by smaller regional auction houses, particularly the French auctioneers associated with the Hotel Drouot sales. Historically, European auction houses have configured sales to include a mixture of furniture, decorative art and objects, and fine art. However, increasingly auction houses are selling works in specialty sales targeted to a defined collecting audience, such as Old Master paintings or drawings, modern and Impressionist, or Chinese works of art. Smaller regional auction houses still tend to have more general sales with a wider range of types of lots for sale. Probably half or more of the investment-grade art passes through auctions.

The buyers at auction are a mix of dealers, collectors, museums, and casual buyers so that the price of any particular item could reflect a wholesale level, retail, or even a nearly random price, depending on the mix of bidders at the time. No reliable figures are available for direct Internet sales and online auction sales, but generally works of art do not lend themselves to entirely Web-based transactions. Digital images, though good and improved, might never substitute for seeing the object in the flesh.

Although auction houses have increasingly styled themselves as retailers of art, most auction houses, including Sotheby's and Christie's, specifically disclaim all but minimal warranties and guarantees as to authenticity and condition. This is a major distinction from dealers who do not disclaim these kinds of warranties. In France the *expert de douane* is a state-authorized expert who can be personally liable for the authenticity of works sold at auctions in which he is the official expert, and this warranty extends to the purchaser for decades; however, French auction houses also have disclaimers. As a practical matter both Sotheby's and Christie's will informally stand behind many works they sell, whereas many dealers are very unwilling to stand behind works that they sell, even when they are legally bound to do so, and it can be very difficult, if not impossible, to return works that are not as represented.

The major auction houses have specialist departments employing true experts, and they will often turn to outside specialists for opinions. Nonetheless, auction catalogue descriptions can be inaccurate, incomplete, and even totally wrong. This is the result of a small staff having to see an enormous number of objects during the year in consideration for possible sale, only a few of which will actually be submitted to auction, coupled with the genuine difficulty of quickly getting a totally certain identification, even from the finest and most venerable scholars.

Investors

Pure investors are undoubtedly the smallest discernable group among buyers and sellers and do not play an important role in the overall market. Investors will sometimes operate in conjunction with dealers, helping to fund the purchase of works of art for a share of the profit—essentially financing a work until a buyer can be found but not actually incurring the direct expense or daily operational involvement of the dealer. Other investors will purchase and hold works of art that are either out of favor or that the investor believes will benefit by long-term inflation, a diminishing supply, an upward change of attribution, or a coming change in taste, such as buying ahead of an anticipated change of taste.

Hypothetically, investors should not be concerned at all with the aesthetic merits of art but only the potential for profit; however, as a practical matter, these judgments required to purchase a work of art for investment overlap. The key difference between collectors and investors is probably the price they are willing to pay, not which work of art they are buying. Unlike dealers, investors do not have their own distribution facilities or sales and marketing resources of their own, but neither do they have the expenses of a dealer's overhead. Generally, investors should be expected to have a much longer expected holding period than dealers.

Art Investment Funds

In recent years, after seeing the success of private equity and venture capital funds, a few investment partnerships have been formed, styled like private equity funds. The prototype was the modestly successful British Rail Pension Fund's £40 million investment in art in the 1970s that was formed to provide a hedge during a period of exceptionally high inflation. The idea was both novel and controversial at the time, but today it looks rather prescient, since art values generally are dramatically higher at much lower levels of inflation. Key to the fund's financial success was buying Impressionist paintings before the Japanese bubble and selling around the peak of that bubble; without this category the investment would likely have been deemed unsuccessful.

The fund diversified across many sectors and received advice from specialists, many of whom probably had significant conflicts. Undoubtedly many advisors and dealers profited directly and indirectly from their involvement with the fund; consequently the embedded overhead and management costs created an additional hurdle. The financial performance by sector varied greatly, with many categories not meeting their investment targets. Generally, the quality of the works was very high, but many of their purchases were at high prices relative to the market at the time, which is not surprising given their high profile, the number of intermediaries involved, and the lack of a truly independent structure for evaluating purchases. The portfolio did not directly track inflation *per se*.

Modeled on private equity funds, art investment funds today would typically have a management fee of 1.5 to 2.0% of assets and a carried interest of 20% of the profits, after taking out direct costs of acquiring and selling the objects, other than the overhead costs of the managing general partner. Some of these funds have a general partner or advisors to the general partner, consisting of dealers or auction specialists. The conflicts of interest are substantial in these cases. It would be the unusual dealer advising an art fund, who on finding a seriously undervalued work of art, would step aside in favor of the fund making the purchase. Art funds that have close affiliations with auction houses also have serious conflicts of interest by potentially encouraging the fund to buy otherwise difficult works to be sold at auction or to sell works of art at auction that actually might be better suited to private sales.

The limited partners in such investment funds get none of the enjoyment of the property but do have to absorb the storage, transportation, and insurance costs. Some funds are rumored to store the art in Switzerland, in free-trade warehouses, which eliminates local tax; however, it is very difficult to show the works to prospective purchasers who would rarely make the trip unless they were already somehow highly motivated. If art is left in dealer galleries, there can be issues of keeping the works free of claims from potential creditors of the gallery. The art funds themselves are rarely set up to be dealers (or an auction house). Art funds that are only allocators of capital and selectors of works to buy do not have the marketing and distribution exposure of a gallery or auction house. It is hard to see how an art fund, with its high cost structure, limited distribution, prolific conflicts of interest, and a fixed finite life, is well suited as a structure for investing in art.

Consultants and Advisors

As art has become more expensive and buyers less willing to spend the time and energy necessary to canvas the galleries, auctions, and art fairs, a small informal industry of advisory services has grown up. Some of these are affiliated with major banks that want to service their private client business as a full-service financial advisory operation. Some consultants deal primarily with corporations that want a prestigious corporate collection or simply to decorate offices with fine art, almost always contemporary. Other consultants help collectors locate, assess, value, and negotiate their purchases. Many of the consultants also become involved in overseeing conservation, cataloguing, framing, and hanging the art of their clients. On an informal basis, many museum curators also help collectors by giving professional advice, usually to create goodwill in the hopes of eventually receiving works of art as donations. These intermediaries play an important behind-the-scenes role in guiding taste and providing confidence to buyers who are spending large sums on often little understood art.

What Transaction Costs Are Associated with Art?

In the typical business world, there are clear differences between retail and wholesale prices, and there are volume discounts. In the art world there is very little by way of counterpart. Auction prices reflect a shifting mix of wholesale and retail buying so that the prices are not reliable as an indicator of either. Profit margins for dealers vary widely, from as little as 5 to 25% for consignments (usually in the lower part of the range for the high-turnover modern and contemporary markets) and 200 to 300% markup or more for some Old Masters and decorative arts owned as inventory. Dealer gross margins have to cover the fixed overhead of the dealer's operations, which include the gallery space, travel, marketing, framing, restoration and conservation, and research. The two main auction houses, Sotheby's and Christie's, have a quasi-retail business model with commensurately high overhead costs, including expensive salesroom facilities, branch offices in cities for finding property to sell, lavish sales catalogues, and extravagant entertaining of clients. Each specialty department has experts, assistants, and administrative personnel. Even with many artworks commanding stratospheric prices, it can be difficult for the two main houses to generate adequate profits. In contrast, smaller auction houses can operate with minimal overhead and marketing costs, allowing them to have acceptable net margins.

The standard commission rates for the main auction houses of Sotheby's and Christie's are a good proxy for general transaction costs in the art world. These commission costs have risen dramatically over the years and, as expected of a duopoly, commission costs are closely aligned. The stated retail commission charges are a percentage of the *hammer price*, the price the winning bidder announces before commissions are applied. There are separate commissions payable by the seller and the buyer, which makes the percentages appear much lower than they really are and allows separate negotiations for reductions of the two commissions. Over the past few decades commission rates have approximately doubled.

At the time of this writing, Sotheby's and Christies have similar buyers commissions of 25% on the first $50,000, 20% on the next amount to $1 million, and 12% on any amount above $1 million. The stated rate for the seller's commissions is 10%. For example, if a buyer bids $1.5 million, he will pay an additional $262,500, for a total of $1,762,500. The seller, net of the seller commission, will receive $1.35 million (less, perhaps, additional insurance charges of about 1.0% and minor other charges, usually waived at this level). The auction house will receive a total of $412,500 ($1,762,500 – $1,350,000), which is 23.4% of the buyer's total cost, equivalent to gross margin. If the new buyer tries to resell the lot, then just to reach break even, the net to the seller will have to be $1,762,500, which means that the next buyer will have to be willing to pay the auction house $2,275,833, which is 1.29 times what the first buyer paid and 1.69 times what the original seller received.

Less valuable lots incur higher percentage transaction costs. A lot sold for $15,000 hammer price will incur combined commissions of 28% of the final cost. However, many sellers do not pay the full listed rates, because these can be heavily negotiated. In fact, Sotheby's reports average commission margins that are a little more than half the combined buyer and seller undiscounted rates. For very expensive lots or for entire collections, the seller might pay no commission and might even get a rebate of part of the buyer's commission. For the most expensive lots, prospective buyers might be able to negotiate a reduction in the buyer's commission, although this is more unusual. These rates are for U.S. sales but are approximately the same in other worldwide locations, with variations due mostly to currency conversion relative to the breakpoints. In addition to commissions, there can be separate charges for insurance and illustration costs, as well as shipping and local sales or value-added tax (VAT), where applicable. The effect of this commission structure is that a one-way transaction cost for the vast majority of lots, that is, those less than $1 million, will be between 23.4% and 28.0% of what the buyer paid in total. Low-value lots incur even higher transaction costs because the proportionate effect of the additional charges for insurance and illustration is significant. For an investor who both buys and resells a work at auction, the transaction costs will be double these amounts. By financial market standards, the gross margins are substantial and a high bar to clear for investors. If the global stock markets had transaction costs anywhere near this order of magnitude, there would be no public markets.

Public auctions give comfort to many buyers who feel that they are paying only one bid more than someone else who was interested. Furthermore, the time pressure and excitement of bidding at auction can create premium prices that are way above normal market value. Because the value of any particular work of art can be very subjective and uncertain, buying at auction seems to convey information about value (or at least the illusion of information) because the auction house is providing seemingly unbiased estimates of value and other bidders (or the absence of bidders) also convey information about value.

For example, if you are highly uncertain about what to pay for a particular work of art, other bidders are unlikely to know less than you, so the fact that at least one other person is bidding can be reassuring that you are paying only one bid more than they thought it was worth. As with all auctions, the buyer has the "winner's curse," having paid more than anyone else was willing at that that moment. Although undoubtedly there is useful price information in the public bidding, it is impossible to know whether the other bidders are indeed knowledgeable, are bidding with similar informational disadvantage, or are simply caught up in the excitement of the moment. Many if not most bidders do not have a firm maximum price in mind that is inviolate when they walk into the auction room, which leaves them vulnerable to the emotion of the moment.

Consignment to dealers might be less expensive as a percentage of the sale, and normally the seller pays the entire commission, typically about 20% of the gross sales price. For some works of art, dealers are better positioned to take the time to market to specific customers and have the advantage of allowing a more leisurely decision period. But dealers do not have the broad marketing range and reach of the auction houses; a typical dealer will have only a fraction of the clients seen by the auction houses, and many dealers say that there are auction buyers who will never set foot in an art gallery. This might be due to time constraints, shyness or embarrassment, or the belief that public auction prices are more nearly fair value.

It takes significant time and expense to cover the for-sale market of auctions, galleries, and art fairs. There are thousands of dealers (sometimes dozens or even hundreds in any particular field); there are auctions almost every week just in New York, Paris, and London, not counting the many secondary city auctions; and there is a constant calendar of art fairs around the globe. Travel is essential but costly, since works of art cannot be prudently purchased from photographs or digital images.

How Is Art Taxed?

Each country has a different scheme for taxation of works of art; it is beyond the scope of this book to do a country-by-country review. However, most tax regimes are variations of taxation of profits, taxation of fair market value, or taxation of value added.

For a U.S. taxpayer, the federal tax rate on the profit from "collectibles" is currently 28%, which is much higher than the long-term capital gain rate for financial investments but lower than the tax on ordinary income or short-term capital gains. Expenses generally are not deductible against income but sometimes can be added to the cost basis, thereby reducing the taxable gain on sale. Qualifying as an investor requires being able to demonstrate investment intent; it is not automatically assumed. Aside from federal taxation, each state has its own rates for taxing profits on art and may impose sales tax on the full value of purchases. For dealers, operating expenses are deductible, but the tax rate on earned income (net profit) is higher than the special capital gains rate for collectibles. In contrast to investors or dealers, buyers without a primary profit motive cannot take net losses against nonart income tax liabilities.

Some countries, such as the United Kingdom, have special rules that reduce or eliminate capital gains tax for sales to public institutions. Switzerland generally taxes the value of art, whereas in France art is exempt from wealth tax. Within the European Union (EU) is the complex scheme of VAT, which varies by country and which has different rates for art purchased within the EU and works purchased outside the EU but imported.

What this means for an investor is that the choice of taxing jurisdiction can make a big difference in the after-tax profits. Various tax schemes can also affect the choice of where the art is stored, and this also works as a barrier to the globalization of the art markets because the demand in some countries can be affected by the tax incentives and disincentives applicable to the buyers and sellers.

Can the Financial Performance of the Art Market Be Measured?

Most academic studies of art as an investment have looked only at the gross returns or have given inadequate weight to the practical costs of art investing. The major indexes, such as Mei Moses Family of Indexes, report gross prices only. Because transaction costs are formidable, the comparison with returns in the public markets, where transaction costs are low, is inapposite.

There are many impediments to accurately measuring financial returns in the art market. Chief among these are:

- Only a small fraction of prices for works of art are publicly known at any point in time. Dealers do not make their sales public information.
- Transaction costs create enormous differences between gross and net prices, which materially distort the meaning of the returns data.
- The art market has no natural or theoretically justifiable index composition for the market as a whole that's analogous to, say, the capitalization weighted indices of the stock markets, which are derived from the Capital Asset Pricing Model, or CAPM.
- Unlike the stock market indices, which can actually be purchased for investment because the underlying stocks can be purchased, there is no such counterpart for the art market.
- There is significant survivorship bias in the publicly reported (auction) data because lots that failed to sell cannot be valued and some works that were valuable in prior centuries are no longer of interest to current buyers.
- Although broad measures of art sales can convey a sense of the magnitude of financial performance, the more specific the measure, the less likely it will capture useful information; for example, data on a particular artist is almost meaningless because, unlike the price of a share of stock, two works will have different prices because they are unique, not necessarily because of a change in the artist's value.

In theory, financial markets could create a derivative security based on a published index, but it is unclear who would be interested in it and it is not likely to be suitable as a hedging instrument due to extreme basis risk. Particular art holdings might have a limited pricing relationship, that is, a correlation, with the indices.

Campbell (2005) identified four major methodologies for measuring art market performance: geometric means, average prices, repeat sales regressions, and hedonic regressions. To the extent there is a systematic market factor, as with the public stock and bond markets, various methods should yield results in the same order of magnitude, but precision would be elusive. She also summarized 59 published studies covering various sectors, such as prints, Old Masters, and modern art, and various time periods, some going back as far as the 17th century.

Table 5.2 shows a number of studies listed by Campbell for nominal returns and real returns, grouped in 2% increments. The modal return is in the 0 to 2% range both for nominal and real returns. Interestingly, two thirds of the real returns from the various studies fall in the range of 0–4%, but nominal returns are more dispersed. This suggests relationships between real and nominal returns that are partly idiosyncratic, conditional on the types of art and the time periods, which may themselves interact idiosyncratically. It is also noteworthy that only one study showed negative returns. There may be no "natural" rate of return for the art market, and if the systematic market factor is not significant relative to variance, it is difficult to assign practical or theoretical meaning to a market measure.

Table 5.2 Studies with Results in Each Category for Nominal and Real Rates of Return

Return Range	Nominal	Real
%	Number of Results	Number of Results
< 0	1	1
0–2	13	19
2–4	6	11
4–6	3	7
6–8	9	9
8–10	8	1
10–12	7	3
12–14	4	2
14–16	0	1
16–18	0	1
18–20	2	1
20–22	1	1
22–24	2	0
24–26	1	0
> 24	2	2

Note: The studies tabulated here involve different types of art and different time periods studied.

Which Strategies Might Be Successful for Art Investments?

Simply buying and holding a random or casual selection of art, in and of itself, is not likely to be a profitable strategy. There is no general market basket of art like stocks or bond index funds. The following sections describe, with pros and cons, some of the more commonly suggested strategies.

Broker-Dealer Strategies

It is possible to create enormous wealth by owning art but difficult for investors not actively participating in the business. Two of the greatest success stories were both dealers who also collected: Ernst Beyler and Heinz Berggruen. Both of these men started their careers in the early part of the 20th century when then-modern art was inexpensive, and they participated in the stunning rise in value of 20th-century art. Being active dealers, they were able to see thousands of works and select from that supply. They kept for themselves large numbers of exceptional works that they retained for decades. Both had extraordinary taste and a deep understanding of the art that would be hard to duplicate for the typical buyer. Each amassed collections that were likely worth in excess of a billion dollars. Interestingly, both donated substantial parts of their collections rather than selling. Whether this success can be duplicated today is an open question, but the examples suggest that an ultra-long-term buy-and-hold strategy for museum-quality works might be viable.

Blue-Chip Strategies

Most dealers counsel clients to "buy the best." Counterintuitively, the academic evidence shows this is not likely to be a winning strategy. Studies are fairly consistent that the top works do not produce the top returns and might even be counterproductive (Pesando, 1993; Pesando and Shum, 2007; Mei and Moses, 2002; Skaterschikov, 2006). Although this finding might be specific to time periods and types of works studied, it certainly goes against the common wisdom. However, the best works of art do have more liquidity, albeit at a price, than less desirable works, and this is particularly true for works of interest to museums.

Although there is no practical limit to the price of works of art, since some have sold for more than \$100 million, the number of buyers is very limited for works that sell for tens of millions of dollars. The list of artists that have made it into the stratosphere of prices over \$10 million is relatively short, which suggests a very limited and narrow market for the top tier. Table 5.3 shows, for European and American paintings, the small number of subsectors with many of the names of the small number of artists who reach lofty price levels. Probably there are not many more than 100 artists of all schools and centuries for which there are works that might plausibly come on to the market and sell at this level. Most of the buyers capable of spending the enormous sums required

Table 5.3 Categories of Ultra-High-Value Art, with a Partial Listing of Artists

- Early Italian Old Masters (Mantegna, del Sarto, Il Duccio)
- Italian Renaissance (Michelangelo, Raphael, Correggio)
- Venetian 16th century (Titian, Tintoretto, Veronese)
- Dutch 16th century (Rembrandt, Vermeer)
- Venetian 18th century (Canaletto, Guardi)
- 18th-century British Old Masters (Constable, Turner)
- American 19th and early 20th century (Bellows, Hopper, Homer, Church)
- 20th-century German-Austrian (Kirchner, Klimt)
- Impressionists (Van Gogh, Gauguin, Cezanne, Seurat, Toulouse-Lautrec)
- Post-Impressionists (Manet, Monet, Renoir, Degas)
- 20th-century Moderns (Picasso, Matisse, Leger, Modigliani, Mondrian, Kandinsky, Brancusi, Giacometti, Malevich, Miró)
- Post-War American (Pollock, Rothko, Newman, Johns, de Kooning, Warhol)
- Post-War British (Bacon, Freud)
- Contemporary (Koons, Murakami, Richter)

for top works by the most desirable artists are interested solely in the 20th and 21st centuries. There is a developing market for multimillion-dollar Chinese works, primarily ceramics of the Yuan and Ming periods and particularly those with Imperial provenance. It is the rare antiquity that becomes available at these levels that has marketable provenance.

Momentum Strategies

One strategy is to buy ahead of developing or changing taste. This works particularly well with contemporary art because tastes develop and change very rapidly, similar to fashion. Monitoring cutting-edge exhibitions, cultivating relationships with leading dealers, and visiting active artists for intelligence as to who is currently very influential are ways to get an informational edge. However, the gross profit margin of primary dealers has been in the range of 30–60% for contemporary artists, although less for the most famous and expensive artists' works. Price appreciation with this strategy would likely be relatively short term—three to seven years. Long holding periods will be at risk for reversals of taste. What is "hot" can change in a matter of a few years.

Emerging Market Strategies

Global trends in developing economies show a long-term growth in wealth. Luxury goods markets in Asia and the Middle East are robust, as is demand for works of art, particularly works of the buyers' region of domicile (objects of nationalist interest) and certain types of modern and contemporary signature pieces, usually easily recognizable with an international reputation (such as Picasso and Renoir) and not culturally offensive (for example, not overtly sexual or scatological). As wealth develops and becomes more diffuse, it is logical to assume that the taste for art will expand to a larger pool of buyers. Although these markets, like their stock markets, can be rampant with speculation and manipulation, careful focus on the taste trends in these markets should produce intermediate-term price appreciation in works that would specifically appeal to the newly wealthy in those booming markets, particularly works that have not yet appreciated to the point of severe overvaluation.

Value Strategies

Even in a booming art market, there are always areas that become undervalued as they fall out of favor. French 18th-century furniture, Barbizon paintings, and most British 18th-century portraits are examples of specialty areas that were once of high relative value and now, although not inexpensive, have shown little or even negative real appreciation since their peak. Certain artists who were extremely famous and whose works were expensive in their lifetimes, such as William Bouguereau, fell very far out of favor until they were "rediscovered," sometimes after decades of price decline. Buying out-of-favor art is similar to deep-value investing in the stock market but with very long holding periods that can last decades, even a generation or more. For long-lived investment plans this can be a suitable strategy if attention is paid to when the markets recover their luster, presenting a selling opportunity.

Supply/Demand Imbalance Strategies

Certain fields of art have foreseeable changes of supply reduction, particularly for objects that are covered under international patrimony and cultural property laws. Examples might be Khmer stone figures and almost anything Egyptian or from ancient Iraq, where the market for pieces with impeccable provenance has jumped significantly and pricing is very different for pieces with acceptable provenance than for those without. However, there are counterexamples, such as medieval works of art, where a highly limited supply has contributed to an overall lack of collecting interest in the field for all but the most stellar pieces.

Arbitrage Strategies

Because, unlike public securities markets, information as to what is for sale globally in the art market is often hard to come by and not timely, there are arbitrage opportunities in finding works of interest in obscure auctions, works in seemingly poor condition that are simply in need of restoration, or works that are being sold in one country when the market is mostly based in another country. A large number of works sold actually fit this category, but it requires time and perseverance. In addition, in some obscure sales the prices achieved can actually be higher than what would be reached at Sotheby's or Christie's. Important works that show up in remote sales can often be identified by a line of expensive cars at the venue because dealers know that few of their clients will know of the sale or what they paid, since these results are not well published.

Conclusion

The art market is not at all homogenous. The buyers and sellers are varied and are a mix of profit seekers and others for whom profit or good value are not key decision factors, such as museums. What constitutes a work of art is difficult to define, and what makes some works "investible" is even more difficult to define, but as a practical matter, the market participants in each specialty field seem to self-define. Although the art market is large, the distribution channels are varied and make for a fragmented, nonintegrated marketplace, very unlike the public securities market. Information flow, though improving, is still limited. What makes any work of art have a particular value is a combination of factors that have variable weightings but include scarcity, subject and color, recognizability, status, liquidity, provenance, publication, size, affinity, currency, quality, and condition. A multitude of factors—macroeconomic and market specific—affect supply and demand. Transaction costs are substantial, often so high as to make investments prohibitive in the absence of special circumstances. Although there can be viable strategies, it is unlikely that a passive index-like approach or a "buy the best" strategy will be successful.

References

Campbell, Rachel A. J. (2005) Art as an Alternative Asset Class (February 2005), Maastricht University/LIFE; available at SSRN: http://ssrn.com/abstract=685982.

Kinsella, E. (2008) $25 Billion and Counting, *ArtNews*, May:122–131.

McAndrew, C. (2007) *The Art Economy*, The Liffey Press.

Mei, J., and Moses, M. (2002) Art as an Investment and the Underperformance of Masterpieces, *American Economic Review* 92(5):1656–1668.

Pesando, J. (1993) Art as an Investment: The Market for Modern Prints, *American Economic Review* 83(5):1075–1089.

Pesando, J., and Shum, P. M. (2007) Investing in Art: A Cautionary Tale, *Journal of Wealth Management*, Spring:80–87.

Skaterschikov, S. (2006) *Skate's Art Investment Handbook*, KunstAM.

Veblen, T. (1994) *Theory of the Leisure Class*, reprint (first published in 1899), Dover Publications.

6 Art as a Financial Investment

Rachel J. Campbell

-University of Maastricht

The comparatively poor performance of traditional asset classes in recent years has driven the search for greater returns via alternative asset classes. The desire to reap higher risk-adjusted returns from diversification into assets that offer low and even negative correlation with equities and bonds is extremely desirable. There has been a huge growth in the traditional alternative investments such as real estate, commodity futures, private equity, and hedge fund investments. Additionally, a number of funds specializing in art have recently emerged. These also appear to offer a highly beneficial diversification strategy with extremely low correlation with traditional asset classes. It is important for investors to understand the risk and return characteristics of this new alternative asset class.

In this chapter we take a closer look at art as an alternative asset and look specifically at how this new alternative asset is expected to perform, also during bear markets, when the benefits of diversification are most needed. We look at the risk and return characteristics of art using art market indices, and the prospects for portfolio diversification in the art market using a variety of data across art market sectors, including the Old Masters, European Impressionists, Modern and Contemporary art markets. Due to the low correlation of art with other asset classes, we find opportunities for portfolio diversification across art markets and across asset classes. The results hold, even allowing for the high transaction costs, which are encountered when trading art, when spread over a longer time horizon.

The vogue for investing in art has received a boost from the availability of art price data. In any market, knowledge empowers the consumer and the proliferation of information sources in the art market is testimony to this. Databases, indices, and market reports are now essential analytical tools with which art investors can assess financial performance. A number of indices show average returns for artists and market sectors with data ranging from the 17th century until today.

Collectible Investments for the High Net Worth Investor

We will focus on the use of available indices for various art markets to give us an indication of art's performance in a diversified portfolio. These provide a good impression of the risk/return profile for art funds.

The difficulty with these tools is that the information on which they are based is neither consistent nor complete, and this may distort results when they are compared to indices for more transparent markets. It is therefore useful to examine briefly the methods currently employed by these information sources to gain an informed perspective of the results they provide.

The rest of the chapter is outlined as follows: In the following section we discuss the current data on art indices and the surrounding methodologies. In the section thereafter we look at the risk and return characteristics of fine art markets. We then analyze art as an alternative asset class in an international diversified portfolio. We take into account the high transaction costs encountered when auctioning fine artworks, as well as the implications of smothered returns, which occurs for assets which are appraisal based. Due to the moderate return found for art in the last 30 years, and the low correlation that art appears to exhibit with other asset classes, including more alternative assets, we find there is a serious case for holding a small percentage of the investment portfolio in art. At present it is inconceivable to hold an index tracking fund; however, there are a number of alternative means to hold a diversified art portfolio as part of an overall wealth management strategy. We conclude in the final section.

Data and Methodology

Art Indices

The Mei Moses and Art Market Research art indices are the two most widely quoted indicators of art market performance. Both are reliant on data from sales at the main auction houses. However, auction results alone provide an incomplete picture of the market performance because they are only a portion of the whole market.

The dealer market is largely ignored due to an absence of obtainable data. There is some disagreement as to the percentage of the market that dealers comprise. Figures from two recent studies range from a 50–50 split between auction houses and dealers to 70–30 split in favor of dealers. In any event, it cannot be denied that dealers have a significant, albeit unquantifiable, impact upon the art market. The absence of dealers' transactions from the art indices may have a bearing upon the rate of return indicated by the indices. This is due to the fact that dealers may buy at lower prices but sell at higher prices transactions costs, thereby reducing the art investors' rate of return (Frey and Eichenberger). It is likely that art funds, which act more like private dealers than auction houses, adopt a similar strategy and use their insider knowledge and expertise to exploit inefficiencies in the market. This is likely to produce art market returns much larger than the benchmark used here.

There are four main methodologies for producing art price indices: geometric means, average prices, repeat sales regressions (RSRs), and hedonic regressions. Chanel, Gerard-Varet, and Ginsburgh's (1996) study indicates that over long periods the respective methodologies are closely correlated. Issues regarding the various index pricing methodologies are extremely well highlighted in a recent paper by Ginsburgh, Mei, and Moses (2006), which specifically compares hedonic to repeat sales regression. Ashenfelter and Graddy (2003) provide an excellent survey of average returns estimated from art price data, currently in the academic literature. We have extended the Exhibit with a few additional studies.

For the purpose of this comparison we shall focus on the data from Art Market Research since it provides a wider and more frequent source of information. We also provide some comparison with the Mei Moses All Art index.

These indices show that historically, average real returns for art are moderate. Returns are above inflation and tend to be greater than for government bonds but less than for equities. There has been a general upward trend of art price increases in the market. See Exhibit 6.1 for the performance of a $1000 investment in the art market over the period 1976–2006. This is purely theoretical, since trading such an index is not presently possible.

The survey of art pricing methodologies in Exhibit 6.2 tends to indicate that the repeat sales methodology provides slightly higher estimates of average returns than the other methodologies for similar time periods. For example, Anderson (1974) provides RSR and hedonic price indices for the periods 1780–1970 and 1780–1960 and Chanel, Gerard-Varet, and Ginsburgh (1996) for the period 1855–1969. It is of interest to observe the long-run trend in the market and to note that there have been periods in which art returns have been substantially higher than average.

To evaluate the various index methodologies, we use both data from Art Market Research (AMR) and Mei Moses (MM) All Art Index. AMR data is available monthly but only goes as far back as 1976. We include data for the 100% range for each sector. It is important to include the entire distribution in the indices because this takes into account the extreme price movements in the market, which are vital in correlation estimation and the analysis of diversification benefits. AMR data uses average returns on a 12-month moving average.

The MM series for the All Art Index dates from 1875 measured on an annual basis and from 1965 on a semiannual basis. The MM All Art Index is computed using repeat sales initially sold at auction by Sotheby's and Christie's.

In Exhibit 6.3 we have provided the summary statistics for two types of price index methodology. To compare the two series we use semiannual data

Exhibit 6.1 Estimated Fine Art Market Performance as Reported by Various Academic Papers by Period of Study, 17th–21st Centuries

Author	Sample	Period	Method	Nominal Return	Real Return	Standard Deviation
Baumol (1986)	Paintings in General	1652–1961	RSR		0.60%	
Frey and Pommerehne (1989)	Paintings in General	1635–1949	RSR		1.40%	
		1653–1987	RSR		1.50%	5.00%
		1950–1987	RSR		1.70%	
Buelens and Ginsburgh (1992)	Paintings in General	1700–1961	Hedonic		0.91%	
	Paintings in General	1780–1970	RSR	3.70%	3.00%	*
Goetzmann (1993)	Paintings in General	1716–1986	RSR	3.20%	2.00%	* 5.65%
		1850–1986	RSR	6.20%	3.80%	6.50%
		1900–1986	RSR	17.50%	13.3%	5.19%
Anderson (1974)	Paintings in General	1780–1960	Hedonic	3.30%	2.60%	*
		1780–1970	RSR	3.70%	3.00%	*
Chanel, Gerard-Varet and Ginsburgh. (1996)	Paintings in General	1855–1969	Hedonic		4.90%	
		1855–1969	RSR		5.00%	
Mei and Moses (2002)	American, Impressionist, and Old Masters	1875–1999	RSR		4.90%	4.28%
		1900–1986	RSR		5.20%	3.72%
		1900–1999	RSR		5.20%	3.55%
		1950–1999	RSR		8.20%	2.13%
		1977–1991	RSR		7.80%	2.11%
Goetzmann (1996)	Paintings in General	1907–1977	RSR		5.00%	
Fase (1996)	19th Century	1946–1966		11.00%	7.50%	
		1972–1992		10.60%	1.10%	
Stein (1977)	Paintings in General	1946–1968	Geometric Mean	10.47%		

Exhibit 6.1 (*Continued*)

Author	Sample	Period	Method	Nominal Return	Real Return	Standard Deviation
Barre, Docclo and Ginsburgh (1996)	Great Impressionist	1962–1991	Hedonic	12.0%	5.00%	*
	Other Impressionist	1962–1991	Hedonic	8.00%	1.00%	*
Czujack (1997)	Picasso Paintings	1966–1994	Hedonic		8.30%	
Deutschman (1991)	Old Masters	1971–1991		12.30%	6.04%	
Angnello and Pierce (1996)	19th-century United States	1971–1992		9.30%	3.25%	
Campbell (2005)	Paintings in General	1976–2004	Average prices	5.73%	1.44%	8.27%
	U.S. Paintings	1976–2004	Average prices	7.94%	3.66%	8.73%
Pesando (1993)	Modern Prints	1977–1992	RSR		1.51%	19.94%
Pesando and Shum (1996)	Picasso Prints	1977–1992	RSR	12.00%	2.10%	23.38%
Frey and Serna (1990)	Old Masters, Modern, Contemporary	1981–1988	Hedonic	10.59%	3.20%	
Candela and Scorcu (1997)	Paintings	1983–1994		3.89%	0.21%	

*Real returns estimated additionally by Ashenfelter and Graddy.

from 1976 to 2002.[1] Using semiannual data rather than monthly increases the series' annual volatility, and the shorter time period results in a slightly lower average annual return.

For all indices we calculate the return of the market, i, by the continuously compounded return. This is commonplace in financial economics and more appropriate than measuring cumulative returns. The return is the natural log return of the price index at time, t, such that $\Delta p_{i,t}$ denotes the rate of change of $p_{i,t}$:

[1]Data is only available until December 2002 on the All Art Index.

Exhibit 6.2 Performance of the Fine Art Market Based on the General Art Index (AMR), January 1976–February 2006

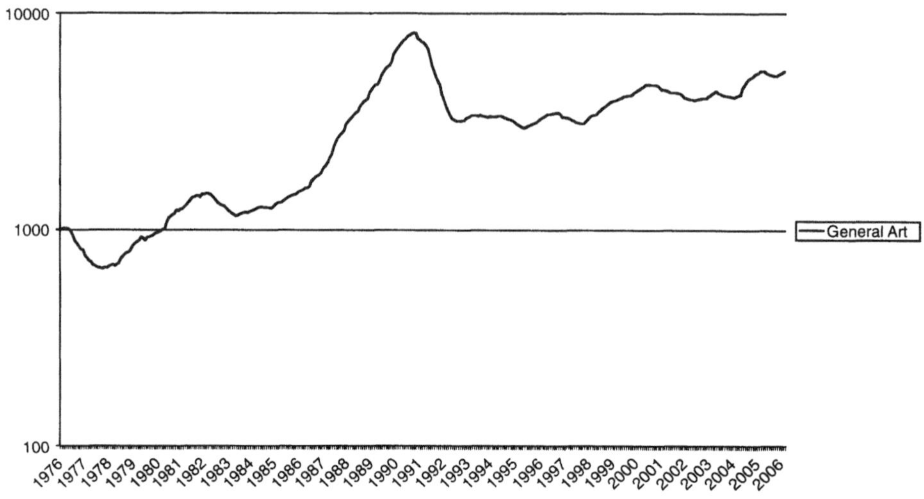

Note: The General Art Index comprises all art indices from Art Market Research.

$$\Delta p_{it} = \ln\left(\frac{p_{i,t}}{p_{i,t-1}}\right) \times 100 \qquad (6.1)$$

From Exhibit 6.3 we can see that the average return on the MM data series for the 27-year period has been much higher than when using the AMR data. Using repeat sales the average return on an annual basis is over 10%, whereas the AMR general art index was just over 5.25% (8% for U.S. artists and 5% for artists in the United Kingdom).[2] Stein (1977), Goetzman (1993), and Ginsburgh (2006) all acknowledge the selection bias that occurs from focusing on repeat sales. To be included in the calculation, repeat sales regression requires artworks to be offered for sale at auction more than once. It is thought that artworks that fall drastically in value tend not to be resold at auction.[3]

Computing the correlation statistics for the two different index methodologies shows us that at first glance the Art 100 methodology from Art Market Research is only 20% correlated with the Mei Moses All Art Index (Exhibit 6.3B). This is due to smoothing in the AMR index.

[2]Descriptions of the artists included in the various indices are given in the appendix.
[3]Similar survivorship bias is also apparent in other financial indices.

Exhibit 6.3 Comparison of AMR Average Price Data and MM Repeat Sales Indices, 1976–2002

Semiannual log return data, 1976/01–2002/12

A.	**Average Prices**			**Repeat Sales**
	Art 100	**U.S. 100**	**U.K. 100**	**All Art Index**
Annual average return	5.27%	8.26%	5.12%	10.07%
Annual average standard deviation	17.11%	15.86%	11.10%	21.88%
Average	0.026	0.041	0.026	0.050
Standard deviation	0.121	0.112	0.078	0.155
Skewness	−0.837	−0.817	−0.097	−0.277
Kurtosis	1.694	1.029	−1.083	−0.395

B.		**Correlation**		**Matrix**
	Average Prices			**Repeat Sales**
	Art 100	**U.S. 100**	**U.K. 100**	**All Art Index**
Art 100	1.000			
U.S. 100	0.822	1.000		
U.K. 100	0.651	0.565	1.000	
All Art Index	0.210	0.221	0.250	1.000

Semiannual log returns; two-period moving averages, 1976/01–2002/12

C.		**Correlation**		**Matrix**
	Average Prices			**Repeat Sales**
	Art 100	**U.S. 100**	**U.K. 100**	**All Art Index**
Art 100	1.000			
U.S. 100	0.871	1.000		
U.K. 100	0.716	0.644	1.000	
All Art Index	0.857	0.714	0.342	1.000

Taking a two-period moving average for the return series increases the correlation dramatically. This is especially true for the All Art Index and the U.S. 100 indices, which have a correlation coefficient of 86%. The larger number of observations used for the moving averages provides correlation coefficients nearing 90% (Exhibit 6.3C).

Exhibit 6.4 Comparison of Art Price Indices, Repeat Sales versus Average Price Indices, Semiannual Data, 1976–2002.

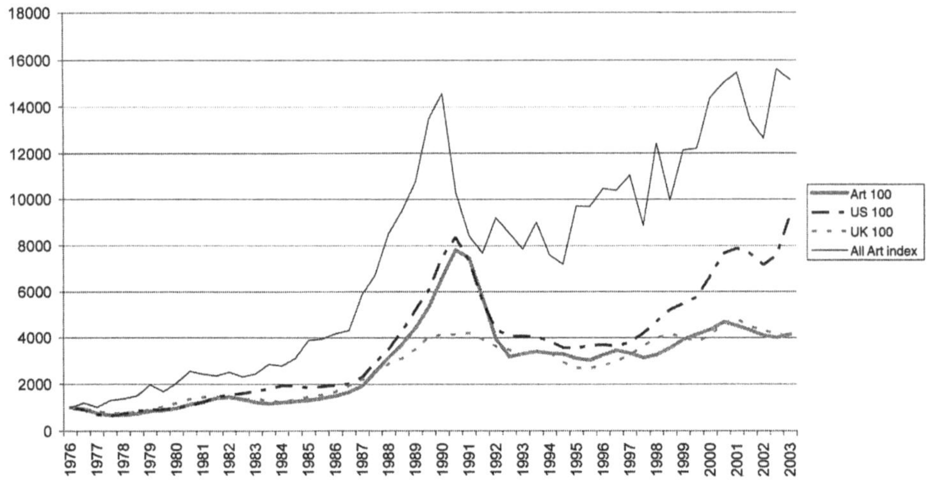

Note: Repeat sales All Art Index versus the average price indices from Art Market Research for the general art market (Art 100), a basket of U.S. artists (U.S. 100), and a basket of British artists (U.K. 100).

The above results indicate that the two methodologies result in indices that are both good proxies of art market prices of auction sales data.

The collection of information from databases is. however, problematic for a number of reasons (see Ashenfelter and Graddy, 2003). Ashenfelter and Graddy's (2003) study contends that an empirical discrepancy in one year can materially alter the overall rate of return by up to 5%. We also find evidence of this phenomenon when the Mei and Moses All Art Index is compared to the General Art Index of Art Market Research for the period 1976–2002. A difference in their estimations of the return after the art market bubble burst in 1991 results in a significant difference between the average return figures thereafter. This can be observed in Exhibit 6.4, where both indices are plotted together. We see that the repeat sales index does not capture as significant a downturn as the AMR data does.

This difference also indicates the importance of liquidity during downturns in the art market. The number of art sales is likely to be greatly reduced in downturns, with the market becoming more illiquid. There is a greater degree of liquidity risk facing the art investor than with other financial assets. With artworks not reaching their reserve prices and not being sold, this will have an effect on the prices included in the price indices. Fewer transactions result in larger estimation errors. At present little information is available on market liquidity over the empirical time series. This problem is especially significant for the case of repeat sales regression estimations, which are constructed with fewer observations. It is likely that the price estimation error that occurred after the art market crash in the early 1990s was due to this issue with repeat sales estimation. Mei and Moses suggest that art does significantly better during wartime, using the example of four U.S. wars this century (Forbes, 2001). During these periods art appears to outperform stocks. This may also be due to the lack of liquidity during these periods and is a highly interesting point that requires further investigation.

Evidently, fundamental problems exist with art databases and indices. However, both are becoming more sophisticated and accurate at providing objective information on what is a notoriously difficult asset to value. Comfort can be taken from the fact that the Standard & Poor's was recently overhauled. If well-established, traditional investment indices are still tweaking their assumptions, art indices may also be forgiven for refining their models over time.

Although the information provided by the databases and indices is not complete, it is the best market information that is currently available. The information provides us with a good indication of the general trends in the market. Moreover, market anomalies and inefficiencies may lead to much higher realized returns.

Investment skill lies in interpreting the available information, assessing whether the risk-return ratio is acceptable, and deciding whether the investment is appropriate to an existing portfolio. Taste adds an additional, unquantifiable element of risk to art investment, even after market analysis has been undertaken. Art as a direct investment presents a risky investment opportunity, although purchasing according to personal taste results in an aesthetic benefit that can potentially outweigh any financial benefit or loss incurred.

When considering art as an indirect investment, where the nonpecuniary benefits are not obtained, then an investor would be advised to opt for an alternative investment vehicle (AIV) or art mutual fund (AMF) where risk diversification through the securitization of artworks is more likely to result in greater financial returns.

Fine Art Market Performance

To analyze the performance of a variety of art markets, we focus on the data indices produced by AMR. These indices also allow for a breakdown of the fine art market into various sectors.

For the various schools, movements, and periods, the average prices of sales by individual artists are combined to form an equally weighted portfolio. For the purpose of this analysis we use the General art index as well as the following four sectors of the art market: Old Masters, European Impressionists, Modern, and Contemporary.

The General art index contains a mixed basket of over 100 well-known artists ranging from Basquiat to Canaletto. The index covers a variety of artists from different sectors and countries, constituting a diversified index of art. The index comprises art sales data from over 109,000 auction sales.

The Old Masters index consists of European artists until the 18th century. There are over 25,000 sales included in the index, with artists from Brueghel (1568–1625) to Constable (1776–1837).

The index for European Impressionist art contains a smaller sample of 25 artists—for example, Manet (1832–1883) and Matisse (1869–1954). The period includes European Impressionist artists in the late 19th century and also some Post-Impressionists. The number of sales included in the index is lower than for other sectors, with just over 22,000 prices included.

Modern art contains a higher number of artists and sales prices, with over 63,000 transactions included. These range from Kandinsky (1866–1944) to Bacon (1909–1992). There may be some disagreement among art historians about the exact definitions of the classification of "Modern" art.

The final sector is Contemporary art, for which there are over 21,000 sales included in the data. The index is newer, with data starting in 1985. Artists covered include Freud (1922–) and Hirst (1965–).

The choice of artists, which is shown in the appendix, is highly subjective but representative. The indices, therefore, provide a general indication of art sector price movements.

In Exhibit 6.5 we see that prices over the past 30 years in the various sectors at times have diverged quite substantially, particularly during the period of the

Exhibit 6.5 Performance of Various Fine Art Markets, January 1976–February 2006

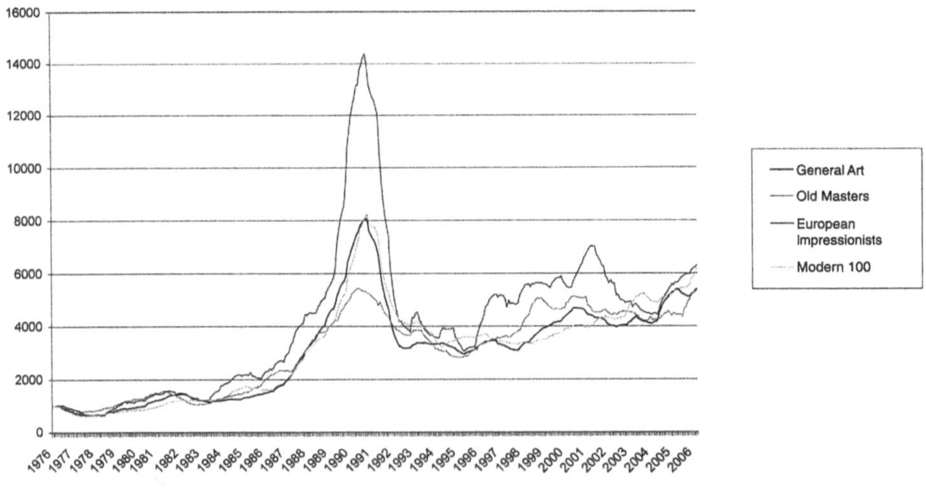

bubble (1988–1991), which affected Impressionist art more than other sectors. Starting at 1000 in 1976, the indices today range between the 5400 level for general art index and the Old Masters market to the 6300 level for European Impressionists.

Including contemporary art and rebasing the indices from January 1985, we can see that this sector has outperformed all others over the past 20 years. Impressionists were the lowest performers, with their greatest returns having been made in the late 1970s. This can be seen in Exhibit 6.6.

Risk and Return

Fine Art Markets

Using data from January 1980 until February 2006, we have 25 years' worth of monthly return data for a variety of sectors. In Exhibit 6.7, we can see that the general art index has given an average annual return of 6.5%. More specifically, Old Masters have generated 5.5%; European Impressionists, 6.3%; and Modern averaging around 7.5%. Contemporary (data starts in 1985, so we take the slightly shorter 20-year period) offered the highest returns, at a 9% annual basis.

Taking a representative, hypothetical fund that holds a composition of 30% Old Masters, 15% European Impressionists, 15% Modern, and 40% Contemporary, the average return using data from the various sectors is 7.05%. This is for the 20-year period, since data on Contemporary art starts in 1985.

Exhibit 6.6 Performance of Various Fine Art Markets, January 1985–February 2006

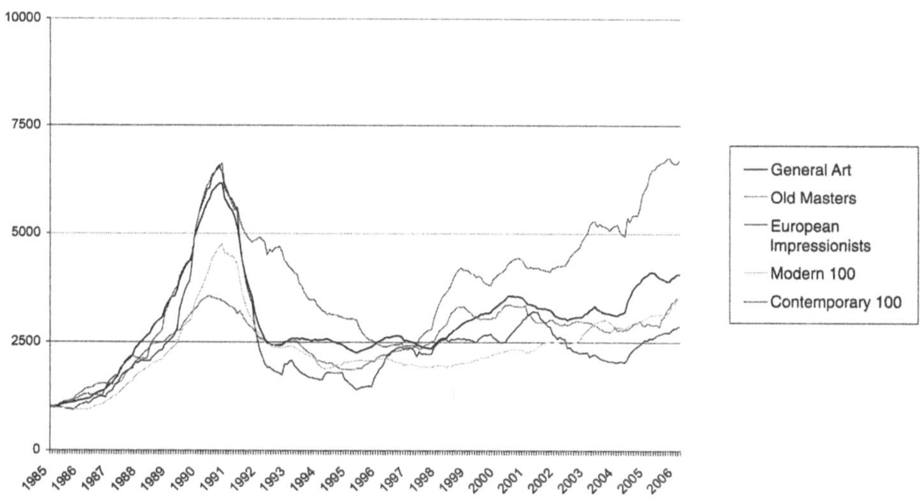

Exhibit 6.7 Average Annual Returns for Fine Art Markets Based on Monthly Data, January 1980–February 2006

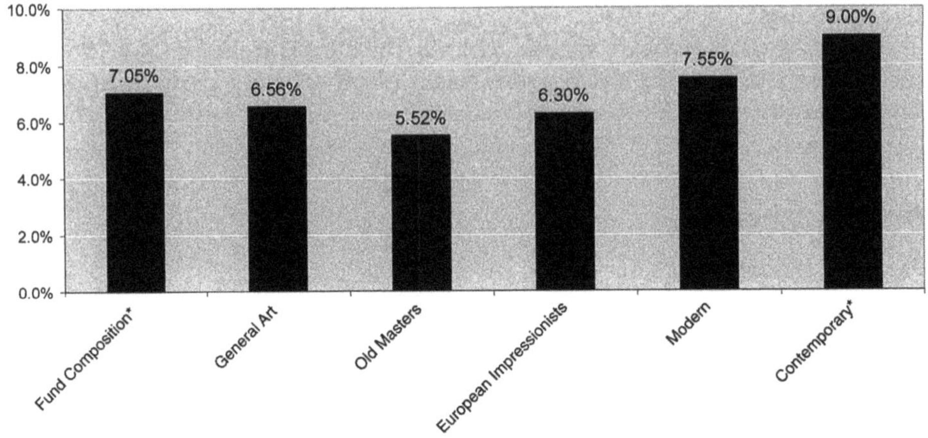

Note: Data starts in 1985.

Exhibit 6.8 Descriptive Statistics for Fine Art Markets, January 1980–February 2006

	Fund Composition*	General Art	Old Masters	European Impressionism	Modern	Contemporary*
Average annual return	7.05%	6.56%	5.52%	6.30%	7.55%	9.00%
Average annual standard deviation	6.92%	8.08%	7.09%	13.12%	7.38%	9.90%
Average monthly return	0.006	0.005	0.005	0.005	0.006	0.007
Average monthly standard deviation	0.020	0.023	0.020	0.038	0.021	0.029
Skewness	0.544	–0.518	0.149	–0.112	–0.146	1.048
Kurtosis	2.099	3.583	0.469	3.510	3.113	3.562

*Data starts in 1985.

Descriptive statistics are shown in Exhibit 6.8. The European Impressionists have been the most volatile market with an annual average standard deviation of the series of more than 15%. Old Masters have been the least volatile with only a 7% average annual standard deviation.

In this section we take a closer look at the risk and return characteristics of the sectors, focusing specifically on the 25-year period from 1980–2006. This period is chosen since other asset class data in the later section is only available from 1980.

The fine art indices are themselves not highly correlated. This gives an indication of the potential benefits from holding a diversified art portfolio across artists and across various art sectors. The highest correlation over the period is between the general art index and all other sectors, most likely because each of the individual sectors feeds into the general art index. The correlation coefficients range between 27% and 53% for the four individual art sectors. Modern art and the general art index are 76% correlated.

Looking at the return-risk ratio of the various sectors we see that Modern and Contemporary art offer the highest return for a unit of risk, where risk is measured by the standard deviation of returns. Per unit of risk the fund composition also offers an attractive return of 1.02. Though the average return is slightly less than for the Modern and Contemporary markets the risk is allevi-

Exhibit 6.9 Correlation Statistics for Fine Art Markets, January 1980–February 2006

	General Art (%)	**Old Masters (%)**	**European Impressionists (%)**	**Modern (%)**	**Contemporary (%)**
General art	100.0				
Old Masters	43.0	100.0			
European Impressionists	74.0	33.8	100.0		
Modern 100	76.1	29.9	61.1	100.0	
Contemporary 100	53.4	27.9	34.6	53.0	100.0

Exhibit 6.10 Return Per Unit of Risk for Fine Art Markets, January 1980–February 2006

	Fund Composition	**General Art**	**Old Masters**	**European Impressionists**	**Modern**	**Contemporary**
Return/risk	1.02	0.81	0.78	0.48	1.02	0.91

Exhibit 6.11 Risk-Return Ratios for Fine Art Markets Based on Monthly Data, January 1980–February 2006

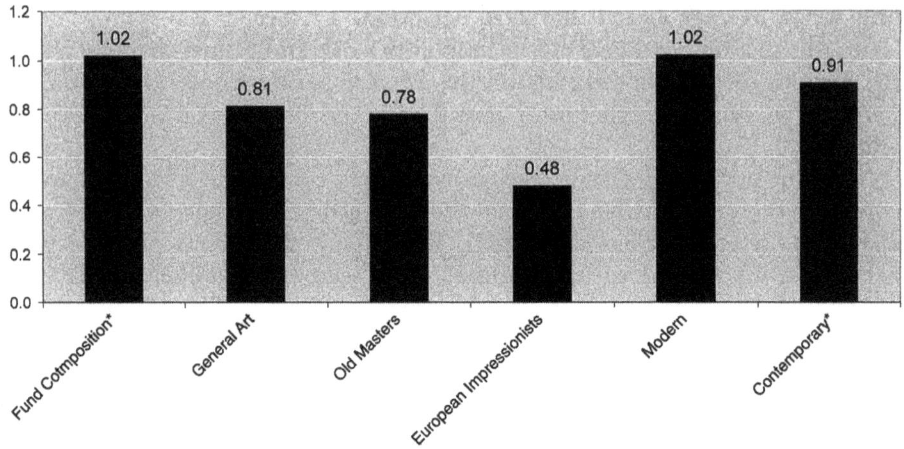

*Data starts in 1985.

ated through a well diversified portfolio where returns per unit of risk are as high as for Modern art.

The risk-return trade-off can also be depicted graphically, as shown in Exhibit 6.12. Generally, there is a positive trade-off between risk and return. The relationship of a higher expected return required for an investor to face greater risk underpins modern finance theory. The higher the return and the lower the risk, the more desirable the index from a financial point of view. In this case the most attractive point from a financial point of view is the top left hand corner of the graph. This is illustrated for both the Modern and Fund composition markets.

Asset Class Framework

The financial markets analyzed represent the major asset classes. We use the Morgan Stanley Capital Indices[4] for U.S. equity (MSCI U.S.), U.K. equity (MSCI U.K.), and world equity (MSCI World); Lehman Brothers Aggregate Corporate Bond Index (available only for the U.S.) and North American Real

[4]The MSCI indices are extremely highly correlated with the national stock market indices—for example, the S&P 500 and the FTSE 100. Data on the MSCI indices are available on a monthly basis for the whole sample.

Exhibit 6.12 Risk and Return Trade-Off for Fine Art Markets, January 1980–February 2006

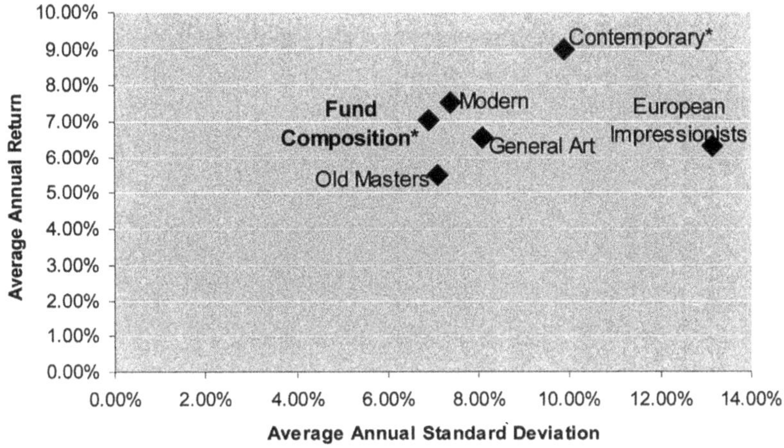

*Data from 1985

Estate Investment Trust Index (NAREIT). For the Hedge Fund data series we use the Credit Suisse/Tremont Hedge Fund data series dating from 1994. We use the U.S. and U.K. 10-year Government Bond Indices, and U.K. Government Treasury Bills, which have only been available on a monthly basis from 1980. Data is collected from Datastream, Global Financial Data, NAREIT, and Credit Suisse/Tremont. Descriptive statistics are given for a variety of time horizons for all asset classes in Exhibit 6.13.

In Exhibit 6.14 we have plotted the risk and return trade-off for the variety of asset classes. We see a general trade-off between risk and return. Due to the smoothed nature of the art market return series we have also included a desmoothed art index, which accounts for the moving average in the series. The risk is substantially higher for the same level of return and hence should be more reflective of the true volatility in the market. This desmoothing process is common in the finance literature for real estate and hedge funds. We shall use this desmoothed data later in our analysis on optimal portfolio allocation.

In Exhibit 6.15, correlation statistics are given for the 25-year horizon. Art has a low correlation with other asset classes; the highest being with commodity futures, with a monthly 9% correlation, and the most negatively correlated with North American real estate investment trust whose returns are correlated at –8%. Domestic real estate and art's correlation tends to be higher.

Exhibit 6.13 Descriptive Statistics for Fine Art and Financial Markets: Five, Fifteen, and Twenty-Five Years

Twenty-Five Years

A. 1980–2006	World Equity	U.S. Equity	U.K. Equity	U.S. Corporate Bonds	Commodities Futures	U.S. 10-Year Government Bonds	U.K. 10-Year Government Bonds	NAREIT	Art
Annual average return	10.88%	12.39%	13.27%	14.91%	8.42%	8.36%	11.00%	11.98%	6.56%
Annual standard deviation	13.93%	15.16%	16.63%	22.72%	17.44%	8.62%	8.57%	12.88%	8.08%
Average	0.009	0.010	0.011	0.012	0.007	0.007	0.009	0.010	0.005
Standard deviation	0.040	0.044	0.048	0.066	0.050	0.025	0.025	0.037	0.023
Skew	−1.175	−0.847	−1.270	3.174	0.071	0.138	−0.211	−0.766	−0.518
Kurt	3.866	3.404	5.755	50.560	1.252	1.274	1.413	2.918	3.583

Fifteen Years

B. 1990–2006	World Equity	U.S. Equity	U.K. Equity	U.S. Corporate Bonds	Commodities Futures	U.S. 10-Year Government Bonds	U.K. 10-Year Government Bonds	NAREIT	Hedge Funds	Art
Annual average return	6.78%	10.28%	8.60%	8.33%	7.36%	6.52%	9.02%	12.10%	10.31%	1.26%
Annual standard deviation	14.00%	14.35%	14.27%	4.53%	19.38%	6.99%	6.75%	12.89%	7.79%	7.54%
Average	0.006	0.009	0.007	0.007	0.006	0.005	0.008	0.010	0.009	−0.001
Standard deviation	0.040	0.041	0.041	0.013	0.056	0.020	0.019	0.037	0.022	0.022
Skew	−0.827	−0.589	−0.491	−0.376	0.247	−0.444	−0.076	−0.669	−0.035	−1.459
Kurt	1.277	0.935	0.623	0.590	0.910	0.829	0.631	2.123	2.367	4.751

Five Years

C. 2000–2006	World Equity	U.S. Equity	U.K. Equity	U.S. Corporate Bonds	Commodities Futures	U.S. 10-Year Government Bonds	U.K. 10-Year Government Bonds	NAREIT	Hedge Funds	Art
Annual average return	0.06%	−1.28%	0.93%	7.18%	13.11%	6.19%	6.35%	19.10%	7.53%	3.56%
Annual standard deviation	14.23%	15.29%	14.14%	4.20%	22.55%	7.64%	4.62%	14.06%	5.09%	5.17%
Average	0.000	−0.001	0.001	0.006	0.011	0.005	0.005	0.016	0.006	0.0030
Standard deviation	0.041	0.044	0.041	0.012	0.065	0.022	0.013	0.041	0.015	0.0149
Skew	−0.596	−0.274	−0.896	−0.967	−0.188	−0.773	−0.338	−1.488	0.204	1.3833
Kurt	3.885	3.381	5.480	42.897	1.190	1.274	1.413	2.823	2.367	4.9021

Exhibit 6.14 Risk and Return Trade-Off for Financial Asset Classes, January 1980–February 2006

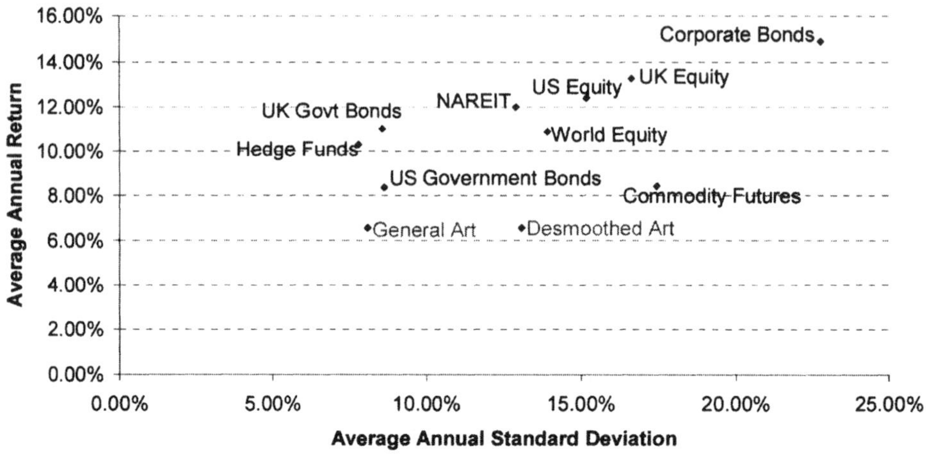

Correlations with other asset classes remain low, even after accounting for various time horizons (see Exhibit 6.16). During the recent bear market for equities, when commodity futures prices, government bond indices, and real estate markets have all risen the correlations between art and other asset classes has been positive, albeit quite low.

The return per unit of risk for the various asset classes shows that over the past 20 years, hedge funds have offered the most attractive returns, with U.K. government bonds also offering a good return per unit of risk. NAREIT, art, and equity also offer attractive investment opportunities. The level to which these assets can reduce risk in an asset portfolio depends crucially on the extent to which the returns are correlated with each other. The lower the correlation, the higher the diversification benefits, and the greater the ability of the portfolio to maintain returns while reducing risk. This results in more moderate returns being made with a lower standard deviation around the expected mean.

For the lowest 10% of returns on the U.K. equity market for the last 25-year period, the average return on other financial assets varied between −6% for world equity and 1.4% for U.S. corporate bonds. U.K. government bonds also provided good protection with returns close to the average 9% over the same period (see Exhibit 6.13A).

Art provides significantly greater monthly returns during these months than the other asset classes. This is, of course, affected by the smoothing process inherent in the data.

Exhibit 6.15 Correlation Statistics for Fine Art and Financial Markets, January 1980–February 2006

	MSCI World (%)	MSCI U.S. (%)	MSCI U.K. (%)	U.S. Corporate Bond (%)	GSCI (%)	U.S. 10-Year Government Bond (%)	U.K. 10-Year Government Bond (%)	REIT (%)	Hedge Fund (%)	General Art (%)	Old Masters (%)	European Impressionism (%)	Modern (%)	CON
MSCI world	100.0													
MSCI U.S.	89.5	100.0												
MSCI U.K.	78.6	70.9	100.0											
U.S. corporate bond	9.2	14.4	3.2	100.0										
GSCI	2.7	0.5	2.4	−0.4	100.0									
U.S. 10-year government bond	5.9	14.9	3.4	71.1	−1.6	100.0								
U.K. 10-year government bond	17.4	16.2	29.1	22.9	3.0	39.1	100.0							
NAREIT	47.7	49.1	41.0	19.4	1.3	18.5	13.2	100.0						
Hedge fund	55.1	48.6	40.9	20.0	16.7	11.0	19.7	24.9	100.0					
General art	4.7	−3.2	3.2	−1.3	9.1	−3.0	−6.3	−7.5	−5.3	100.0				
Old Masters	6.2	3.3	0.3	4.3	9.2	6.7	−10.4	−2.2	7.7	43.0	100.0			
European Impressionists	6.9	0.1	4.6	−5.8	8.2	−6.7	−8.4	−0.2	0.3	74.0	33.8	100.0		
Modern	1.3	−3.6	−0.7	−0.4	4.9	−4.5	−8.8	−6.7	3.6	76.1	29.9	61.1	100.0	
Contemporary	3.2	2.3	1.5	1.3	3.9	−1.4	−8.8	−12.1	−0.8	53.4	27.9	34.6	53.0	100.0%

Exhibit 6.16 Correlation Statistics for Fine Art and Financial Markets: Five, Fifteen, and Twenty-Five Years

Time Frame	MSCI World (%)	MSCI U.S. (%)	MSCI U.K. (%)	U.S. Corporate Bond (%)	GSCI (%)	U.S. 10-Year Government Bond (%)	U.K. 10-Year Government Bond (%)	REIT (%)	Hedge Fund (%)	General Art (%)
1980–2006	4.7	v3.2	3.2	−1.3	9.1	−3.0	−6.3	−7.5	−5.3	100.0
1990–2006	2.0	−4.2	−0.7	−11.8	7.1	−5.4	−6.7	−7.0	−5.3	100.0
2000–2006	−6.1	−5.0	v2.9	−2.5	10.1	3.8	11.5	4.4	−8.9	100.0

Exhibit 6.17 Risk-Return Ratios for Fine Art and Financial Markets Based on Monthly Data, January 1980–February 2006

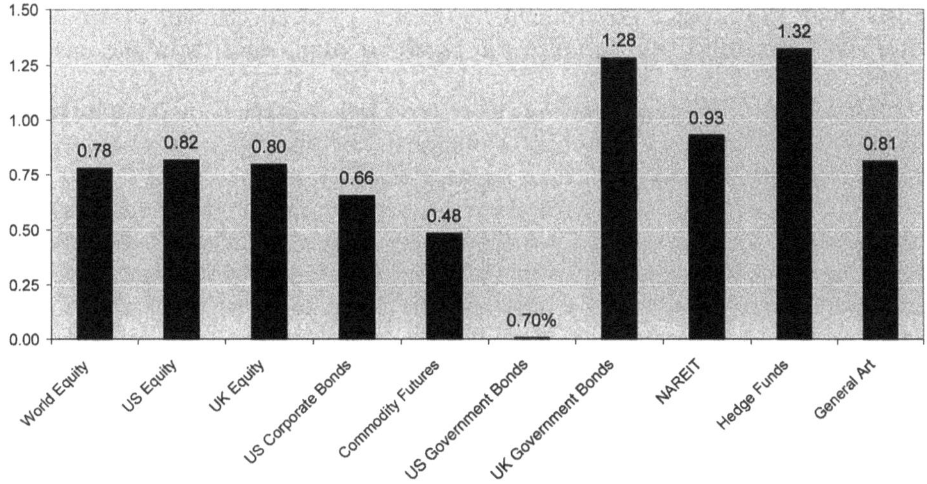

Exhibit 6.18 Fine Art Market Performance During U.K. Equity Bear Markets, Based on Monthly Data, January 1980–February 2006

Portfolio Diversification

To determine optimal portfolio allocations, we need to make an assumption about the expected return distribution of asset classes. Our best prediction of the future is helped by looking at the historical distribution of returns as an estimate of future expected returns. This, of course, depends on the time horizon chosen in the past. We have provided a number of descriptive statistics as well as correlation coefficients for the time horizons of 25 years, 15 years, and 5 years. Data on U.K. government bonds are only available on a monthly basis since 1980. Since government bonds are a crucial element of any well-diversified portfolio, we optimize the portfolio using data from the past 25 years.

Importantly, investing in art has large transaction costs, sometimes as much as 30% of the sale price. This can be minimized by taking a long time horizon. For this reason, we suggest a time horizon of 25 years.

In Exhibit 6.19 the risk-return trade-off between the various asset classes is shown along with the optimal portfolio when art is also included. Also shown is the capital market line where the risk-free rate (where the risk is assumed to be zero) intercepts with the y axis and the optimal portfolio of assets. The investor can obtain any position along the capital market line by holding a proportion of his wealth in cash, with an expected return equal to the risk-free rate and the optimal portfolio.

The optimal portfolio is derived from the perspective of a U.K. investor who has the possibility of investing in the following indices: World, U.S., and U.K. equity; U.S. corporate bonds; Commodity Futures Index; North American Real Estate Investment Trusts (NAREIT); 10-year U.K. government bonds; Art Index; and hedge funds.

We first optimize the portfolio excluding an investment in art. This assumes the risk-return profile from the past 25 years and generates the following combination of these assets held as given in Exhibit 6.20.

Exhibit 6.19 Risk-Return Trade-Off: Optimal Portfolio Allocation, January 1980–February 2006.

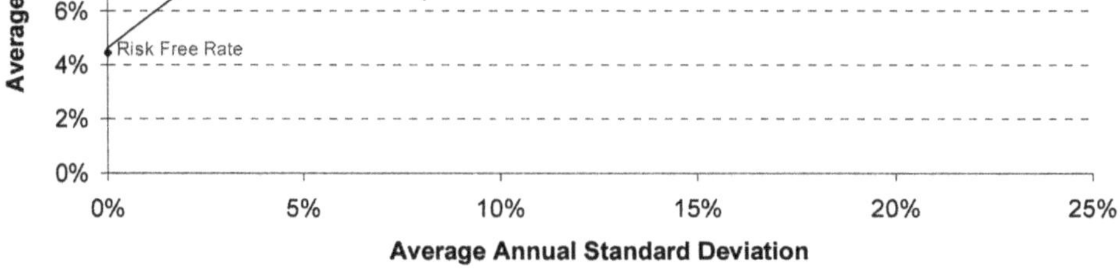

Including General Art in the portfolio, we find that the low correlation with the other asset classes results in a high allocation of art into the portfolio: over 20%. This is derived using the General Art index rather than the fund composition, which would be an even higher percentage allocation in the optimal portfolio. Therefore the more conservative return from the General art index does not overemphasize the art allocation.

Exhibit 6.20 Optimal Portfolio Allocation, Excluding Art, Based on Monthly Data, January 1980–February 2006

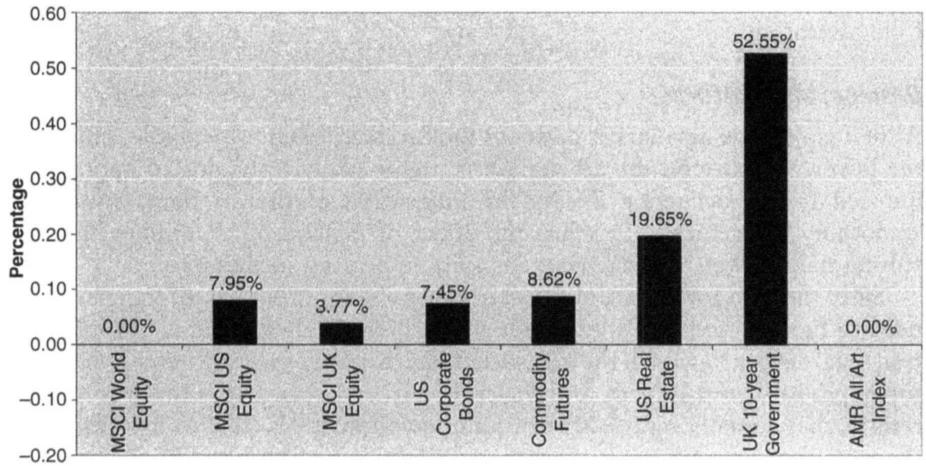

Exhibit 6.21 Optimal Portfolio Allocation, Including Art, Based on Monthly Data, January 1980–February 2006

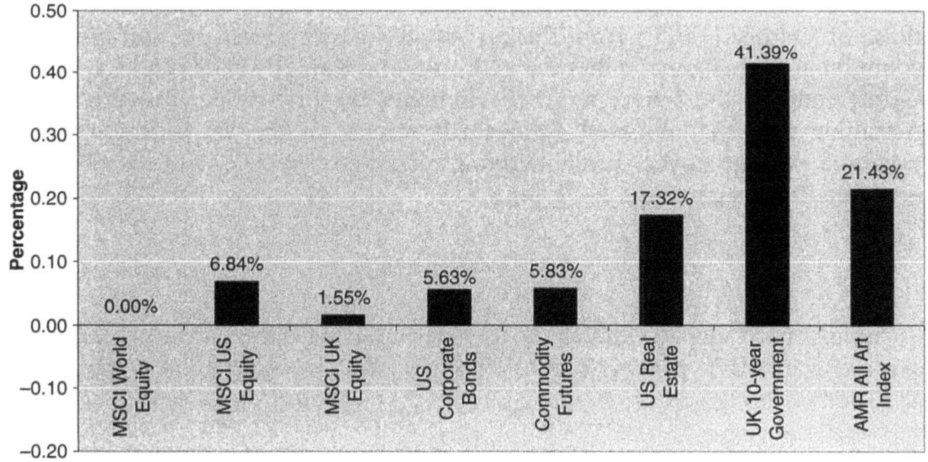

An important feature of the data methodology behind the indices is the moving average, which results in a positively autocorrelated series. It is important in the analysis on risk and return and on portfolio diversification that the true market risk and return levels are calculated. In the next section, the desmoothed data results in a more volatile return series that is more in line with the true art market volatility.

The section from this point on will take transaction costs into account, which has the effect of reducing the returns made on the series. We will look at how these two effects of greater risk and lower return affect the optimal portfolio allocation. Finally, we will include hedge funds in the optimal portfolio allocation.

Desmoothing Returns

At first glance the art market does not look to have been too volatile. However, the lower volatility on the art market is highly likely to be due to appraisal—induced biases, occurring during the indexation of the art data, and hence smoothing the returns. This has the effect of generating volatilities that are substantially lower than the true volatility appearing in the market.

Since the data for the art indices are generally appraisal based, they therefore need to be analyzed carefully. While it is a highly valuable source of information regarding behavior in the art market, there is of course a difference between the appraisal-based returns and the true market returns. It is the true market returns that actually represent the economic opportunity cost to investors, and the statistical properties of which are directly comparable to alternative asset classes. The illiquid nature of the art market, with infrequent valuations, and averaged price quotes, leads to a smoothing in the returns. It is therefore imperative that the series are "desmoothed" so as to eliminate, as far as possible, any underlying autocorrelation that tends to be characteristic of these smoothed series of appraised returns. The most widely used approaches are those of Geltner (1993), from the real-estate finance literature, and now also common in the hedge fund literature (Brooks and Kat, 2001; Kat and Lu, 2002). Geltner adjusts the return series to eliminate the first-order autocorrelation. Assuming that the observed (smoothed) return on the art index, r_t^*, is a weighted average of the true underlying return at time t, r_t, and the observed (smoothed) return at time $t - 1$, r_{t-1}^*:

$$r_t^* = (1-\alpha)r_t + \alpha r_{t-1}^* \tag{6.2}$$

Simply rearranging enables us to determine the actual return that if we assume is an AR(1) process acts to eliminate the first-order autocorrelation.

$$r_t = \frac{r_t^* - \alpha r_{t-1}^*}{1-\alpha} \tag{6.3}$$

If the first-order autocorrelation of the smoothed series is positive, then the standard deviation of the actual return series will be greater. However if the first order autocorrelation of the smoothed series is negative, then the standard deviation of the actual series will be lower. If the autocorrelation structure is more complicated, then the more rigorous process developed by Okunev and White (2003) can be adopted to remove higher levels of autocorrelation in the smoothed series.

$$\alpha = \frac{(1 + a_{0.2} - 2d_1 a_{0.1}) \pm \sqrt{(1 + a_{0.2} - 2d_1 a_{0.1})^2 - 4(a_{0.1} - d_1)^2}}{2(a_{0.1} - d_1)} \qquad (6.4)$$

where the constant, α, to desmooth the series, is a function of higher orders of autocorrelation.[5] This approach is directly applicable for art indices, which also exhibit exceptionally high autocorrelations in reported returns. There is indeed evidence of smoothing in the returns and for these series that are positively autocorrelated has the effect of diminishing the risk apparent in the asset class; hence, we need to correct for the smoothing, resulting in a more volatile "desmoothed" return series.

We find that using the more simplified approach from Geltner does not completely eliminate the first-order autocorrelation in the time series for art. The more sophisticated approach from Okunev and White (2003), which takes into account higher orders of autocorrelation, does result in a desmoothed series that no longer suffers from first-order autocorrelation. The high positive autocorrelative structure present in the art series results in the desmoothed series exhibiting significantly higher volatility.

By desmoothing the returns to account for the autocorrelation in the data, we find that the risk increases substantially from 6.5% to 11.5%.[6] By taking a universal 5% increase in the monthly standard deviation for the art series, we see how this affects the optimal portfolio allocation. This reduces the allocation in art substantially, by roughly half, from over 20% to just under 10%, with the 10% reduction in art roughly equally spread among the other asset classes in the portfolio. The low correlation still results in art providing a highly attractive portfolio investment. World equity still remains unattractive given the slightly lower return-risk ratio than the other asset classes and the relatively high correlation with the U.S. equity market; in this case, 90% correlation. This is seen in Exhibit 6.22.

Transaction Costs

Art's high transaction costs spread over 25 years equals 1.5% per year. Despite these costs, art still remains an attractive, but small portfolio allocation.

[5]See Orkunev and White (2003) for greater detail on the conditions that the autocorrelation function must fulfill and on the application to remove higher orders of autocorrelation.
[6]See Campbell (2005) for a detailed analysis on desmoothing art series data.

Exhibit 6.22 Optimal Portfolio Using Desmoothed Art Returns Based on Monthly Data, January 1980–February 2006

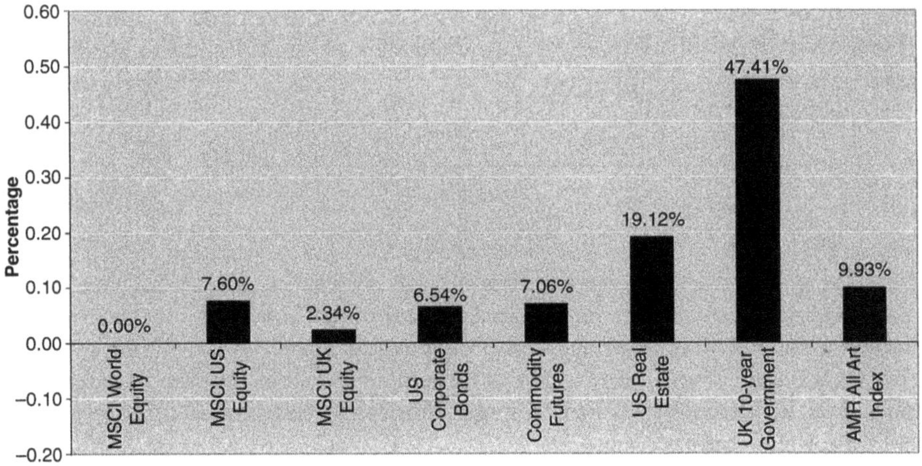

Exhibit 6.23 Optimal Portfolio Allocations Using Desmoothed Art Returns and Transaction Costs Based on Monthly Data, January 1980–February 2006

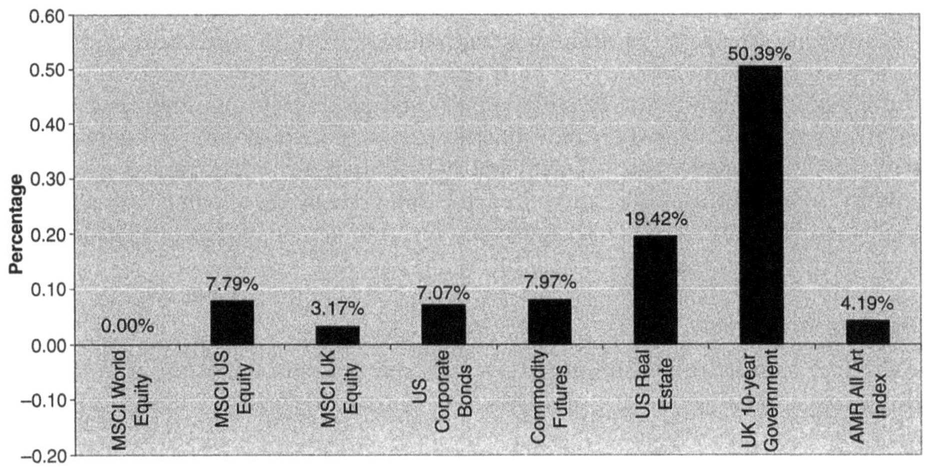

Including Hedge Funds

Hedge funds provide an attractive return per unit of risk. This means that hedge funds also provide an interesting asset to include in a diversified portfolio. Including them in the portfolio allocation analysis, we find a much higher allocation into hedge funds and art's allocation reduced to only 3%. From Exhibit 6.15 we saw that the correlation of hedge fund returns and mainstream asset classes was higher than between other alternative asset classes. This is because hedge funds, rather than being an alternative asset class, offer investment strategies for investing in mainstream assets, mainly equities.

We find that optimizing the portfolio with the inclusion of hedge funds in the four previous scenarios: (i) without art, (ii) with art, (iii) with desmoothed art, and (iv) with desmoothed art and transaction costs, produces the following portfolio allocations.

For each of the four scenarios, the allocation into art is increasingly lower and there is a large percentage allocation into hedge funds. Hedge funds over the period analyzed here have been the preferred investment to equity.

Summary and Conclusions

Faced with underperforming portfolios, investors are continually seeking alternative assets and sophisticated solutions to reap high returns while minimizing risk. In this chapter, we have taken a close look at the financial implications of including art as an alternative asset class. This previously nontransparent market is becoming more accessible via the increasing availability of indices and data on the art market. Additionally, art funds offer investors the opportunity to invest indirectly into the art market.

Indirect investment into the art market results in losing the aesthetic pleasure from holding the art; however, financial gains can be made through pooling resources with the help of experts while gaining from diversification benefits. The art fund market is still in its infancy. There are few alternatives, and these are only available to investors willing to invest at a substantial level. Entry levels are at present still high. In time, these funds may become more accessible to the mainstream investor through pooling joint interests.

The results in this chapter show that art's low correlation with other asset classes offers diversification benefits from holding art in an investment portfolio. Optimal portfolio allocations using empirical returns over the past 25 years provide support for investors to consider art an attractive, albeit small, addition to their investment strategy.

Exhibit 6.24 Optimal Portfolio Allocation, Including Hedge Funds, 1980–2006

Portfolio	MSCI U.S. Equity (%)	MSCI U.K. Equity (%)	U.S. Corporate Bond (%)	Commodities Futures (%)	U.S. Real Estate (%)	U.K. 10-Year Government Bond (%)	AMR All-Art Index (%)	Hedge Funds (%)
No art	0.00	0.00	2.96	3.04	10.20	42.55	—	41.25
With art desmoothed	0.00	0.00	2.47	1.92	9.89	35.60	15.91	34.21
Art	0.00	0.00	2.67	2.34	10.84	39.17	7.04	37.94
Desmoothed art and transaction costs	0.00	0.00	2.80	2.74	10.74	41.04	2.82	39.87

References

Anderson, R. C. (1974) Paintings as an Investment, *Economic Inquiry* 12(1):13–26.

Ashenfelter, O. (1989) How Auctions Work for Wine and Art, *Journal of Economic Perspectives* 3(3):23–36.

Ashenfelter, O., and K. Graddy (2003) Auctions and the Price of Art, *Journal of Economic Literature* 41(3):763–788.

Bauer, R., R. Molenaar, T. Steenkamp, and E. Vrugt (2004) Dynamic Commodity Timing Strategies, LIFE Working Paper, No. 04–012.

Baumol, W. J. (1986) Unnatural Value: Or Art Investment as Floating Crap Game, *American Economic Review* 76(2):10–14.

Bogle, J. C. (2005) The Mutual Fund Industry 60 Years Later: For Better or Worse? *Financial Analysts Journal* 61(1):15–24.

Campbell, R. (2005) Art as an Alternative Asset Class, Working Paper, Maastricht University.

Chanel, O., L. A. Gerard-Varet, and V. Ginsburgh (1996) The Relevance of Hedonic Price Indices, *Journal of Cultural Economics*, 20(1):1–24.

Frey, B. R., and R. Eichenberger (1995) On the Return of Art Investment Return Analyses, *Journal of Cultural Economics* 19:207–220.

Geltner, D. (1993) Smoothing in Appraisal Based Returns, *Journal of Real Estate Finance and Economics* 4:327–345.

Genesove, D., and C. Mayer (2001) Loss Aversion and Seller Behaviour: Evidence from the Housing Market, *The Quarterly Journal of Economics* 116(4):1233–1260.

Ginsburgh, V. A., J. Mei, and M. Moses (2006) The Computation of Price Indices. In V. A. Ginsburgh and D. Thorsy (eds.), *The Handbook of Economics Art and Culture*, North-Holland/Elsevier.

Grampp, W. (1989) *Pricing the Priceless: Art, Artists and Economics*, Basic Books Inc.

Keynes, J. M. (1947) *The General Theory of Employment, Interest and Money*. MacMillan and Co.

Kochugovindan, S. (2005) *Barclays Capital Equity Gilt Study*. Barclays Bank

Mei, J., and M. Moses (2002) Art as an Investment and the Underperformance of Masterpieces, *American Economic Review* 92(1):1656–1668.

Mei, J., and M. Moses (2005) Vested Interest and Biased Price Estimates: Evidence from an Auction Market, *Journal of Finance* 60(5):2409–2435.

Odean, T. (1998) Are Investors Reluctant to Realise their Losses? *Journal of Finance* 53(5):1775–1798.

Okunev, J., and D. White (2003) Hedge Fund Risk Factors and Value at Risk of Credit Trading Strategies, Working Paper, University of New South Wales.

Rouwenhorst, K. G. (2004) The Origins of Mutual Funds, Yale ICF Working Paper No. 04–48.

Stein, J. P. (1977) The Monetary Appreciation of Paintings, *Journal of Political Economy* 85(5):1021–1035.

Appendix
Index Constituents

General All Art

Pierre ALECHINSKY, Helen ALLINGHAM, Sir Lawrence ALMA-TADEMA, Michael ANCHER, Karel APPEL, Georg BASELITZ, Jean Michel BASQUIAT, Albert BIERSTADT, Pierre BONNARD, Fernando BOTERO, Francois BOUCHER, Eugene BOUDIN, Arthur Merric Bloomfield BOYD, Georges BRAQUE, Bernard BUFFET, Sir Edward Coley BURNE-JONES, CANALETTO, Marc CHAGALL, Sandro CHIA, Giorgio de CHIRICO, Pieter CLAESZ, Jean Baptiste Camille COROT, Gustave COURBET, Salvador DALI, Montague DAWSON, Otto DIX, Jean DUBUFFET, Max ERNST, Henri FANTIN-LATOUR, Lyonel FEININGER, Lucio FONTANA, Myles Birket FOSTER, Jean Honore FRAGONARD, Sam FRANCIS, Thomas GAINSBOROUGH, John William GODWARD, Jan van GOYEN, Jean-Baptiste GREUZE, Atkinson GRIMSHAW, Francesco GUARDI, Keith HARING, Henri HARPIGNIES, Childe HASSAM, Paul-Cesar HELLEU, John Frederick (snr) HERRING, Ferdinand HODLER, Antonio JACOBSEN, Johan-Laurents JENSEN, Johan Barthold JONGKIND, Asger JORN, Jan van KESSEL, Ernst Ludwig KIRCHNER, Moise KISLING, Paul KLEE, Gustav KLIMT, Willem KOEKKOEK, Oskar KOKOSCHKA, Willem de KOONING, Nicolas de LARGILLIERE, Carl LARSSON, Marie LAURENCIN, Fernand LEGER, Lord Frederic LEIGHTON, Sir Peter LELY, Bruno LILJEFORS, Nicolaes MAES, Rene MAGRITTE, Michele MARIESCHI, Ben MARSHALL, Henri MATISSE, Sir John Everett MILLAIS, Joan MIRO, Claude MONET, Giorgio MORANDI, Sir Alfred MUNNINGS, Emil NOLDE, A R PENCK, Pablo PICASSO, Serge POLIAKOFF, Pierre Auguste RENOIR, Sir Joshua REYNOLDS, Jean-Paul RIOPELLE, Diego RIVERA, Hubert ROBERT, Dante Gabriel ROSSETTI, Salomon van RUYSDAEL, Gino SEVERINI, Dorothea SHARP, Leon SPILLIAERT, Carl SPITZWEG, Alfred STEVENS, Marcus STONE, Abraham STORCK, Antonio TAPIES, David (younger) TENIERS, Fritz THAULOW, Archibald THORBURN, Giovanni Battista TIEPOLO, James Jacques Joseph TISSOT, Maurice UTRILLO, Louis VALTAT, Edouard VUILLARD, Andy WARHOL, Tom WESSELMANN, Jack Butler YEATS, Anders ZORN

Old Masters

Osias I BEERT, Nicolaes BERCHEM, Louis Leopold BOILLY, Francois BOUCHER, Jan (elder) BRUEGHEL, Jan (younger) BRUEGHEL, CANALETTO, Annibale CARRACCI, John CONSTABLE, Aelbert CUYP, Arthur DEVIS, Carlo DOLCI, Sir Anthony van DYCK, Jean Honore FRAGONARD, Frans I FRANCKEN, Thomas GAINSBOROUGH, Theodore GERICAULT, Luca GIORDANO, Jan van GOYEN, Jean-Baptiste GREUZE, Francesco GUARDI, Giacomo GUARDI, Giovanni Francesco GUERCINO, Jan Davidsz de HEEM, Egbert van HEEMSKERK, Meindert HOBBEMA, William HOGARTH, Melchior de HONDECOETER, Jean Baptiste HUET, Jacob van HULSDONCK, Jan van HUYSUM, Julius Caesar IBBETSON, Antonio JOLI, Jacob JORDAENS, Jan van I KESSEL, Nicolas LANCRET, Nicolas de LARGILLIERE, Sir

Thomas LAWRENCE, Sir Peter LELY, Carle van LOO, Nicolaes MAES, Alessandro MAGNASCO, Michele MARIESCHI, Ben MARSHALL, Adam Frans van der MEULEN, Jan Miense MOLENAER, Klaes MOLENAER, Joos de MOMPER, Peter MONAMY, Jean Baptiste MONNOYER, George MORLAND, Alexander NASMYTH, Charles-Joseph NATOIRE, Jean Marc NATTIER, Aert van der NEER, Adriaen van OSTADE, Isaac van OSTADE, Jean Baptiste OUDRY, Giovanni Paolo PANINI, Jean Baptiste PATER, Giambattista PIAZZETTA, Giovan Battista PIRANESI, Guido RENI, Sir Joshua REYNOLDS, Marco RICCI, Sebastiano RICCI, Hubert ROBERT, George ROMNEY, Salvator ROSA, Thomas ROWLANDSON, Sir Peter Paul RUBENS, Jacob van RUYSDAEL, Salomon van RUYSDAEL, Paul SANDBY, Francis (elder) SARTORIUS, John Nott SARTORIUS, Jan STEEN, George STUBBS, Giovanni Battista TIEPOLO, Giovanni Domenico TIEPOLO, Jacopo TINTORETTO, Joseph Mallord William TURNER, Lucas van UDEN, Willem van de (elder) VELDE, Simon VERELST, Nicolas van VERENDAEL, Joseph VERNET, Paolo VERONESE, David VINCKEBOONS, Simon de VLIEGER, Sebastian VRANCX, Jean Antoine WATTEAU, Jan WEENIX, Adam WILLAERTS, John WOOTTON, Philips WOUWERMAN, Joseph WRIGHT OF DERBY, Jan WYNANTS, Johann ZOFFANY, Francesco ZUCCARELLI

European Impressionists

Laureano BARRAU, Jean BERAUD, Eugene BOUDIN, Gustave CAILLEBOTTE, Paul CEZANNE, Edgar DEGAS, Jean Louis FORAIN, Paul GAUGUIN, Armand GUILLAUMIN, Albert LEBOURG, Stanislas LEPINE, Max LIEBERMANN, Edouard MANET, Henri MARTIN (French), Henri MATISSE, Maxime MAUFRA, Claude MONET, Berthe MORISOT, Roderic O'CONOR, Camille PISSARRO, Pierre Auguste RENOIR, Theodore ROUSSEAU, Alfred SISLEY, Max SLEVOGT, Joaquin SOROLLA Y BASTIDA

Modern Artists

Pierre ALECHINSKY, Karel APPEL, Fernandez ARMAN, Edouard ARROYO, Frank AUERBACH, Francis BACON, Willi BAUMEISTER, William BAZIOTES, Max BECKMANN, Joseph BEUYS, Max BILL, Jules BISSIER, Fernando BOTERO, Louise BOURGEOIS, Alberto BURRI, Reg BUTLER, Alexander CALDER, Giuseppe CAPOGROSSI, Anthony CARO, Baldaccini CESAR, Lynn CHADWICK, John CHAMBERLAIN, Eduardo CHILLIDA, CHRISTO, CORNEILLE, Joseph CORNELL, Richard DIEBENKORN, Jim DINE, Piero DORAZIO, Jean DUBUFFET, Jean FAUTRIER, Lucio FONTANA, Sam FRANCIS, Helen FRANKENTHALER, Alberto GIACOMETTI, Arshile GORKY, Adolph GOTTLIEB, Hans HARTUNG, Dame Barbara HEPWORTH, Patrick HERON, Eva HESSE, David HOCKNEY, Hans HOFMANN, Friedrich HUNDERTWASSER, Robert INDIANA, Asger JORN, Wassily KANDINSKY, Paul KLEE, Yves KLEIN, Franz KLINE, Willem de KOONING, Wilfredo LAM, Peter LANYON, Roy LICHTENSTEIN, Richard LINDNER, Richard LONG, Morris LOUIS, Piero MANZONI, Giacomo MANZU, Marino MARINI, Agnes MARTIN, Georges MATHIEU, MATTA, Joan MITCHELL, Henry O M MOORE, Robert MOTHER-

WELL, Ernst Wilhelm NAY, Louise NEVELSON, Ben NICHOLSON, Isamu NOGUCHI, Jules OLITSKI, Victor PASMORE, Serge POLIAKOFF, Jackson POLLOCK, Arnaldo POMODORO, Arnulf RAINER, Martial RAYSSE, Ad REINHARDT, Germaine RICHIER, Bridget RILEY, Jean-Paul RIOPELLE, Diego RIVERA, James ROSENQUIST, Mark ROTHKO, David SIQUEIROS, Pierre SOULAGES, Daniel SPOERRI, Nicolas de STAEL, Rufino TAMAYO, Antonio TAPIES, Wayne THIEBAUD, Mark TOBEY, Gunther UECKER, Emilio VEDOVA, Bram van VELDE, Maria Elena VIEIRA DA SILVA, Andy WARHOL, Tom WESSELMANN

Contemporary Artists

Carl ANDRE, Richard ARTSCHWAGER, Miguel BARCELO, Matthew BARNEY, Georg BASELITZ, Jean Michel BASQUIAT, Vanesa BEECROFT, Ross BLECKNER, Christian BOLTANSKI, Maurizo CATTELAN, Sandro CHIA, Francesco CLEMENTE, Tony CRAGG, Enzo CUCCHI, Olivier DEBRE, Wim DELVOYE, Thomas DEMAND, Rineke DIJKSTRA, Peter DOIG, Stan DOUGLAS, Marlene DUMAS, Tracey EMIN, Luis FEITO, Rainer FETTING, Eric FISCHL, P. & Weiss FISCHLI, Dan FLAVIN, Gunther FORG, Lucian FREUD, GILBERT and GEORGE, Robert GOBER, Nan GOLDIN, Felix GONZALEZ-TORRES, Douglas GORDON, Dan GRAHAM, Andreas GURSKY, Keith HARING, Damien HIRST, Jenny HOLZER, Gary HUME, Jorg IMMENDORF, Jasper JOHNS, Donald JUDD, Alex KATZ, Mike KELLEY, Ellsworth KELLY, Anselm KIEFER, Martin KIPPENBERGER, Jeff KOONS, Jannis KOUNELLIS, Sol LEWITT, Robert LONGO, Sarah LUCAS, Robert MANGOLD, Brice MARDEN, Mario MERZ, Juan MUNOZ, Bruce NAUMAN, Shirin NESHAT, Chris OFILI, Claes OLDENBURG, Gabriel OROZCO, Nam June PAIK, Mimmo PALADINO, PANAMERENKO, A R PENCK, Michelangelo PISTOLETTO, Sigmar POLKE, Richard PRINCE, Robert RAUSCHENBERG, Charles RAY (American), Gerhard RICHTER, Pipilotti RIST, Mimmo ROTELLA, Susan ROTHENBERG, Thomas RUFF, Edward RUSCHA, Niki de SAINT-PHALLE, David SALLE, Antonio SAURA, Jenny SAVILLE, Julian SCHNABEL, Thomas SCHUTTE, Sean SCULLY, George SEGAL, Richard SERRA (American), Andres SERRANO, Joel SHAPIRO, Cindy SHERMAN, Jose Maria SICILIA, Frank STELLA, Thomas STRUTH, Donald SULTAN, Rosemarie TROCKEL, Luc TUYMANS, Cy TWOMBLY, Jeff WALL, Franz WEST, Christopher WOOL

7 Art Investing and Wealth Accumulation

A. Petterson and O. Williams

-ArtTactic.com; Cambridge University

Introduction

As high net worth individuals' (HNWIs') personal wealth has increased, so has their interest in fine art. Once viewed almost exclusively as the pastime of connoisseurs, art collecting is increasingly seen as an alternative asset class. This, in turn, is helping fuel a large international art market that has been setting record prices, not just for the scarce work of Old Masters and Impressionist painters, but also for the works of contemporary artists.

A significant increase in global wealth over the past 10 years has arguably helped fuel the current boom in the international art market. We have seen prices rise not only among Western artists but across most emerging markets, such as Russia, China, India, the Middle East, and Southeast Asia. Intuitively this suggests that art market performance might be linked to the growing HNWI wealth in the world, a relationship we aim to explore further in this chapter.

Our approach is to attempt to partially explain art price developments using asset market factors that relate to wealth and unearned income, such as the price of gold and interest rates. To incorporate some measure of investors' prospects for future wealth, we also include forecast HNWI wealth growth. We carry out the investigation in a modeling framework that is somewhat *ad hoc* but that intentionally avoids imposing too much formal structure. In particular, our approach allows for the possibility of *long-run* relationships between the variables, since by its very nature art is typically held for relatively long holding periods: transaction costs are notoriously high and reputations of young artists take time to develop (or deteriorate, as the case may be). On short-term time horizons, low correlations can be observed between art and conventional asset returns, but this could obscure important long-run comovements, which especially capture our interest.

Collectible Investments for the High Net Worth Investor

The organization of this chapter is as follows. We begin with a brief review of key literature and recent market developments, then discuss theoretical frameworks for approaching analysis. Next we review data sources, and finally, we report empirical findings.

We emphasise that our analysis was carried-out during summer 2008 and our results and discussion reflect events up to that point, prior to the downturn experienced in autumn 2008.

Literature Review

Art as an asset class has many attractive characteristics that make it suitable for investment. Many of these have already been mentioned in other chapters of this book, particularly in Chapter 5, "An Overview of the Art Market," by Jeffrey E. Horvitz, and Rachel J. Campbell's chapter on "Art as a Financial Investment," Chapter 6.

Besides looking at return and risk characteristics of art as an asset class (Baumol, 1986; Pesando, 1993; Goetzmann, 1993; and Mei and Moses, 2002), an increasing amount of literature has been written on the relationship (or lack thereof) with other asset classes. Numerous studies by, for instance, Pesando (1993), Mei and Moses (2002), and Campbell (2005) have established the low correlation between art and other asset classes, which has become one of the primary arguments by the advocates of art for its viability as an investment with portfolio diversification benefits.

Global Wealth Effects

> *The broad long term story of global wealth creation continues unabated and the economic elite continue to drive our business, many of them somewhat insulated from the subprime credit crunch we read and hear about all day long in New York City.*
>
> —*William Ruprecht, President and CEO of Sotheby's, Investor Call, May 9, 2008*[1]

Although the value of other asset classes has been deteriorating significantly on the back of slowing U.S. and European economies, and with inflation on the rise, the art market has continued unabated because the wealthy are taking a fancy to (or maybe refuge) in art as a hard, physical asset. According to recent studies by McAndrew (2008), the size of the art market has roughly doubled in the last seven years. The estimated turnover in 2006 was €50 billion. Total auction value for Sotheby's as of the end of June 2008 was \$2.83 billion,[2] 4.5% higher than the same period last year. In 2008 a number of auction records were established for Western artworks, such as Francis Bacon's *Triptych* (1976),

[1] *Source:* Conference Call Transcript from Seeking Alpha, www.SeekingAlpha.com.
[2] Throughout this chapter we quote all auction prices including buyer's premium.

which sold for $86 million, and Lucian Freud's *Benefits Supervisor Sleeping* (1995), which achieved a record $33 million. However, emerging markets, such as India, have also seen record prices being paid for contemporary artists, as for Subodh Gupta's painting *Untitled* (2006), which sold for $1.43 million in June 2008—a record for an Indian contemporary work of art. China has seen a similar development: In May 2008 the 44-year-old artist Zeng Fanzhi sold his *Mask Series No. 6* (1996) for $8.6 million—a record for a contemporary Chinese work of art. Recent record prices are a testimony to the interest that the high end of the art market is generating among ultra-HNWIs.

Arguably, the art market is currently riding on a "global wealth effect." According to the *Capgemini Merrill Lynch World Wealth Report, 1999 to 2008* (WWR), the HNWI accumulated wealth grew approximately 88% from 1998 to 2007, in a period in which the overall art market increased 199% in nominal terms.[3] This hints at the possibility that the value of the stock of art worldwide might have some relationship to the overall growth in HNWI wealth—a relationship we explore in more detail in the proposed model described later in this chapter.

It is also clear from the two most recent WWRs that HNWIs and ultra-HNWIs allocate and spend a significant portion of their wealth on investments of passion, defined as art collections, luxury cars, yachts, sports teams, memorabilia, wine collections, luxury travel, and health/wellness. Indeed, the 2008 report found that 15.9% of HNWI "investment in passion" is invested in art, the second largest category after luxury collectibles such as private jets, yachts, and high-end automobiles.

It is difficult to assess how much of the investment in art comes down to vanity and fashion versus a question of strategic asset allocation. However, with the growth in value of art, combined with the strong "positional/status" effect that art has, one can safely assume that art is increasingly being regarded as a very attractive alternative asset for more and more HNWIs, regardless of their motivations.

The Model

We now outline the structure of the modeling framework that we apply.

Overview

Relating art price data to financial asset price series is a challenging prospect, and the diversity of existing literature in this area reflects the range of alternative asset pricing paradigms of financial economics. In general we might distinguish among three major asset pricing frameworks, as follows.

A frequent approach, popular with investors considering incorporation of art into diversified portfolios, is to examine the performance of art within a

[3]Measured by the Art Market Research (AMR) Art 100 Index.

capital asset pricing model (CAPM) context. The low correlation of art with conventional financial assets suggests that the CAPM efficient frontier can be shifted in a northwesterly direction in risk/return space, which is clearly an attractive prospect for investors. This is an effect that art investments have in common with other "alternative" assets such as private equity, hedge funds, and infrastructure projects. An attraction of the CAPM framework is that it is inherently static and stresses the diversification benefits of the asset class while remaining silent on such contentious issues as time horizon involved and how art prices could evolve over time in relation to other assets (that is, price dynamics). The focus of CAPM theory is that all asset returns share a *single* component of common randomness (known as *systematic risk*) that imposes a significantly constraining overall structure on the joint distribution of returns.

An alternative approach to modeling returns that somewhat generalizes CAPM (although from a markedly different theoretical basis) is the Arbitrage Pricing Theory (APT) of Ross (1976). This model posits that asset returns can be represented by a linear combination of weighted returns on *multiple* common risk factors plus idiosyncratic noise. Researchers investigating APT empirically have considerable freedom to identify appropriate common factors. The theoretical backbone of APT is that it should be impossible to make systematic risk-free profit over time by combining appropriate long and short positions in available assets; in other words, the linear factor model should hold true for all assets in the available universe. Empirical testing and estimation of APT require contemporaneous returns time series for assets and associated risk factors. One of the drawbacks of incorporating art returns in this framework is that art index data is relatively low frequency and heavily aggregated (for example, monthly index data reflects a wide range of heterogeneous transactions at random times during the month); it seems doubtful that a single linear specification could be compatible with such underlying heterogeneity.

A third asset pricing paradigm is the concept of the state price deflator as described by Duffie (2001). In this case we have the existence of a probability measure, and loosely speaking, the equilibrium price of any asset is computed as the expectation of its discounted future value taken under this probability measure. This is equivalent to discounting the future value at a suitable interest rate, including an appropriate risk premium. Although this approach is well suited to the valuation of well-defined future cash flows (e.g., the coupons and redemption payments of a bond), it is less immediately useful for assets (such as art) that pay no *money* income but do nevertheless provide a stream of *utility* income (such as aesthetic pleasure).

Given the drawbacks that become apparent when investigating art in heavily formalized theoretical settings, the approach we take in this chapter is to examine art index returns in an econometric setting that makes minimal theoretical assumptions and is not overly dependent on high-quality, high-frequency data. At the same time, we seek to remain focused enough to highlight potential relationships. This is intended to give us some sense of which asset pricing framework might be most suitable while keeping an open mind. We look forward to further, more rigorous analysis in future papers.

Risk Factors

If we attempted to model art returns in a rigid APT framework, we would conduct a thorough search for common factors employing statistical methods such as factor analysis. Though we refrain from publishing exhaustive results here, we find disappointing relationships between art markets and either worldwide equity returns or bond returns (both conventional and index-linked). Indeed, it is the apparent lack of correlation with these asset classes to which art owes some of its popularity as an investment vehicle. However, one time series that appears to have some nontrivial relationship with the overall index and its subcomponents is the USD-denominated price of gold. Although we report and discuss this relationship in more detail later in the chapter, the connection seems intuitively reasonable; for instance, it is popularly assumed that real assets in general (including art and gold) become jointly relatively attractive in times of high inflation (see, for instance, Chua and Woodward, 1982) and times when the safety offered by hard-currency deposits is questionable (as in periods of foreign exchange volatility).

A secondary factor that we find to have some explanatory power is the level of yields of the 10-year maturity U.S. Treasury bond; we also consider this in our regressions. (We stress that this is very much a proxy for global low-risk investment returns, and there is no particular significance to the choice of the U.S. Treasury as opposed to, say, a German bund). It is conceivable that interest rates could influence art prices via two complementary channels: a substitution effect (in which higher interest rates reduce the attractiveness of art in comparison to interest-bearing securities) and an income effect (in which higher interest rates can increase attractiveness of art as it becomes more affordable to those receiving interest income from savings). In common with the overall theme of our analysis, we have no preconceptions about which of these effects might be dominant. It is worth noting in this context that the vast majority of art transactions might be assumed to be settled using the buyer's own cash rather than with bank lending. Although credit facilities secured against art collections are available from a number of private banks, this tends to be confined to some of the most developed segments of the market in which valuation is relatively transparent. By contrast, for instance, it is hard to obtain loans against the purchase of contemporary art, which is harder to value conservatively (from a banker's point of view), and in emerging markets such facilities remain very undeveloped.

Global Wealth Growth

In a naïve model, we might suggest that the value of the stock of worldwide art would simply equal a constant proportion of HNWI wealth. From a statistical point of view this would mean fairly smooth growth in the value of any art indices, albeit with some noise. However, in reality we observe that art price indices are subject to relatively frequent downturns, which in fact occur significantly more frequently than we would expect from comparison with the growing stocks of global wealth (or indeed growing GDP).

Instead we propose a more anticipatory notion. It seems intuitively quite reasonable that art market prices could somehow incorporate a forward-looking component of value, which we tentatively suggest represents *expectations of future growth* in HNWI wealth. For instance, when the market is bullish on future wealth, there might be a tendency for art prices to rally (and do the opposite when wealth growth forecasts are more downbeat).

We therefore propose the following model: We denote by W_t the total wealth of HNWIs at time t. On aggregate, HNWIs are expected to allocate a fixed proportion of this wealth to art at time t, and we denote this proportion by θ_t. For generality at this stage we allow θ_t to be a time-dependent function of wealth W_t, which we denote by $\theta_t(W_t)$. Suppose that we assume a certain annual growth rate of HNWI wealth g^e_{HNW} with a time horizon of H years into the future (that is, at time t we forecast wealth growth up to $t + H$). Beyond this point we assume that HNWI wealth grows at the same rate as the risk-adjusted discount rate. We also introduce the notation $\mathbb{P}[\text{reputation maintained}]$ to represent the joint probability that the reputations of today's "basket" of artists will be maintained for the next H years.

We now denote the spot market value of the stock of all outstanding art at time t by $P_{ART,t}$ and this is given by the probability-weighted present value

$$\begin{aligned} P_{ART,t} &= \mathbb{P}[\text{reputation maintained}]PV[\theta_{t+H}(W_{t+H})W_{t+H}] \\ &= \mathbb{P}[\text{r.m.}]\theta_{t+H}(W_{t+H})W_t\left[\frac{(1+g^e_{HNW})^H}{(1+r_f+\pi)^H}\right] \end{aligned} \tag{7.1}$$

where r_f is the risk-free discount rate and π is an appropriate risk premium (which we assume is constant, independent of time horizon, and therefore treat as a component of investors' required return or yield).

As regards reputation effects: Clearly, derivation of a series of $\mathbb{P}[\text{reputation maintained}]$ is somewhat impractical, although in future work we intend to investigate the quantity more formally by use of latent reputation variables $R_t^{(i)}$ with $R_t^{(i)} = 1$, indicating that artist i can be considered established at time t and therefore suitable auction material. We would expect that $R_t^{(i)}$ would evolve differently over time, depending on sector—for example, if comparing an emerging artist with an established artist, we would expect that

$$\lim_{h\to\infty}\mathbb{P}[R_{t+h}^{(\text{contemporary})} = 0] > \lim_{h\to\infty}\mathbb{P}[R_{t+h}^{(\text{established})} = 0] \approx 0$$

Now we pose the question: What happens to the equilibrium price in Equation 7.1 if the assumed rate of wealth growth g^e_{HNW} changes? We hence calculate the derivative

$$\frac{\partial P_{ART,t}}{\partial g^e_{HNW}} = \frac{H}{(1+g^e_{HNW})} P_{ART,t} + \Pi[\text{r.m.}] \frac{\partial \theta_{t+H}}{\partial g^e_{HNW}} W_t \left[\frac{1+(g^e_{HNW})^H}{(1+r_f+\pi)^H} \right]$$

$$\frac{\partial P_{ART,t}}{\partial g^e_{HNW}} = \frac{H}{(1+g^e_{HNW})} P_{ART,t} + \frac{\partial \theta_{t+H}}{\partial g^e_{HNW}} \frac{1}{\theta_{t+H}} P_{ART,t} \tag{7.2}$$

$$\frac{\left(\frac{\partial P}{P}\right)}{\partial g^e_{HNW}} = \frac{H}{1+g^e_{HNW}} + \epsilon_{\theta_{t+H}, g^e_{HNW}}$$

where we use $\epsilon_{\theta_{t+H}, g^e_{HNW}}$ to denote the semielasticity of the allocation proportion θ_{t+H} with respect to the expected growth rate g^e_{HNW}. Hence the percentage change in art price for a 1% change in expected wealth growth rate will approximately equal the time horizon H divided by $1+g^e_{HNW}$ plus $\epsilon_{\theta_{t+H}, g^e_{HNW}}$ (and if the allocation proportion is constant, of course this second term will be zero). Similarly, we can derive a sensitivity between prices and the discount rate as follows:

$$\frac{\partial P_{ART,t}}{\partial r_f} = -\frac{H}{(1+r_f+\pi)} P_{ART,t}$$

$$\frac{\left(\frac{\partial P}{P}\right)}{\partial r_f} = -\frac{H}{1+r_f+\pi} \tag{7.3}$$

We note in passing that both Equations 7.2 and 7.3 are somewhat similar to the concept of modified duration, which is used in the analysis of fixed income securities as a measurement of the sensitivity of bond prices to yield (see, for instance, Fabozzi, 2005).

Data

Our analysis is based on data gathered from a selection of diverse sources and we carefully explain these next.

Art Prices

Our art price data are indices calculated by Art Market Research (AMR), which uses average auction returns on a three-month moving average; however, it's important to emphasize that these do not use the Case-Schiller repeat-sales methodology, which is considered more robust because it compares identical pairs of data rather than averages. AMR provides indices calculated for the overall art market as well as separate indices for particular segments, such as Old Masters. According to availability of data, for some segments of the market we use data that AMR designates the "central 80%" price bracket of the market, which indicates that the highest and lowest 10% of sales have been removed from calculations. However, in other cases (such as the Art 100 Index), we are able to use the 100% price bracket, which includes all sales.[4] The artists who are included in the various AMR indices are listed in the appendix to this chapter.

It is important at this stage to draw attention to the problem of *survivorship bias* that plagues art auction data. This bias arises as a result of several factors:

Reputation. Major auction houses, the source of the data used to calculate the index, do not typically accept work by artists who don't have an established reputation. Though this factor might be relatively insignificant in the indices of, for instance, Old Masters and Impressionists, the effect is highly material in the case of contemporary work.

Editing. Auction houses might have a tendency to edit their sales depending on the outcome of the last auctions, that is, select those artworks that are selling well. Works that are losing value or are not selling are likely to be edited out of forthcoming sales, or sellers will be discouraged/advised not to consign. Similarly, Goetzmann (1993) argues that the decision by an owner to sell a work of art in the first place could be conditional on whether or not the work's value has increased.

Reserve prices. Ashenfelter, Graddy, and Stevens (2001) point out that not all items that are put up for sale at auctions are sold, because some final bids might not reach the reservation prices. The price data of these "failed" lots are normally not recorded.

All these factors would tend to bias estimated returns upward, so we view affected index returns as approximate or as an upper bound on the average return obtained by investors over the period. The return could be further reduced by transaction costs. Finally, it should be noted that art auction data only represent around 47% of the total art market (McAndrew, 2008).

Wealth Growth and Financial Returns

Data on expected wealth growth rates have been compiled from the *Capgemini Merrill Lynch World Wealth Report*, which has provided forecasts of future expected annual growth in global HNWI wealth every year since 1999. These forecasts have typically been proposed for four- to five-year time horizons. To make this series more comparable with the monthly art data, we interpolated monthly forecasts using a cubic spline methodology, as illustrated in Figure 7.1. We recognize the potential distortions that interpolation can introduce; however, we feel relatively comfortable with this approach in this case because the series is inherently rather qualitative. Our aim is to create a monthly series that to some degree captures the *zeitgeist* of the HNWI world.

Due to the lack of availability of suitable alternatives, when analyzing geographical segments of the market, such as contemporary Chinese, we use global HNWI growth rates, irrespective of the fact that regional forecasts would be preferable.

[4]Further details of the AMR methodology can be obtained from Art Market Research via *www.artmarketresearch.com.*

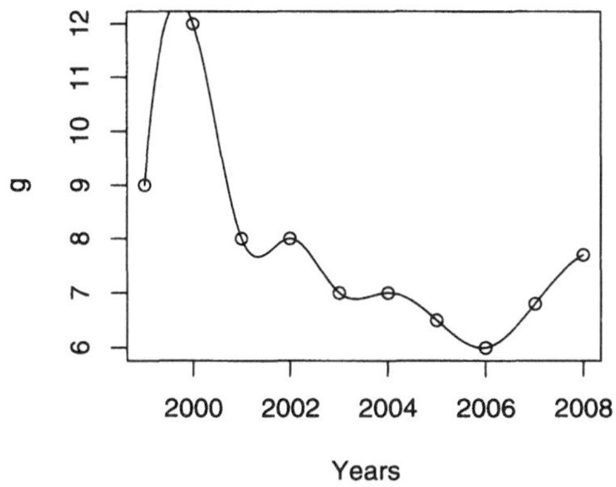

Figure 7.1 HNWI Wealth Forecast Growth Rates. *Note:* Small circles represent the original annual data points from the *Capgemini Merrill Lynch Wealth Report,* and the plotted line shows the intermediate points interpolated by cubic spline

Monthly U.S. Treasury 10-year yields originate from the Federal Reserve H.15 report. For all analysis, we consider monthly data from June 1999 to April 2008 (107 observations).

Empirical Analysis

We now apply the model to our chosen dataset and discuss our findings.

Methodology

As our most general specification we make the simplifying assumption that $\epsilon_{\theta_{t+H},g^e_{HNW}} = 0$ and propose that returns on the asset from $t - 1$ to t might be represented as follows:

$$r_{ART,t} = \beta_{gold}\gamma_t + \beta_{HNW}\frac{\Delta g^e_{HNW,t}}{1+g^e_{HNW,t-1}} + \beta_r\frac{\Delta r_{ft}}{1+r_{f_{t-1}}+\pi} + \epsilon_t \tag{7.4}$$

where the second and third beta coefficients can be interpreted as

$$\begin{aligned}\beta_{HNW} &= H \\ \beta_r &= -H + \beta_r^{wealth}\end{aligned} \tag{7.5}$$

where (in the latter case) we distinguish between the discounting effect (H) and the wealth effect, which we denote by β_r^{wealth}.

We denote the gold return from $t - 1$ to t by γ_t, $\Delta g^e_{HNW,t}$ is the change in the expected wealth growth rate from $t - 1$ to t, Δr_{f_t} is change in risk-free rate from t – 1 to t and ε_t is some noise term. Summing both sides of Equation 7.4 from time 0 to *t* provides a formulation in terms of log prices (which we denote by *p* with appropriate subscripts):

$$p_{ART,t} = \alpha + \beta_{gold} p_{GOLD,t} + \beta_{HNW} \sum_{\tau=1}^{t} \frac{\Delta g^{e}_{HNW,\tau}}{1 + g^{e}_{HNW,\tau-1}} + \beta_r \sum_{\tau=1}^{t} \frac{\Delta r_{f_\tau}}{1 + r_{f_{\tau-1}}} + \sum_{\tau=0}^{t} \varepsilon_\tau \quad (7.6)$$

where α is some constant. As a simplification, we have also taken the bold step of setting risk premium $\pi = 0$. Our justification for this is to suggest that the utility of incremental return expected to compensate for risk should be offset, to some degree, by the nonfinancial benefits of art ownership (such as aesthetic pleasure), which we do not explicitly model. Determination of the "correct" risk premium here therefore remains an open question.

Having established the proposed specification we proceed to empirical investigation with a view to testing appropriateness of the model and estimation of the key unobservable parameters.

At first glance it would appear that the obvious course of action is to estimate the regression in Equation 7.6 by conventional ordinary least squares (OLS). However, as first highlighted by Granger and Newbold (1974), caution is required in applying this technique to variables that might be *nonstationary* (loosely speaking, these are series that do not have a fixed mean and variance/covariance structure over time; it is generally the case that asset prices such as ours *do* follow nonstationary processes such as the random walk). In such cases it is frequently possible to obtain OLS estimation results that are apparently an excellent fit (measured in terms of R^2) with highly significant β coefficients, although inspection of the regression residuals indicates that they themselves are also nonstationary, which invalidates the results. This phenomenon is known as *spurious regression.*

In a major econometric advance however Engle and Granger (1987) introduced the concept of *cointegration* and demonstrated that regression results remain valid in the special case where residuals are stationary. In this case, significant estimated β values can be interpreted as characterizing a *long-run* equilibrium relationship between the nonstationary series. In the short term, the series could diverge from one another for prolonged periods of time, but nevertheless, over longer time horizons, there is a fundamental tendency for a linear relationship to persist. We believe that these dynamics might well characterize the long-term relationships among art prices, wealth, and financial returns, so we proceed to estimate the model in Equation 7.6, being alert to the pitfalls of spurious regression and the need to test carefully for nonstationarity of series and residuals.

Compute the summation terms in Equation 7.6 as:

$$\lambda_t \equiv \sum_{\tau=1}^{t} \frac{\Delta g^e_{HNW,\tau}}{1+g^e_{HNW,\tau-1}}$$

and

$$\omega_t \equiv \sum_{\tau=1}^{t} \frac{\Delta r_{f_\tau}}{1+r_{f_{\tau-1}}}$$

before estimating the regression composed of

$$\hat{p}_{ART,t} = \alpha + \beta_{gold} p_{GOLD,t} + \beta_{HNW} \lambda_t + \beta_r \omega_t \tag{7.7}$$

Results

As a first step we test for nonstationarity of our data series using Augmented Dickey Fuller (ADF) tests. The results of these tests appear in Table 7.1 and indicate that we cannot reject the null hypothesis of a "unit root" (nonstationarity) in any of the series in Equation 7.7.

When testing for nonstationarity, it is important to consider whether a time series may indeed be a random walk or, alternatively, an autoregressive process with many lags. For a pure random walk, we would find that each change in the level of the series persists permanently (there is no tendency for the series to revert to a long-run mean). However, this can be mistaken (both visually and statistically) for a series that does revert to a long-run mean, only very slowly. Therefore, in testing for nonstationarity, the ADF tests require that we specify a certain number of lagged series values that help determine whether

Table 7.1 Unit-Root Test Results

Series	Lags	ADF Stat	*p*-Value
Art 100 Index	2	0.18	0.97
Old Masters 100	13	1.84	1.00
European Impressionist art	3	0.451	0.98
Contemporary Art 100	12	1.67	1.00
Contemporary Chinese art	3	0.910	1.00
Indian 20th-century painting	2	–0.515	0.88
Gold	6	1.588	1.00
λ_t	17	–1.48	0.54
ω_t	1	–1.76	0.40

there might be a significant degree of mean reversion. In our testing process we determine the appropriate number of lags by application of the Akaike Information Criterion (a method of comparing the relative goodness of fit of alternative model specifications, which guides us on how many lags appear to provide useful information).

Our approach for each segment of the AMR index is to estimate the cointegration regression in Equation 7.7 by means of ordinary least squares. If a valid cointegration relation is present, we should find that the residuals from this regression are stationary. For each regression estimated, we test for the stationarity of residuals using both ADF tests (with lags selected by AIC) and the test of KPSS (where the null hypothesis is stationarity). Overall results are presented numerically in Table 7.2; Figures 7.2 through 7.6 show plots of actual series compared with fitted series and residuals. Because the results of each of these regressions are subtly different for each segment of the market, we discuss our results case by case.

One common theme throughout the estimation is significant serial correlation in residuals, as evidenced by the Breusch-Godfrey Lagrange Multiplier tests reported in the results table. As well as indicating the possibility of a cycle in the data or lack of long-run equilibrium, this could also be an artifact of the moving average method of construction used by AMR or the cubic spline method we applied to generate monthly $g^{e}_{HNW,t}$ series.

Table 7.2 Results of Estimation of Cointegrating Regression

					Residual Tests		
Series	β_{gold}	β_{HNW}	β_r	R^2	**KPSS**	**ADF**	**Serial Correlation**
Art 100 Index	0.824	7.18	0.72	0.72	0.11	−2.98	580.4
	(15.8)	(4.44)	(0.214)			[0.04]	[0.00]
Old Masters 100	0.574	7.12	−1.01	0.83	0.16	−1.87	204.3
	(22.5)	(8.98)	(−0.610)			[0.35]	[0.00]
European Impressionist art	0.730	10.02	−1.97	0.58	0.12	−2.44	668.9
	(11.8)	(5.20)	(−0.487)			[0.13]	[0.00]
Contemporary art 100	0.873	8.70	−17.7	0.88	0.07	−2.55	122.9
	(22.8)	(7.30)	(−7.09)			[0.11]	[0.00]
Contemporary Chinese art	3.35	10.9	34.2	0.91	0.13	−2.84	161.4
	(30.1)	(3.16)	(4.71)			[0.06]	[0.00]
Indian 20th-century painting	2.25	−14.7	38.9	0.93	0.10	−3.15	164.3
	(27.3)	(−5.72)	(7.23)			[0.03]	[0.00]

Note: KPSS asymptotic critical value is 0.463 at the 5% level. *t*-ratios appear in parentheses and *p*-values in square brackets. Serial correlation test is the Breusch-Godfrey Lagrange Multiplier test.

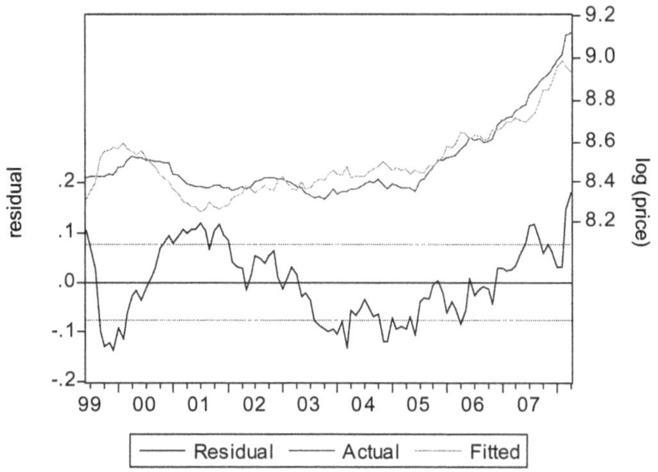

Figure 7.2 Old Masters 100

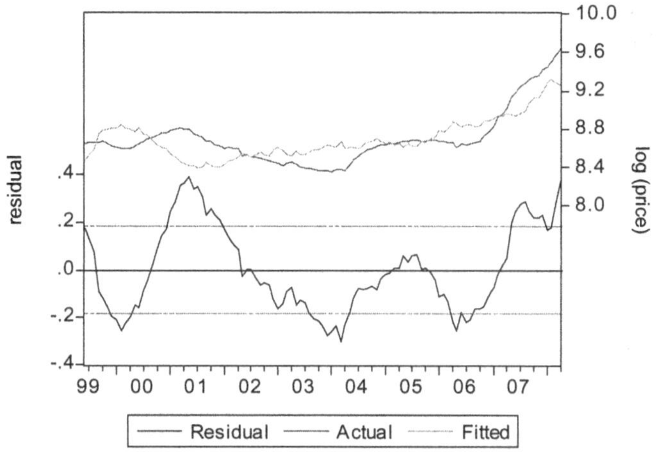

Figure 7.3 European Impressionist Art

Old Masters and Impressionists

For Old Masters our empirical findings show relatively poor evidence of cointegration compared to other segments. In the case of Impressionists, results are even less compelling, both statistically and visually, when we compare the fit of the regression with actual data series. In both cases the null hypothesis of a unit root in residuals cannot be rejected by ADF tests (although we concede that the null of stationarity is not rejected by KPSS). Here we consider a number of factors that could partially explain this phenomenon.

The prices of Old Masters have been lagging behind those of contemporary art, despite the fact that the supply of Old Masters is shrinking. Between April

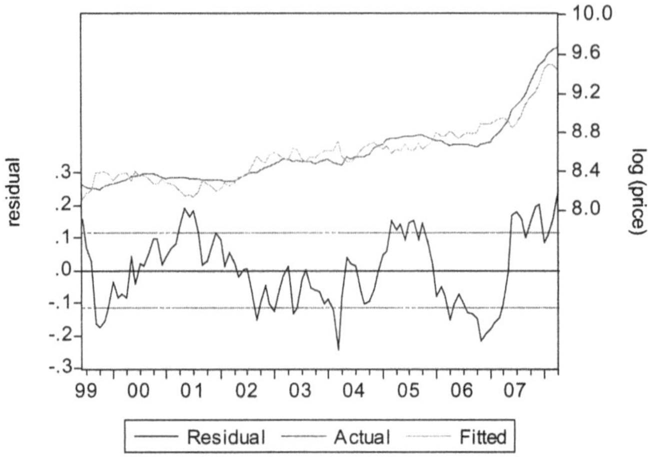

Figure 7.4 Contemporary Art 100

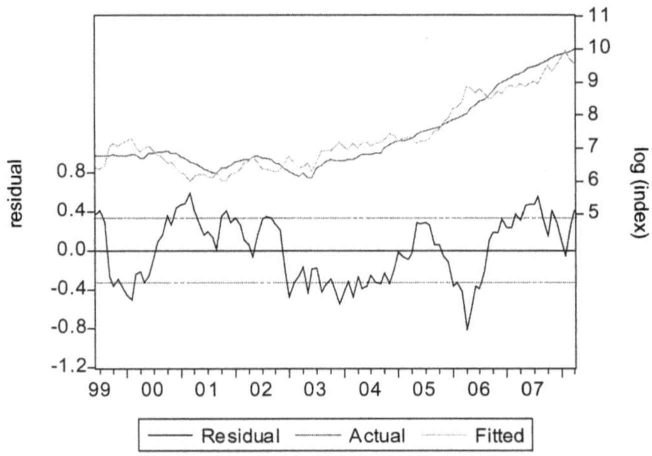

Figure 7.5 Contemporary Chinese Art

1998 and April 2008, according to the AMR index, the Old Masters market had a total return of 115%, versus 346% for the contemporary art market. There appear to be a number of reasons for this difference. First, the Old Masters market is a specialist/connoisseur market compared to that of contemporary art. With museums around the world hunting for the last remaining treasures, there are increasingly fewer opportunities to be found. Both strict deaccession policies for museums as well as national patrimony laws prevent these masterpieces being moved freely across borders. For the new wealth that has recently entered the art market, the lack of quality supply and the characteristics of the Old Masters market make it very difficult for any new entrant to build a first-rate collection of Old Masters today.

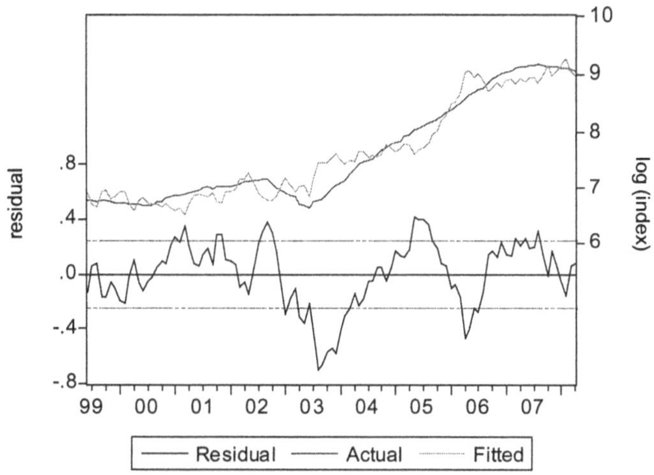

Figure 7.6 Indian 20th-Century Painting

The second factor behind the lag of the Old Masters market can be attributed to a generation shift and a change of taste in our society, coupled with a lack of art-historical knowledge. The new generation of art collectors are less or not at all familiar with the classical art-historical education that many Old Masters dealers used to be able to take for granted. Hence there is a huge knowledge gap in the Old Masters market today. Efforts by dealers, such as the London-based Colnaghi, to attract younger clientele through their mixed contemporary/Old Masters exhibitions are signs that the trade is realizing the challenge ahead.

Although very different from the Old Masters market, the traditionally biggest-grossing sector, the Modern and Impressionist market has been overtaken by the contemporary art market since 2007. Lack of quality supply has forced major dealers to look for opportunities in the contemporary sector, another sign that the "older" markets are offering fewer opportunities, pushing the trade and hence its clients into the contemporary market, where supply is still ample.

In 2007, Christie's and Sotheby's total USD auction volume for Old Masters was above $700 million, dwarfed by the size of contemporary art sales of $3.1 billion and Modern/Impressionist auctions of $2.6 billion.[5]

Contemporary

For the case of Contemporary Art 100, we find rather more persuasive evidence of cointegration. Again we are unable to reject the unit root hypothesis in residuals via ADF tests, but KPSS provides relatively strong support for stationarity, and visual inspection of the actual and fitted lines suggests a plausible common trend. Both R^2 and coefficient t-ratios are high, which can be loosely

[5]Source: Sotheby's and Christie's.

indicative of cointegration. The pattern of the residuals here suggests that our regression systematically underestimates for prolonged periods during approximately 2001, 2005, and 2008; however, establishing a missing factor to explain these potential regime shifts could help improve the fit statistically.

Considering the results more closely, we find a positive coefficient on gold returns that is a little less than unity, an estimated value of approximately 8.7 years for β_{HNW} (which we take to equal the wealth growth time horizon H) and a significant negative coefficient for β_r. This latter coefficient is somewhat surprising since, according to our suggested decomposition in Equation 7.5, we would expect $|\beta_r| < H$. However, there are various relevant complexities here that we have deliberately abstracted away from in our model, such as our assumptions of zero semielasticity of allocation ϵ and constant risk premium π. At the expense of statistical precision, we prefer to simply highlight these factors here rather than dwell on further exhaustive analysis, and we look forward to considering these effects more closely in future research.

The improved fit in this case is reassuring since the contemporary art market has arguably received the most intense media and research scrutiny of recent years, and it is well known that this segment has recently attracted significant and conspicuous new investment by HNWIs. Indeed, in 2007 the contemporary art market (measured by Sotheby's/Christie's sales) overtook the Modern/Impressionist market for the first time. In particular there has been much recent media focus on the ultra-high end of the contemporary market with the arrival of new ultra-HNWI buyers keen to establish new collections rapidly.

It seems particularly important to note here that in contrast to Old Masters and Impressionists, an important feature of the contemporary segment is that there is good liquidity on the supply side in the form of an ever-expanding stream of new work by both established and promising young artists alike. This makes it realistically possible for an HNWI to establish a sizeable and important collection of contemporary work far more rapidly than would ever be possible in the more traditional segments, although, of course, collectors must take account of the probability of "reputation maintenance," as we discussed earlier.

Emerging Markets

Again, for the cases of Chinese and Indian art, we find more persuasive evidence of cointegration. In the case of India, the unit root residuals hypothesis is clearly rejected at the conventional 5% level and for China at the 6% level.

Interestingly, in the cases of both markets, we find β_{gold} significantly higher than unity and high-positive coefficients on β_r, which suggest a dominant wealth effect of interest rates in these markets. (The very large extent of China's state lending in the U.S. Treasury market is well documented, as is the extremely high level of household holdings of gold in India.) For China we find a plausible significant value for β_{HNW}, indicating a wealth growth time horizon H of approximately 11 years. For India, however, we estimate β_{HNW} to be significantly negative—a curious result that should again be taken as evidence of the limitations of our simplified model and that serves as a reminder of the importance of using a g^e_{HNW} series that captures geographical variations in expected wealth growth.

From the perspective of goodness of fit, emerging markets give the impression of perhaps having more in common with the Contemporary Art 100 segment than the traditional Old Masters and Impressionists. This is a revealing reflection of the nature of these markets and the rapid pace with which their structure and valuations are catching up with more established segments. We provide some background commentary on this trend in the discussions that follow.

India

The Indian art market grew from about $2.3 million in 2001 to approximately $144 million in 2006. At the beginning of 2007, the market saw a significant slowdown in the Modern Indian art segment, leading to an overall fall in total sales volume of 32%, to $98 million. The Modern Indian art market has seen average prices coming down, from $107,000 in September 2006 to $70,000 in September 2007 (a drop of 34%). In the same period the contemporary Indian art market saw an increase in average prices of 30%, from $31,000 to $40,000, closing the average price gap between the modern and contemporary artists to only $30,000 from $77,000 the year before. There has been a clear change in focus among art buyers, who are now looking for a more contemporary aesthetic but also see an opportunity to ride the next art market wave.

In 2008, prices of both modern and contemporary Indian art have strengthened further, and there are clear signs that the modern Indian art market is again attracting interest after the speculative bubble deflated toward the end of 2006. Furthermore, both the modern and contemporary Indian art markets have seen an increasing demand at the top end ($500,000 and above), a trend that is driving higher volumes and is likely to drive further price increases. We are starting to see a similar trend in the emerging markets to that of the Western markets, where the very high end of the market is performing strongly, regardless of the economic circumstances, mainly as a result of this end of the market appealing to the super-wealthy, recession-proof buyers. Tina Ambani, the wife of Anil Am-bani (who ranks number six among *Forbes'* world billionaires), paid a record $2.5 million for F. N. Souza's *Birth* at Christie's Indian auction in London in June 2008. The top end of the market accounted for 38% of total value in modern Indian sales (up from 19% in March 2007) and 28% in contemporary Indian sales (there was no contemporary sale above $500,000 in March 2007).

China

In 2007, China became the third largest art market in terms of turnover. The Chinese market generated no fewer than 75 sales above the million-dollar threshold, with top prices paid for works by the contemporary artists Cai Guoqiang, Zheng Fanzhi, Yue Minjun, and Zhang Xiaogang.

In 2007, 36 Chinese artists featured in the Artprice Index for the top 100 contemporary artists in terms of sales revenue. Since the summer of 2005, Chinese contemporary art auction sales in China have entered a phase of rapid development. The results from the auction house China Guardian (established in 1993 and the first auction house to sell oil paintings and sculptures on mainland China) is evidence of this development. Prior to 2003, its sales generally reached no more than 5 million RMB yuan (less than $2 million). During the following two years, volumes rose rapidly, and in the autumn of 2005, the volume broke through 100 million RMB yuan (approximately $13 million) for the first time.

Fueling the market is not only speculative fever but also China's own economic growth—eight of the 10 buyers of Christie's Asian art "top lots" last fall were believed to be Chinese. Globally, there is a widespread belief that this collecting field is one of the few in which masterpieces, both new and old, are still available for sale.

China ranked second in HNWI population growth, advancing 20.3% in 2007—more than two-and-a-half times greater than its 2006 pace. Market capitalization and real GDP growth rates exploded last year, at 291%[6] and 11.4%, respectively. Fueled by impressive price increases and strong IPO activity, the Shanghai Exchange grew to be the sixth largest exchange in the world in terms of total market capitalization. Yet despite rapid growth in its financial services sector, China's economy is still built on its manufacturing capacity. This helps explain why its HNWI population growth is slower than that of India—and why the gap continues to widen between China's richest citizens, a group with a particularly high concentration of wealth, and the middle class, which continues to grow in size but remains largely unable to cross the HNWI threshold. Nonetheless, 2007 HNWI growth in China greatly exceeded its 2006 performance of 7.8% rate, reflecting strong economic fundamentals and great potential for future gains.

Conclusion

Establishing robust relationships between asset prices is a tenuous undertaking in general. In handling art price data, this task becomes necessarily even more approximate. In the course of writing this chapter we have attempted to steer a cautious course away from tentative assertions that can only be weakly supported by actual data. On the other hand, we have chosen to highlight apparent features of the data that are somewhat consistent with stylized facts and deserve further technical consideration.

[6] According to Artprice Art Market Trends 2007.

The overwhelming majority of published art market research is qualitative in nature, and our primary aim in this chapter has been to demonstrate how quantitative treatments might be applicable to reinforce anecdotal evidence in a framework that helps bridge the gap between art markets and financial assets.

From the point of view of investors and their advisers, our results represent an initial step at clarifying risk differences between alternative segments of the art market. It is, of course, always possible to carry out more thorough statistical treatment, however, and we have also identified specific areas of further technical analysis that seem worthwhile. Consequently we first summarize here our preliminary hypotheses for *investors;* we then conclude by discussing potential *econometric* refinements.

Investor Perspective

We note first the apparent differences between price dynamics in emerging/contemporary and those in mature art market segments. Our analytical method has focused on detecting whether long-run equilibria might exist among art, HNWI wealth growth, and certain asset markets. Though we feel there is a tolerable body of evidence to support the existence of relationships in contemporary and emerging markets, we have had less success in examining segments such as Old Masters and European Impressionists. This partially corroborates existing literature that advocates the use of art for portfolio diversification; however, our findings suggest that mature market segments might be more effective in this regard.

Where our analyses *do* support the possible existence of long-run equilibria, we find that long-run returns in particular segments are similar to weighted portfolios indexed to the price of gold, U.S. Treasury interest rates, and HNWI wealth growth expectations. Various market segments appear to place different weightings on these components, somewhat in line with our intuition, at least from a directional point of view. For example, Contemporary Art 100 appears to have long-run price performance similar to gold but overlaid with positive exposure to HNWI wealth growth (explained by buying pressure from collectors) and negative exposure to interest rates (explained by the relative attractiveness of the asset class in low-yield environments). By contrast, Chinese and Indian art markets appear more highly leveraged to the price of gold and have positive dependency on interest rates (both likely to be the result of wealth effects).

We have already drawn attention to the limitations of using art index data for our analysis, in particular highlighting the problem of survivorship bias. Taking into consideration this bias plus the effect of transaction costs would materially reduce actual realized market returns. This means that investors with neutral views on interest rates and HNWI growth should perhaps consider whether a position in gold bullion might be a more liquid and cheaper alternative to the art markets we have examined. Of course, the positive utility benefits of art ownership must always be considered an offset to this position.

For all segments we examined (apart from Indian 20th-century painting),[7] there is evidence of positive sensitivity to HNWI wealth growth. This suggests that a suitable portfolio of art investments could also commend itself as a long-term "hedge" of forecast global HNWI wealth growth. It seems likely that such a position could be of value to a range of institutional and private investors.

Finally, we emphasize that the relationships we propose are fundamentally long run by nature and of most interest to collectors and investors as opposed to speculators. Inspection of the plots of our regression residuals very much reinforces the fact that speculative trends can drive divergence from long-run "fundamental" levels for prolonged periods of time. Our analysis is not intended to provide a model for trading art markets; rather, we want to shed light on its intricate connections with the rest of the economy.

Econometric Perspective

In the course of our analysis we have necessarily made a number of simplifying assumptions. To begin with, our simple theoretical model raises various specific issues, which include (1) How might portfolio allocation proportions behave as wealth levels change? (2) How should future expected values of art be discounted back to spot? (3) How do interest rates affect art demand from the perspective of substitution and wealth effects? (4) How might we handle probabilities of "reputation maintenance" more rigorously? Each of these elements of the model can be enhanced and would help us relate intuition more closely to the effects we estimate.

From a data point of view, we are acutely conscious that throughout we have used global data series, although it would be highly preferable to incorporate local data series for markets, where relevant (particularly China and India). Although mature art market segments are essentially global by nature, there are clearly more regional influences in contemporary and emerging segments. As far as interest rates are concerned, we recognize that there is considerable international investment in the U.S. Treasury market and that there is a degree of dependency between interest rates in international markets. However, we look forward to carrying out further analysis in the future, with more focused local series. Forecasting wealth growth is, on the other hand, a more subjective exercise, but generating local series should also prove worthwhile.

Our main concern from an econometric perspective is the presence of significant serial correlation in regression residuals. This has the effect of understating standard errors in our results, which overstates the significance of estimated β coefficients. Because our analysis in this chapter is preliminary, we have erred on the side of transparency in methodology and have stopped short of computing serial-correlation robust standard errors, but we realize that there

[7]Although it's worthy of much further scrutiny, we believe the aberration in the Indian case could well be due to the use of global wealth growth forecasts rather than local forecasts.

is a range of alternative methods we could use to treat this problem to ensure greater precision.

References

Ashenfelter, O., K. Graddy, and M. Stevens (2001) A Study of Sale Rates and Prices in Impressionist and Contemporary Art Auctions, CEPR Working Paper.

Baumol, W. J. (1986) Unnatural Value: Or Art Investment as a Floating Crap Game, *American Economic Review* 76(2):10–14.

Campbell, R. (2005) Art as an Alternative Asset Class, Working Paper, Maastricht University.

Chua, J., and R. Woodward (1982) Gold as an Inflation Hedge: A Comparative Study of Six Major Industrial Countries, *Journal of Business Finance and Accounting* 19(2):191–197.

Duffie, D. (2001) *Dynamic Asset Pricing Theory*, 3rd ed. Princeton University Press.

Engle, R., and C. Granger (1987) Cointegration and Error Correction: Representation, Estimation and Testing, *Econometrica* 55(2):251–276.

Fabozzi, F. (2005) *The Handbook of Fixed Income Securities*. McGraw-Hill.

Goetzmann, W. (1993) Accounting for Taste: Art and the Financial Markets Over Three Centuries, *American Economic Review* 83:1370–1376.

Granger, C., and P. Newbold (1974) Spurious Regressions in Econometrics, *Journal of Econometrics* 2:111–120.

McAndrew, C. (2008) *The Art Economy: An Investor's Guide to the Art Market*. The Libbey Press.

Mei, J., and M. Moses (2002) Art as an Investment and the Underperformance of Masterpieces, *American Economic Review* 92:1656–1668.

Pesando, J. (1993) Art as an Investment: The Market for Modern Prints, *American Economic Review* 83(5):1075–1089.

Ross, S. (1976) The Arbitrage Theory of Capital Asset Pricing, *Journal of Economic Theory*, 13:341–360.

Appendix
Art Market Research Index Components

Old Masters 100 Index

Osias I BEERT, Nicolaes BERCHEM, Louis Leopold BOILLY, Francois BOUCHER, Jan (elder) BRUEGHEL, Jan (younger) BRUEGHEL, CANALETTO, Annibale CARRACCI, John CONSTABLE, Aelbert CUYP, Arthur DEVIS, Carlo DOLCI, Sir Anthony van DYCK, Jean Honore FRAGONARD, Frans I. FRANCKEN, Thomas GAINSBOROUGH, Theodore GERICAULT, Luca GIORDANO, Jan van GOYEN, Jean-Baptiste GREUZE, Francesco GUARDI, Giacomo GUARDI, Giovanni Francesco GUERCINO, Jan Davidsz de HEEM, Egbert van HEEMSKERK, Meindert HOBBEMA, William HOGARTH, Melchior de HONDECOETER, Jean Baptiste HUET, Jacob van HULSDONCK, Jan van HUYSUM, Julius Caesar IBBETSON, Antonio JOLI, Jacob JORDAENS, Jan van I KESSEL, Nicolas LANCRET, Nicolas de LARGILLIERE, Sir Thomas LAWRENCE, Sir Peter LELY, Carle van LOO, Nicolaes MAES, Alessandro MAGNASCO, Michele MARIESCHI, Ben MARSHALL, Adam Frans van der MEULEN, Jan Miense MOLENAER, Klaes MOLENAER, Joos de MOMPER, Peter MONAMY, Jean Baptiste MONNOYER, George MORLAND, Alexander NASMYTH, Charles-Joseph NATOIRE, Jean Marc NATTIER, Aert van der NEER, Adriaen van OSTADE, Isaac van OSTADE, Jean Baptiste OUDRY, Giovanni Paolo PANINI, Jean Baptiste PATER, Giambattista PIAZZETTA, Giovan Battista PIRANESI, Guido RENI, Sir Joshua REYNOLDS, Marco RICCI, Sebastiano RICCI, Hubert ROBERT, George ROMNEY, Salvator ROSA, Thomas ROWLANDSON, Sir Peter Paul RUBENS, Jacob van RUYSDAEL, Salomon van RUYSDAEL, Paul SANDBY, Francis (elder) SARTORIUS, John Nott SARTORIUS, Jan STEEN, George STUBBS, Giovanni Battista TIEPOLO, Giovanni Domenico TIEPOLO, Jacopo TINTORETTO, Joseph Mallord William TURNER, Lucas van UDEN, Willem van de (elder) VELDE, Simon VERELST, Nicolas van VERENDAEL, Joseph VERNET, Paolo VERONESE, David VINCKEBOONS, Simon de VLIEGER, Sebastian VRANCX, Jean Antoine WATTEAU, Jan WEENIX, Adam WILLAERTS, John WOOTTON, Philips WOUWERMAN, Joseph WRIGHT OF DERBY, Jan WYNANTS, Johann ZOFFANY, Francesco ZUCCARELLI

European Impressionists

Laureano BARRAU, Jean BERAUD, Eugene BOUDIN, Gustave CAILLEBOTTE, Paul CEZANNE, Edgar DEGAS, Jean Louis FORAIN, Paul GAUGUIN, Armand GUILLAUMIN, Albert LEBOURG, Stanislas LEPINE, Max LIEBERMANN, Edouard MANET, Henri-French MARTIN, Henri MATISSE, Maxime MAUFRA, Claude MONET, Berthe MORISOT, Roderic O'CONOR, Camille PISSARRO, Pierre Auguste RENOIR, Theodore ROUSSEAU, Alfred SISLEY, Max SLEVOGT, Joaquin SOROLLA Y BASTIDA

Contemporary Art 100 Index

Carl ANDRE, Richard ARTSCHWAGER, Miguel BARCELO, Matthew BARNEY, Jean Michel BASQUIAT, Christian BOLTANSKI, Maurizo CATTELAN, Sandro CHIA, Francesco CLEMENTE, Tony CRAGG, Enzo CUCCHI, Wim DELVOYE, Tracey EMIN, Rainer FETTING, Eric FISCHL, David FISCHLI, Dan FLAVIN, Gunther FORG, GILBERT and GEORGE, Robert GOBER, Felix GONZALEZ-TORRES, Douglas GORDON, Dan GRAHAM, Keith HARING, Mona HATOUM, Damien HIRST, Jenny HOLZER, Jorg IMMENDORF, Jasper JOHNS, Donald JUDD, Alex KATZ, Mike KELLEY, Ellsworth KELLY, Anselm KIEFER, Martin KIPPENBERGER, Jeff KOONS, Jannis KOUNELLIS, Sol LEWITT, Robert LONGO, Mario MERZ, Juan MUNOZ, Bruce NAUMAN, Claes OLDENBURG, Gabriel OROZCO, Nam June PAIK, Mimmo PALADINO, PANAMERENKO, A R PENCK, Michelangelo PISTOLETTO, Sigmar POLKE, Richard PRINCE, Robert RAUSCHENBERG, Charles RAY, Gerhard RICHTER, Pipilotti RIST, Mimmo ROTELLA, Edward RUSCHA, Niki de SAINT-PHALLE, David SALLE, Julian SCHNABEL, Thomas SCHUTTE, Sean SCULLY, George SEGAL, Richard SERRA, Joel SHAPIRO, Cindy SHERMAN, Frank STELLA, Donald SULTAN, Rosemarie TROCKEL, Cy TWOMBLY, Jeff WALL, Peter and WEISS, Franz WEST

20th-Century Indian Painting Index

Zainul ABEDIN, K M ADIMOOLAM, J. Sultan ALI, Krishna Hawlaji ARA, Badri Nath ARYA, Narayan Shridhar BENDRE, Ramkinkar BAIJ, Manjit BAWA, Bikash BHATTACHARJEE, Nandalal BOSE, Rameshwar BROOTA, Sakti BURMAN, Allah BUX, Jayashri CHAKRAVARTY, Shiavax CHAVDA, Jogen CHOWDHURY, Abdur Rahman CHUGHTAI, Arup DAS, Sunil DAS, Dharmanarayan DASGUPTA, Shanti DAVE, Vinod DAVE, Biren DE, Mukul DEY, Rajendra DHAWAN, Mahadev Viswanath DHURANDHAR, Atul DODIYA, Hari Ambados GADE, Vasudeo S. GAITONDE, Laxma GOUD, Satish GUJRAL, Sawalaram Laxman HALDANKAR, Asit Kumar HALDAR, Ganesh HALOI, Kattingeri Krishna HEBBAR, Maqbool Fida HUSAIN, George KEYT, Bhupen KHAKKAR, Krishen KHANNA, Sudhir Ranjan KHASTGIR, Ram KUMAR, Nalini MALANI, Hemen MAZUMDAR, Tyeb MEHTA, Anjolie Ela MENON, Dhruva MISTRY, Benode Behari MUKHERJEE, Badri NARAYAN, Shibu NATESAN, Akbar PADAMSEE, Laxman PAI, Madhvi PAREKH, Manu PAREKH, Baiju PARTHAN, Homi B PATEL, Sudhir PATWARDHAN, Ivan PERIES, B PRABHA, Jaggu PRASAD, Ganesh PYNE, Shyamal Dutta RAY, Sayed Haider RAZA, Rekha RODWITTIYA, Jamini ROY, Proshanto ROY, Suhas ROY, Jehangir SABAVALA, SADEQUAIN, Gulam Rasool SANTOSH, Paritosh SEN, SHAHABUDDIN, Lalu Prasad SHAW, Gulam SHEIKH, Lax-man SHRESHTHA, Arpita SINGH, Paramjit SINGH, Satish SINHA, K G SUBRAMANYAN, Jagdish SWAMINATHAN, Abanindranath TAGORE, Gaganendranath TAGORE, Rabindra Nath TAGORE, Ramkinkar VAIJ, Thotha VAIKUNTAM

Contemporary Chinese Index

AI XUAN, CA YU SHUI, CAI CHUFU, CAI GUO QIANG, CAO LIWEI, CHANG FEE MING, CHEN KEZHAN, CHEN XIONGLI, CHEN YANNING, CHEN YIFEI, CHEN YIMING, CHEN YINHUEI, CHENG TSAI-TUNG, CHENG YAJIE, CHIU YA-TSAI, CHUA MIA TEE, CHUANG CHE, CUI RUZUO, FAN ZENG, GU MEI, HE BAILI, HE DAQIAO, HE DUOLING, HE HUAISHUO, HO KAN, HUANG MINGCHUANG, HUANG MINGZHE, HUANG ZHONG YANG, Francisco HUNG, JI DACHUN, JIA YOUFU, JIANG CHANGYI, JIANG MINGXIAN, KWONG-SANG, LI GENG, LI HUASHENG, LI HUAYI, LI HUIFANG, LI QUANWU, LI ZHONGLIANG, LIANG YIFENG, LIN HUKUI, LIU DANZHAI, LIU GUOSONG, LIU XIAODONG, LIU XUN, LIU YE, LIU YINGZHAO, LONG LIYOU, LU JIREN, LUO ZHONGLI, MA CHENGKUAN, MA XIAOGUANG, MAO LIZI, NAMCHEONG, NIE OU, PANG JIUN, QI LIANGZHI, QIN DA HU, SHAO FEI, SHI HU, SONG YUGUI, SONG YULIN, SU LIU PENG, SUN XIANGYANG, SUNQUA, TAN CHOH TEE, TANG MULI, WANG GUANGYI, WANG HUAIQING, WANG JIAN, WANG XIN, WANG YIDONG, WANG YONGQIANG, WANG YUNHE, WANG ZHENGHUA, WANG ZIWU, WEI RONG, WU HAO, WU HSUAN-SAN, WU JIAN, WU TAI, XING BAOZHUANG, XU SHIPING, XU TIANRUN, XU XI, YAN PEI MING, YANG FEIYUN, YANG HSING-SHENG, YANG SISHENG, YANG YANWEN, YE ZIQI, YU PENG, YU SHICHAO, YUAN JINTA, YUE MINJUN, ZHAI XINJIAN, ZHANG LI, ZHANG XIAO GANG, ZHENG ZHIYUE

8 Investing in Rare Books

Andrew Rudd[1]

-Advisor Software, Inc.

Introduction

I suspect most of us formed collections in our youth from such items as baseball cards, stamps, and Dinky Toys, which were dutifully saved by our parents after we grew older in case "we should ever need them." A great many of us never did, but many others graduated into becoming serious collectors. This begs the question: Why do large numbers of people show such an interest in collecting?

Many people spend a great deal of time and money planning and growing their collections, shopping for new items, and generally managing and cataloguing their collectibles. The activity has been described thus:[2] "Collecting is a common, intensely involving form of consumption." A wide variety of objects are collected, including art and related items such as posters, photographs, lithographs and prints, wine and wine bottle labels, coins, antique furniture, antiquities, jewelry, ceramics, rocks, gems, fossils, musical instruments, sporting memorabilia, cars, match book covers, model airplanes, quilts, and metalware, including brass, copper, silver, and gold items—not to mention baseball cards, stamps, and Dinky Toys. It is worth noting that each of these collectible specialties typically support special interest groups and communities, together with a wide variety of commercial activities, including information sources, markets, or exchanges where collectibles are bought and sold and, increasingly frequently, sophisticated ecommerce applications and infrastructure.

An important follow-on area of study relates to the questions: What are the characteristics of items that are "collectible"? If you were to define a collectible,

[1]Chairman and CEO, Advisor Software, Inc., Lafayette, California. Without implicating them in any errors or omissions, which are entirely my responsibility, I would like to acknowledge valuable advice and helpful discussions with Thomas Healey, Kristine Houglet, Abby Schoolman, Lord Robert Skidelsky, Ian Smith, and Nicolo Torre, and excellent research assistance from Maksym Bychkov.

[2]R. Belk, M. Wallendorf, J. Sherry, M. Holbrook, and S. Roberts (1988), Collectors and Collecting, *Advances in Consumer Research* 15:548–553.

Collectible Investments for the High Net Worth Investor

which dimensions would be important to highlight? Perhaps more interesting, if you were to innovate a new collectible, what "product" features should be included?[3] And for our purposes in this chapter, what makes books so interesting? What type of book is of most importance to collectors?

Finally, what are the economics of collectible markets? How liquid are they? Are they informationally efficient? There is very little published work on the investment performance of collectibles, suggesting that an important consideration is the measurement and analysis of rates of return from investing in collectibles generally and, being as it is the main focus in this chapter, rates of return arising from collecting fine books?

Space limitations prevent me from pursuing all these questions. Instead, after a brief review of relevant research on the psychological foundations of collecting, I focus on books as collectibles, the market for books, and some statistical results on the investment performance of fine books as collectibles.

Why Collect?

There is clearly more than one type of collector, potentially a number of disparate motivations for collecting, and more than one model applied in understanding the phenomenon.[4] However, the psychological and sociological literature on collecting shows recurrent themes. First, few collectors explicitly decide to start a collection but instead begin as a result of an incidental or accidental event. Over time, addiction and compulsive aspects can begin to pervade the collecting process, and many collections are seen as becoming an addictive activity in which adding items is likened to a "fix." Most important, any positive recognition of the collection by others reinforces the value of the activity in the collector's mind: Recognition confirms that the collector's activities are now valuable and purposeful. Further, those items in the collection that benefit from contagion or contact through prior ownership with celebrities or famous people (that is, have a good provenance) serve to promote the self-image of the collector and reinforce the significance of the collection, and hence its value.[5] Organized groups of collectors are important in this regard since they support their mutual identity through the opportunity of trading with each other, discussing new acquisitions, and, generally, sharing common experiences.

Other researchers following a sociological approach extend these ideas by suggesting that collecting is related to desires for group membership.[6] Those

[3]Clearly, not all collectibles are antiques or even old: Think of Pet Rocks, Beanie Babies, Swatch watches, Power Rangers, Crocs, Cabbage Patch dolls, and Pokemon trading cards, for example.

[4]See, for example, R. Belk (1995), *Collecting in a Consumer Society*, Routledge; and S. Pearce (1995), *On Collecting: An Investigation into Collecting in the European Tradition*, Routledge.

[5]Not surprisingly, auction and bookseller catalogues typically are careful to explain the price-inflating provenance of an item for sale when it has a famous history.

[6]See, for example, R. Belk (1995), Collecting as Luxury Consumption: Effects on Individuals and Households, *Journal of Economic Psychology*, 16(3):477–490; and A. Olmsted (1993), Hobbies and Serious Leisure, *World Leisure and Recreation* 35(1):27–32.

who are motivated to belong to and attain status within a group of like-minded individuals may achieve this goal as a result of collecting. Any satisfaction gained in the act of collecting is enhanced through the connection of the collector to the collectible's creator or prior owner; it allows the collector to self-aggrandize as a result of owning and handling a celebrated item. As McIntosh and Schmeichel state, "... the collector may accrue self-benefits simply by aligning the self with the object."[7]

As we shall see later, this sense of association is important to the valuation of rare books and the pursuit of book collecting. Over the years, books have been a source of knowledge and innovation, which leads them to have an inherent value. For many centuries books have been collected by institutions such as monasteries and libraries, which have assembled collections not only as a source of learning but also as a source of power and prestige by becoming an attraction and destination for scholars, intelligentsia, and the wealthy. Further, there is a tradition of authors giving their works as gifts and for books to be a universally accepted token of appreciation. As a result, books, unlike many other collectibles, offer the opportunity for a benefit of association and connection with history, which can provide a significant intangible value for book collectors.

Who Collects?

One estimate of the popularity of collecting is that one out of every three Americans collects something.[8] More formally, the items collected are typically a series of related objects of which the principal function is of little or no concern, and the collector has no plan to immediately dispose of the items. Comparatively little survey work has looked at the demographics of collectors.[9] The results suggest that the incidence of collecting rises with age among adults and is not limited to any particular income category, and the time and money spent on collecting rises over time. Other than fine art, which is suggested to be an upper-class, high-net-worth activity, there is little evidence of a connection with wealth levels, although one study of investors did find a positive relationship between investments in collectibles and investments in other financial instruments. More precisely, one survey[10] reported that 35% of respondents

[7]McIntosh and Schmeichel (2004), Collectors and Collecting: A Social Psychological Perspective, *Leisure Sciences*, 26:85–97 (see p. 92).

[8]G. O'Brien (1981), Living with Collections, *New York Times Magazine*, April 26, Section 6, part 2, pp. 25–37.

[9]Examples include M. Schiffer, T. Downing, and M. McCarthy (1981), Waste Not, Want Not: An Ethnoarcheological Study of Reuse in Tucson, in *Modern Material Culture: The Archeology of Us*, R. Gould and M. Schiffer (eds.), Academic Press, pp. 67–86; and T. McInish and R. Srivastava (1982), The Determinants of Investment in Collectibles: A Probit Analysis, *Journal of Behavioral Economics* 11(2):123–134.

[10]W. Pearman, J. Schnabel, and A. Tomeh (1983), Rationalization and Antique Collecting, *Free Enquiry in Creative Sociology* 11(1):55–58.

cited investment as their primary motive for collecting; a later and broader survey reported that 22% of respondents gave financial investment as a motivation.[11]

The collector's motive potentially has an important impact on the pricing of books. For example, given the high and increasing cost of antiquarian first editions, it would be surprising if book collecting, like fine art, were not the province of high net worth investors. If this is true I should expect to observe a positive relationship between returns on the stock market and returns on fine books, since, as the collectors perceived themselves becoming wealthier (poorer), they would purchase (sell) books. As a result it is likely that the returns to book collecting would not have any hedging benefits with other asset markets.

To the extent that it is the love of books and the joy of ownership that are the primary motivation for collecting, owning rare books will offer a "convenience yield," or nonfinancial benefit, possibly as a substitute for some fraction of the investment return. Similarly, the collector's personal valuation of any association benefit may also be a substitute for greater investment return. Additionally, it is likely a collector will perceive some value arising from the scarcity of a rare book, which, being of fixed supply, suggests that given a typical supply/demand relationship, over time the scarcity value will increase as a result of anticipated loss and damage. Bill Gross, CEO of investment management firm PIMCO and well known as a successful rare stamp collector, reinforced these points when recently quoted describing stamps as an "authentic collectible, established over time and appreciating at least at the same rate as the local economy, 5 or 6 percent a year. You don't get rich, but you do have some fun."[12] I report some preliminary empirical results on these issues later in the chapter.

Books as Collectibles

There are several dimensions that are important to consider in understanding the behavior of a serious collector and estimating the value of rare books. Interestingly, the well-known economist Ricardo opined on this issue, writing: "There are some commodities, the value of which is determined by scarcity alone. No labour can increase the quantity of such goods, and therefore their value cannot be lowered by an increased supply. Some rare statues and pictures, rare books and coins, wines of a peculiar quality ... are all of this description. Their value is wholly independent of the quantity of labour originally necessary to produce them, and varies with the varying wealth and inclinations of those who are desirous to possess them."[13] In other words, in the case of rare books,

[11]R. Formanek (1991), Why They Collect: Collectors Reveal Their Motivations, *Journal of Social Behavior and Personality* 6(6):275–286.

[12]Reported in M. Healey, Bond Trader to Sell Rare Stamps for Charity, *New York Times,* April 14, 2008, p. C2.

[13]D. Ricardo (1817), *On the Principles of Political Economy and Taxation*, London, pp. 2–3, as reported in A. Heertje (1990), Collecting Rare Economics Books, *Contributions to Political Economy* 9:99–105.

each transaction is largely independent of others and depends on both the characteristics of the individual book and the preferences and knowledge of the collector.

Which Edition?

As a rule of thumb, collectors find the first printing of the first edition of a book most desirable. It is the first edition that has the greatest probability of representing the author's intentions and perspective, since it appears closest in time to the actual writing. It is also the edition that the author actually saw through the production process. In addition, since there may be more than one printing of the first edition, most attention is paid to the first printing. Of course, the reaction to the edition could cause the author to substantially revise the book, and subsequent editions can differ significantly from the first.[14] This can cause these subsequent editions to be additionally collectible, but the first will typically retain its unique characteristics in the minds of collectors.

Unfortunately, it is not always clear from the book itself what constitutes the first edition. Particularly with books published in the 19th century and earlier, one can determine the edition only by knowing the sequence of changes that took place between printings. These changes can seem relatively minor, such as changes in words in specific locations, a minor change to the title page, type of binding, the color of the wrappers, and so on, but become significant to the collector and to the value of the book. For example, the author might find errors in the manuscript and correct them midproduction, or the publisher may run out of some material and make a substitution such as the color of the cover. Should this occur during the printing, it is said that the edition has another *state* or *issue*. A first edition can, therefore, have several states, each potentially giving rise to different valuations.[15]

Occasionally a first edition may be preceded by a private or *author's edition*, particularly if the author is paying to have the manuscript published. In addition, publishers may issue a *limited edition* of a new book. These are usually issued at the same time as the normal first edition, typically referred to as the *trade edition*. Limited editions are usually signed, numbered, and sold in a slipcase at a price far in excess of the first trade edition. They are typically produced using the same first trade edition sheets but delivered in a more extravagant binding and at greater cost.

Two other publication variants of first editions are worth noting: (1) proofs and advance reading copies and (2) offprints. Prior to the completion of the publishing process, the publishers will make proofs available to authors for corrections and advance reading copies for reviewers. These latter may be actual first trade edition copies but with a slip or letter laid into the book indicating

[14]Malthus's *An Essay on the Principle of Population* was initially published anonymously in 1798. It generated so much controversy that he revised the book substantially, and the second edition was published in 1803. Both editions are collectible.

[15]For example, the first edition of Charles Dickens' *Oliver Twist* had three issues, which refer to slightly different title pages.

that the copy was sent for review in advance of publication. Occasionally, galley proofs or uncorrected proofs of manuscripts will become available, as will advance reading copies. Many collectors of first editions are excited to obtain proofs or advance copies of the first printing, and these frequently bring a premium.

Offprints refer to a part or an excerpt of a book or larger printing, such as specific chapters, individual stories in a collection of short stories, or individual journal articles from a volume of articles. They are usually printed on the same paper and with the same type but bound or stapled separately with a simple paper cover. Journal articles are also sometimes separately paginated rather than carrying the pagination of the journal. Many times a publisher will offer offprints prior to publication, to help the marketing campaign of a forthcoming book, enabling authors to distribute them widely. More important for our purposes, offprints are a very common way of getting first edition publications from the scholarly or scientific community.

The Importance of Signatures and Inscriptions

It is clear from this description that first editions leave the publication process in many different forms. The next important differentiating characteristic relates to any inscription, should it exist, by the author. A signature can appear in a number of forms. For example, as discussed, signed limited editions are routinely produced, and these incorporate by design the author's signature and are initially priced to reflect the special nature of the edition. In addition, signed trade editions are regular trade editions signed by the author. They can also include an inscription. Typically a signed first trade edition is more valuable than an unsigned but otherwise equivalent copy, and an inscription can also add to the valuation differential, even if the recipient is unknown. This effect is reinforced should the author only rarely sign a book or rarely provide an inscription with the signature. Although there is some debate among booksellers, a signed first edition commands a premium over an equivalent unsigned book, and an author's signature plus inscription is usually worth more than equivalent-quality copies with a signature alone.

There are two other variants worth considering. Association copies are books that include a signed inscription from the author to a celebrity or other famous person or to an individual who had some importance in the author's life. As discussed, from a psychological viewpoint, the personalization of the book is very important for many collectors, and it is unsurprising that association copies will be valued more highly than a normal signed first edition. As we shall see later, in many cases association copies can command considerable premium over copies without any explicit connections.

Related to association copies are copies with a valued provenance. The provenance of a book demonstrates its previous ownership, and though it might not have a direct association with the author, there could well be a previous owner who has equivalent value to the collector. For example, the book might have been previously owned by one of the major collections or had an owner who was connected with the author or was influential in the same field of study. Again, the personalization of the book can be very important for some collectors and is often the focus of a collection.

The Types of Binding

Not only are there many variations among first editions, there are also many variations of book production that affect the desirability of a book from the collector's viewpoint. The bindings of most books published over the last 50 to 100 years range from paper covers (with paper of similar quality to the actual pages), called *paperwraps* or *paperbacks,* to completely stiff paper covers, called *boards*, and ultimately to cloth and leather-bound books. In general, if both soft- and hard-backed copies are published, recent practice has been for the paperwrap to be published later, which causes it to be not particularly valuable for collectors unless it contains some new content.[16]

The dust jacket (alternately called a *dustwrapper*), when included with a first edition, is an integral part of the collector's experience. It is also the most fragile part of the book and is frequently creased, torn (chipped), or otherwise damaged, which makes the book less valuable. It is frequently hard to sell recent first editions without their dustjackets, and older books suffer similarly if the dust jacket is not in good condition. Finally, with particularly desirable authors (Fleming, Rowling, Hemingway, etc.), the presence of a fine dust jacket will increase the value of the book enormously. And just as there are different states among first editions of the book itself, dust jackets for first editions can come in different variations.[17]

Assessing Book Quality

A crucial determinant of the desirability of a book is its physical quality. Unfortunately, unlike many other collectibles, there is no generally accepted definition of quality standards. Unless one has had a great deal of experience and has examined (or better, handled) a large number of books, it is very hard to understand and describe the quality of a book. This situation is more acute for antiquarian and rare books; without a standard, it is hard to judge a comparative measure such as quality. More worrying is the fact that, even among experienced bibliophiles, there can be wide differences of opinion. At some level, a statement about quality is subjective and probably more subjective among higher-quality books than lower, since a book with its covers missing, for example, cannot be disguised.

[16]There is a small and separate market for the first printings of these paper reprint editions, which appears to be driven by both the quality of the cover art and the book content.

[17]For example, Ian Fleming's *Casino Royale* has two first edition dustjackets, one with and one without reviews.

Since many books are bought sight unseen with the collector relying on descriptions in a catalogue or on the Internet, this lack of objective standards potentially leads to disappointment or worse. It is becoming more common for catalogue descriptions to include photographs, although not every Internet bookseller is willing or able to send photographs of their stock.

A general grading scheme is used by booksellers to indicate the condition of a book, but unfortunately interpretations of this grading scheme are not standardized and really only apply to books produced after the introduction of edition binding! Moreover, auction records rarely disclose book condition based on the grading scheme, preferring instead a brief description, which makes for an ambiguous assessment of quality unless there are photographs or one has viewed the item. The International League of Antiquarian Booksellers (ILAB) lists a condition scheme on its Web site with the following grades, which are typically represented as _/_ (e.g., F/F), denoting first the book condition and second the dust jacket:[18] Mint (M), Fine (F), Very good, Good, Fair, Poor, w.a.f. ("with all faults").

An example might be helpful. Ian Fleming's first James Bond novel, *Casino Royale*, was published in 1953 and sold for about 50 cents, with a first edition run of 4750 copies. Today a first edition signed by Ian Fleming will cost considerably more. At the end of July 2008, one first edition/first impression copy apparently in fine condition could be found for sale on the Internet at a price of $75,000, with (from simply interpreting the description) a very attractive association. There are at least three more first edition/first impression unsigned copies available in the price range $25,000 to $50,000. If a dust jacket is not wanted, first edition copies can be found at a price of a few hundred dollars or less, which is the asking price of second impression copies. If there is a library stamp, torn or damaged dust jacket, or markings on the text, the price is dramatically reduced from the price of a pristine copy.

The Market for Books

There are currently five interrelated channels for the sale/purchase of first edition books: auctions, bookstores and dealers, book fairs, catalogues, and the Internet. These channels have evolved over approximately the last century since, until about 1900, the auction markets were largely a wholesaling channel, whereas booksellers handled the retailing of books. At auctions booksellers acted both as agents for their customers' bids as well as acting on their own account to purchase inventory. However, starting in the United States approximately 100 years ago, the major auction houses deliberately positioned themselves to directly attract the business of collectors. As a consequence, the market for fine books continues to evolve as roles of the participants change and the influence of the Internet and e-commerce tools strengthens. These changes,

[18]See the Glossary at *www.ilab.org*.

coupled with the increasing scarcity of quality books, seem to have resulted in more common, inexpensive books becoming cheaper (since search costs have decreased, the Internet has made knowledge of the availability of books more accessible, and the competition to sell is more intense) whereas rarer, more expensive fine books have become more expensive (most likely because of increased demand coupled with increasing scarcity; collectors feel that the chance to buy an important rarity could be their last).

The market appears largely oligopolistic; there are only a few major players in each of the channels who coexist in an environment of both cooperation and competition. The interesting special characteristics of this market are (1) the demand for a high level of knowledge and skill in understanding rare books and their content; (2) the fact that each rare book is to a large extent individually unique within a context, providing some degree of comparability; and (3) the evolving structure and relationship between the channels, particularly auction houses. As a result, these characteristics cause the market to display distinct tendencies of monopolistic behavior when one dealer, for example, possesses a rarity for sale. I believe this behavior explains some of the wildly different prices observed for rare books of the same title.

The following sections briefly discuss each of the market channels in turn.

Auctions

Auction houses have repositioned themselves to cater to private clients principally, it is thought, because of the decreasing availability of quality books. They now produce elegant catalogues of auctions, which include helpful information such as estimates to encourage nonspecialists to understand the potential cost of each lot. Many commentators believe these catalogues function partly as advertising material. Just as the auction houses focus on private clients rather than booksellers, they also focus on the seller rather than the purchaser—another indication of the increasing difficulty of getting access to quality books.

One of the most controversial changes over the past 40 years has been the introduction of a buyer's premium at salerooms worldwide. The premium was first introduced in the late 1970s at 10% (although one auction house set the rate at 8% for a while) and subsequently, in 1993, raised to 15% on "bargains" up to $50,000. The bottom rate has risen since to 25%. In many cases, the cost including buyers' premium will also be subject to sales or value-added taxes. On the other hand, the sellers' premium was initially set at less than 10% and is negotiable, depending on the quality of the items. The buyers' premium is nonnegotiable.

As a result of the changing emphasis of auction houses, the saleroom has become the location of price discovery in the fine book market. Nevertheless, for the purchaser, auction houses have certain limitations, most particularly that if the collector is not able to spend the time to examine the sale items on view days, it is not clear that a sufficiently detailed assessment of the item's quality can be gleaned from the auction catalogue. Other than professional ethics, it is not clear that auction houses have a particularly strong incentive not to be too optimistic about the items to be sold.[19]

Booksellers

As auction houses have changed their business models to drive for greater profits by placing more emphasis on private clients, the booksellers have become partially disintermediated. Booksellers have responded by taking a higher-profile market position by being more customer focused, providing more client services, and/or taking on more of a dealing function.

Although price discovery can take place in the auction saleroom, booksellers can fix their prices, thereby eliminating for the collector the risk of price discovery (although presumably for a premium). Booksellers also maintain an inventory, so a collector who is searching for a rare book might have a far better chance of finding it through the skill and knowledge of an experienced bookseller rather than waiting an indeterminate length of time for it to come up at auction. The difficulty is that booksellers are typically undercapitalized and the cost of financing their inventory could be challenging. This suggests that the pricing decision for booksellers carrying specialized inventory is unlikely to be straightforward, with discounting an unsatisfactory outcome except to encourage repeat customers, of whom other booksellers are an obvious target. Not surprisingly, there are reciprocal discounts offered within the trade.

Book Fairs

Many important book fairs[20] are held around the world each year. Historically, these fairs were events that collectors attended and were ways for the booksellers to build clientele and interact with other booksellers. Today sales within the bookseller community are a large part of the transactions that take place at fairs.

Catalogues and Direct Advertising

The distribution of booksellers' catalogues, which used to contain substantial bibliographical and pricing information, was the principal way booksellers promoted their business and established pricing for fine books. Now much of this informational role has been taken over by e-commerce functions. Many specialist booksellers still issue catalogues, though mainly to advertise what they have in inventory; some of the larger, more generalist booksellers have taken a marketing approach with high-quality, glossy brochures. Price discovery has become less important, but building a client base and distribution skills has

[19]One solution to this information problem is to commission a bookseller to act as agent in the saleroom, a standard charge for which is 10% of the sale item.
[20]A list is provided at *www.ilab.org/bookfairs/*.

clearly become more important. At least one major East Coast bookseller even advertises in the Sunday *New York Times.*

Internet and e-Commerce

There are many specialist sites dedicated to helping collectors find the books they want as well as, conversely, helping booksellers sell the books they have in inventory.[21] For example, Abe Books has more than 13,500 booksellers who are attached to their site and who display their inventory. A collector accessing the Abe Books site has access to vastly increased inventory than she would have going to a single bookseller. The common problem is that bookseller descriptions are not standardized and that it is possible to find divergent prices for books that are described as being quite similar. As a result, these sites are most useful for finding books and getting an initial sense of prices for standard first editions. To the extent that a collector either has a specific wish for a rare or unusual book or is looking for unknown titles that can enhance a collection, the Internet has real limitations.

Return and Risk of Book Collecting

Although there has been some prior work with certain collectibles, specifically art and wine, there has not been much work focused on fine books. Here I briefly describe this literature, then discuss the approach taken here, first by describing the data, then the methodology to construct an index of returns, and finally the results.

Survey of the Literature

As indicated, there is not extensive literature on the investment performance of rare books. This is somewhat surprising since there is a long history of eminent bibliophile economists. Adam Smith was a serious book collector, both on his own account as well as on behalf of his university (the University of Glasgow), and there exist two published catalogues of his library. Other important collectors include John Maynard Keynes, who owned a magnificent copy of Virgil, which had once belonged to Adam Smith, and spent considerable effort collecting books originally from Sir Isaac Newton's library,[22] which were in danger of becoming widely dispersed; and William Stanley Jevons, who collected many items of early economic literature.[23] In a short note in *The Contributions to Political Economy,* Giancarlo de Vivo, a professor at the University of Naples,

[21]Sites include *www.alibris.com*, *www.abebooks.com*, *www.bookfinder.com*, and *www.ilab.org*.

[22]See The Newton Project at *www.newtonproject.sussex.ac.uk*.

[23]It is interesting to note, given the comments above concerning collecting as an addiction, that Keynes referred to Jevons as an "economic bibliomaniac" and claimed that Jevons had transmitted "the affliction" to another economist, Herbert Somerton Foxwell. J. M. Keynes, (1936), William Stanley Jevons, in *Essays in Biography*, Vol. 10, of *The Collected Writings of John Maynard Keynes*, Macmillan and C.U.P., 1972.

lists other bibliophile economists and then proceeds to provide an indication of the growth rate of several economics books from 1932 until 1980. He took the pricing data from bookseller catalogues and pointed out the difficulty of not knowing the quality of the books in order to make an accurate comparison over time. During that period, when an index of price levels rose about 25 times, many of the books appreciated several hundredfold.[24]

The danger in these backward-looking studies is selection bias: By focusing on what has done well, one potentially ignores books that have performed poorly or even disappeared. A recent (2008, though undated) French study by Patrick Sourget looks at the performance of seven famous French books over periods ranging up to 193 years. He used auction data collected at a few points in time (10 observations, in the case of the 193-year history) to build his model of returns. Needless to say, this universe of books has performed extraordinarily well, but there is no implication that the average book or any other books chosen at similar times would have performed similarly.

Healey has written two brief notes in the *Rare Book Review*, one in June 2003 and the other in June 2005.[25] In both articles he looked at large universes of modern books, 127 titles in the first study and 244 titles in the second, from predefined universes, with prices taken from catalogues at the beginning and end of two consecutive periods (1982, 1991, and 2001). His results show that over the 20-year period the average annual compound growth rates were in the range of 12.3% to 15.3%, significantly ahead of traditional asset classes of stocks and bonds as well as inflation.

Two other sources may be interesting; Keen reports that returns to "Old Books" delivered an average annual nominal return of 14% over the period 1950 to 1969.[26] However, even at this high rate of return, the "Old Books" underperformed equities, with a difference in annual nominal returns of −0.33%. More recently, Reese compared prices of 71 books common to two sales, one in 1968 and the other in 1999, which increased in price 16.19 times.[27] He notes that four titles accounted for half the total value, whereas the other 67 showed a growth of 10.4 times, which he believes accurately reflects the general market.

Universe Selection and Book Pricing Data

The book data used in this study are based on a sample of 20 frequently traded books extracted from a large sample of auction prices covering the years 1975 to the end of 2007. The prices represent hammer prices (that is, prices without the buyer's premium being added) of actual transactions as recorded by Book

[24]G. De Vivo (1989), *Contributions to Political Economy* 8(March):74–80.

[25]Thomas Healey (2003), An Ancient Pursuit Takes on New Value, *Rare Book Review*, June:44–46; and Thomas Healey (2005), Money Matters, *Rare Book Review*, June:46–48.

[26]G. Keen (1971), *The Sale of Works of Art*, Nelson.

[27]W. Reese (2000), The Rare Book Market Today, *Yale University Library Gazette* 74:3–4.

Prices Current.[28] Each record contained identifying information on the book (its size, date of publication, edition, state, and so on), an indication of its quality, and the location and date of the auction, lot number, and the hammer price. As discussed, each auction price is for an identified asset potentially quite different from an asset with the same title sold but as a different lot. I have attempted to minimize this problem by controlling for the following variables:

- *Edition.* Standardized by edition, printing, size where appropriate, and year of publication. Where relevant I also control for state.
- *Signature/inscription.* I eliminated signed books, association copies, and copies from major libraries.
- *Quality.* I attempted to eliminate books that were described as being of unusually poor quality.

For each title, the goal was to obtain a time series of auction prices that were as representative of a typical copy of the book as possible. In other words, I attempted to eliminate those auction lots for atypical books by removing the lots for unusual copies that should be valued appropriately by collectors using a different valuation model than should be applied to the typical or average copy. My reasoning is that, provided collectors did not change attitudes over time and given the homogeneity of the sample, they could apply the same valuation function at each auction. I expected to observe some variation among auction prices for the same title, but I wanted to minimize the variation arising from having unrepresentative copies of the title in the sample of prices.

Book Index Construction

There are three usual methods of calculating returns on collectibles. One approach is to run a *hedonic* regression in which the price of the item is regressed on its characteristics. The advantage of this approach is that it explicitly takes into account the differentiating characteristics of the collectible. However, for our purposes, though we generally know the differentiating characteristics, we do not know them precisely, and there is no standardized description available that would ensure some comparability. It is hard to see, given the data sets available, how this approach could be used effectively.

A second approach is to use the method of repeat sales. A number of researchers have used this approach, particularly with paintings but also with prints and wine. Although it has a number of methodological advantages, it is inapplicable to the fine book market because no track of repeat sales is kept consistently; consequently almost all the available pricing information would be unusable.

The final and most obvious approach for the book market is to create a composite index by selecting a sample of the collectibles (the market basket),

[28]*www.bookpricescurrent.com.*

each of whose prices can be measured, and then averaging them. Various subtleties can be employed to make the approach more suitable for particular situations, such as varying the basket over time, or in the fixed basket case, randomly choosing the constituents of the basket, forming a broad-based representative basket, or having the basket chosen by experts. Using a fixed basket avoids the problem of varying quality over time, but in a dynamic market it potentially suffers from the drawback that the basket becomes unrepresentative.

My approach is to use a fixed basket, chosen by market experts who are able to provide guidance as to those books that must satisfy two of our criteria: The books must trade frequently, and they must be sufficiently "simple" that straightforward rules will produce the sample of prices for a given title to come from a relatively homogeneous set of books.[29] Table 8.1 gives the details of the titles and other relevant information. For example, I restricted the sample of Audubon's *Birds of America* to sales of the first octavo edition published in seven volumes between 1840 and 1844. There were 144 auction prices recorded over the period, an average of just over four per year.

Methodology and Book Index Performance

For each title, appropriately defined, we retrieve the auction prices. These are grouped by year from 1975 through 2007. For each year and each title, I computed the median auction price, which is the representative price from which I formed the index value for that year. The index value each year is an equal-weighted average of the median book prices. There are a few years for which a title did not trade, in which case I interpolated a price from adjacent prices.

I use the median price each year from the observed set of auction prices to further minimize the impact of the inevitable situation in which one or more of the auction prices for a particular title will be an outlier because of some unusual characteristic that was not reflected in the description of the book. As an example, Figure 8.1 shows the incidence of outliers for one of the basket titles, Audubon's *Birds of America*, where I have graphed the logarithm of the median auction price, which tends to visually emphasize the impact of extreme results. As can be seen, the year-by-year changes are generally smooth except in 1978, when there was an anomalous price, which on further checking was the result of a rich winning bid for what was described as a remarkably good copy of the book.

Figure 8.2 shows the index value over the 33-year period; Table 8.2 contains the statistics on the Book Index performance. Again, the graph is represented on a logarithmic scale versus a regression line. As shown, the index value fell

[29]Employing expert help in choosing the constituents of the basket has the advantage that we ensure that the books are liquid, but there is no certainty that the basket is representative of the totality of the market. We have attempted to ensure a high degree of representation by having exposure to different genres.

Table 8.1 Constituents of the Market Basket

Author	Title	Description	Publication Date	Number of Auction Prices
Audubon, John James	*Birds of America*	First octavo ed., 7 vols.	1840/4	144
Boswell, James	*Life of Johnson*	First ed./first issue	1791	200
Burns, Robert	*Poems*	Second ed./first Edin. ed.	1787	99
Burton, Richard	*Personal Narrative ...*	First ed., 3 vols., 8vo	1855/6	64
Cartier-Bresson, Henri	*The Decisive Moment*	First ed., Folio	1952	119
Catlin, George	*North American Indians*	First ed., 2 vols., 8vo	1841	56
Darwin, Charles	*The Descent of Man*	First ed./first issue, orig. cloth, 2 vols., 8vo	1871	71
Dickens, Charles	*Oliver Twist*	First ed./first issue, illus. by George Cruikshank, 12mo	1838	118
Doyle, Arthur	*Hound of the Baskervilles*	First ed., original cloth	1902	123
Fielding, Henry	*The History of Tom Jones*	First ed., 6 vols., 12mo	1749	94
Fitzgerald, F. Scott	*The Great Gatsby*	First ed./first printing, orig. cloth	1925	123
Fleming, Ian	*Casino Royale*	First ed.	1953	131
Hawthorne, Nathaniel	*The Scarlet Letter*	First ed./first issue, original cloth	1850	52
Hemingway, Ernest	*A Farewell to Arms*	First ed./first issue, without legal disclaimer	1929	121
Johnson, Samuel	*A Dictionary of the English Language*	First ed., 2 vols., Folio	1755	199
Joyce, James	*Finnegan's Wake*	First ed., one of 425	1939	61
Melville, Herman	*Moby Dick*	First American ed., 12mo	1851	101
Milne, Alan	*Winnie-the-Pooh*	First ed., one of 350 L.p. copies, illus. by E. H. Shepard	1926	32
Stanley, Henry	*In Darkest Africa*	First ed., 2 vols., 8vo	1890	86
Stevenson, Robert Louis	*Treasure Island*	First ed.	1883	106
TOTAL				2100

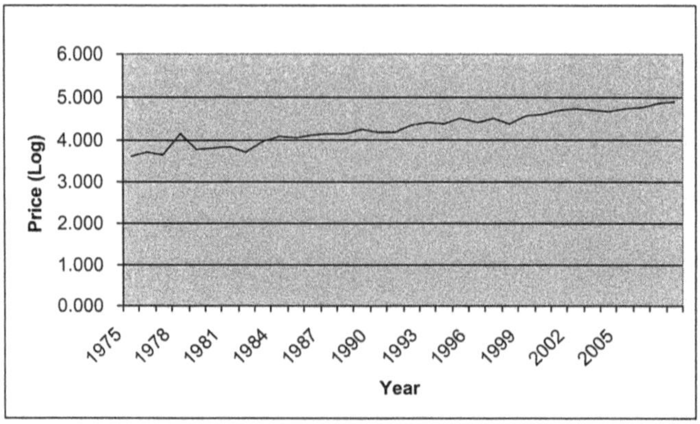

Figure 8.1 Auction Prices (Log) for Audubon's *Birds of America,* 1975–2007

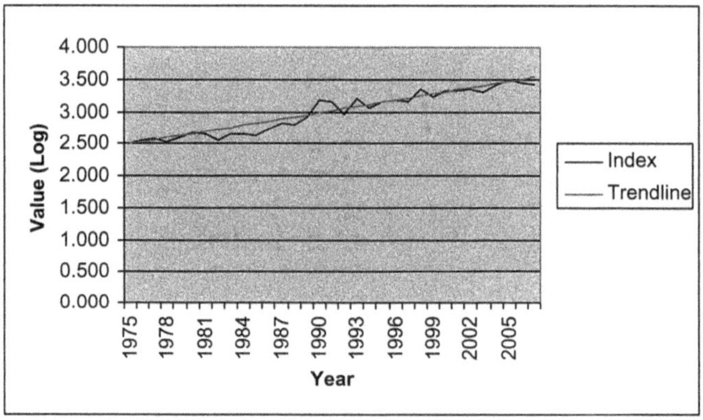

Figure 8.2 Book Index Value (Log)

Table 8.2 Annualized Arithmetic Return on the Book Index, 1975–2007

Mean return	9.64%
Median return	4.63%
Standard deviation	26.09%
Interquartile range	28.89%
Minimum return	–38.02%
Maximum return	78.42%

behind the trend line in the mid- to late 1980s but caught up in the early 1990s. Since that time the index value has not wandered far from the trend line. The statistics on the arithmetic performance show an average 9.64% return per year over the entire 33-year period, whereas the median return is a little less than half the mean return. This relationship suggests that the return distribution has some large positive returns, which is indeed the case, with the largest positive return during one year being almost 80%. The average return per unit of risk (Sharpe ratio) is much smaller than for established traded markets, such as the equity market, suggesting an allocation to fine books could be inefficient relative to the traded markets.

The risk of the index is high, which again is plainly visible from the plot in Figure 8.3 that shows the pattern of annual arithmetic returns. The extreme movements during the early 1990s are clearly apparent and were, according to participants in the market at that time, the result of several auctions containing some exceptional books. The early 1990s were obviously an interesting time in the rare book world!

Finally, Table 8.3 shows the correlations with the major asset classes. The results indicate that books do not covary to any great degree with the established markets, with the largest correlation being with the return on long Treasury bonds. A period of decreasing long-term rates appears beneficial to the book market.

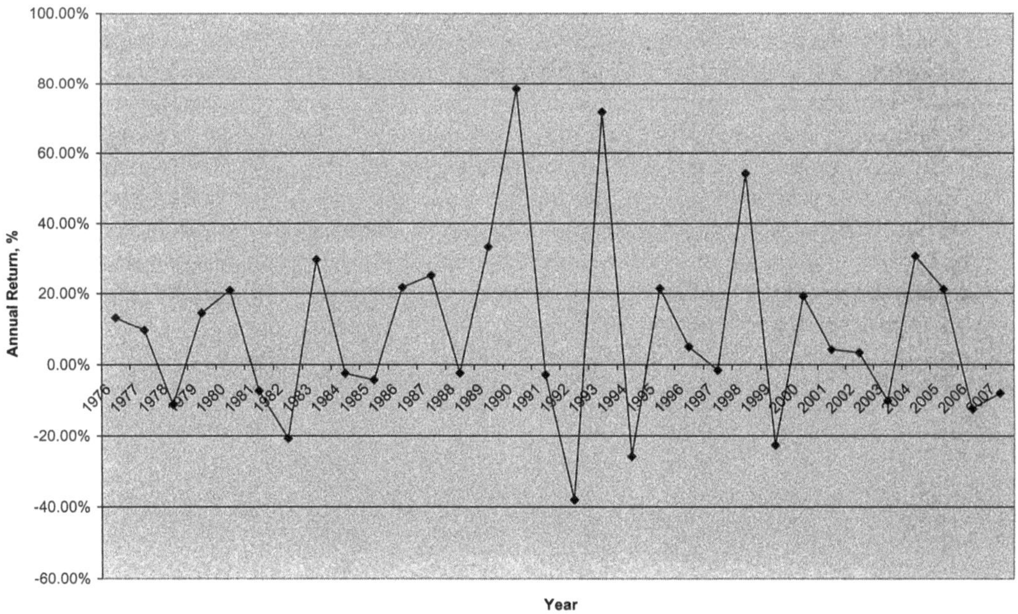

Figure 8.3 Average Annual Arithmetic Index Return (%)

Table 8.3 Correlations with Major Asset Class Indexes: Book Index, 1975–2007

S&P 500	–0.02
EAFE	0.022
Treasury bonds	0.112
Treasury bills	–0.018
Inflation	0.057

Conclusion

The rare book market is a complicated one that has changed structurally quite significantly over the last 50 years or so. The auction houses have become more important players and now appear to be the dominant force in price formation, whereas the major booksellers have typically become more specialized to maintain a "skill advantage." As this change in market structure has occurred, there has been a significant decrease in the availability of quality books, causing rare items to become even rarer, possibly because in the 1970s and 1980s the "industry" was so successful in selling books to university libraries and other institutions, which have effectively taken these books off the market. Finally, the Internet has democratized much of the search, information sourcing, and trading in books, particularly in the less "exotic" rare books. In spite of all these changes, people still want and (possibly) need to collect; demand for collectibles will continue, but will the collectible of choice be rare books?

All the data seem to reinforce the result that rare books have increased in value steadily over the last 30 to 50 years, although short-term risk has been high. The annual return I computed from the 33-year period is similar to that suggested by Bill Gross for the rare stamp market.[30] This does not mean that "trading" in books has necessarily been profitable, because the frictions of trading are truly substantial, but the store of value in a rare book portfolio certainly appears to have increased. Moreover, the increase in value appears not to have been structurally connected with other asset markets or inflation to any great degree. Books appear to have been relatively immune to the risks and episodic crises that have influenced other investment classes.

[30] Ibid.

9 Maps as Collectibles

Adam Jared Apt

-Peabody River Asset Management LLC

> *At noon to the Change a little, and then bespoke some maps to hang in my new Roome ... which will be very pretty ... Home to dinner; and after dinner to the hanging up of maps and other things for the fitting of the room, and now it will certainly be one of the handsomest and most useful rooms in my house.*
>
> —*Samuel Pepys, diary entry for April 27, 1666*[1]

Introduction

Even before Samuel Pepys decorated a room with maps in the year of the great fire of London, others were collecting maps and atlases for their decorative value and the information they contained. It was the technology of mass production through printing that facilitated the collectibility of maps.

Maps, considered as collectibles, have much in common with rare books and prints, but there are differences in kind and degree. Consequently, there are close similarities between the economics of map collecting and the economics of collecting books and prints. Atlases, of course, are books of maps, and throughout this chapter, nearly all references to maps should be understood to encompass atlases, too.

There is an enormous variety of kinds of maps. I will not list all of them here, but even if we consider only maps of regions on the earth's surface, there are political maps, topographical maps, thematic maps (of geology, rainfall, vegetation, and so forth), road maps, and tourist maps. There are maps of the world, maps of the heavens, maps of the oceans, and so on. They can be based on different projection systems. They can be printed on postcards or on huge sheets that hang on walls.

This chapter considers the pricing and valuation of maps, the ways in which maps are bought and sold, the returns that can be realized on them, and the

[1]Pepys (1972), p. 111.

Collectible Investments for the High Net Worth Investor

possibilities for constructing valuation and risk models for maps. Very little has been written about maps as investments, and the pricing data that exist are not in a form that is readily accessible for econometric analysis. This chapter briefly suggests lines of research, but primarily it emphasizes ways of thinking about maps as though they were investment vehicles.

In writing this chapter, I have assumed that anyone who collects maps has been doing so because he appreciates them for what they are. I do not intend to persuade anyone who does not appreciate maps that he should take up map collecting as a hobby or an investment. This chapter contains a few hints of advice, but it is primarily a positive description of the economics of map collecting, organized from the standpoint of a financial economist and with suggestions for further research and analysis.

In most of my discussion of map prices, I rely on Francis J. Manasek's *Collecting Old Maps*.[2] This book contains the most thoughtful and extensive writing to date on maps as collectibles. Dr. Manasek is both a medical researcher (specializing in cardiology), now retired, and a longtime dealer in rare maps, and his book has something of a scientist's approach to its subject, being analytical as well as appreciative. It does not, however, reflect the economist's structured way of thinking in relation to explanatory models. Most other writing on the economics of map collecting consists of little more than tables of some past prices.

Similarities to Books and Prints

Like both books and prints, maps are generally issued through a technology of reproduction; they can occur in different editions, issues, and states[3] produced over a period of years; they are usually but not always on some form of paper; and individual examples can differ widely in condition and associations over their history, leading to widely disparate prices for copies representing even a single edition, issue, or state. (This chapter ignores manuscript maps and others that are unique in construction.)

Some dealers specialize in maps, and dealers in rare books and prints also frequently sell maps. The dealers may present maps at book fairs, and there are five international fairs specifically for maps.[4] Auctions of books often include maps, though auctions of prints only occasionally do so. This is to say, maps are often sold in the same dealer and auction markets as books and prints. Like many books—and maps are often bound into books, such as atlases, histories, and accounts of explorations—maps generally convey information and often have associations with human history and intellectual development. (Far fewer maps than books are intentionally fictional.) Unlike unillustrated books, maps were seldom produced by letterpress and instead were printed using many of

[2]Manasek (1998), Chapter 8, pp. 107–118.
[3]The definitions of the terms *editions*, *states*, and *issues* are not entirely distinct from each other.
[4]In Miami, London, Denver, Paris, and Breda, the Netherlands.

the methods that were used in the production of prints, such as wood, copper, and steel engraving as well as lithographic methods.

Although some books are treasured primarily for their content and the historical significance or associations of that content, others for their aesthetic value, and still others for both their content and their design, antique maps today, like prints, are prized primarily for their aesthetic value in combination with the historical connections represented by their content. Like prints, they are more likely to be displayed than books. Some maps, such as bird's-eye views,[5] can indeed be readily categorized as prints. In addition, because they usually are associated with particular locations, they frequently appeal to buyers other than collectors. An individual can choose to buy just one or two antique and even valuable maps without becoming a collector. Maps in general, but not in particular, have nearly universal appeal.

Seldom does a particular map have association value with a past owner, and in this, maps are different from books. A significant owner may have written his name on the flyleaf of a book, pasted in a bookplate, or annotated the text. There are few equivalent possibilities of memorializing the associations with a particular copy of a map. Still, there are some rare instances where provenance matters. When an especially distinguished private collection is dispersed, those maps can command a premium, perhaps because they have the imprimatur of a connoisseur.

The single most important difference between maps on the one hand and books and prints on the other is that they are bound to locations to a degree that most books and prints are not. Although many books are histories, nearly all of which are associated with particular continents, countries, regions, or cities, and many prints are depictions of particular locations, such books and especially such prints may appeal to buyers and collectors who themselves have no firm connection with these places. In contrast, and with the main exceptions of maps of the heavens above and the globe of the earth below in its entirety, few locations represented by maps have universal appeal. That is, in contrast to the nearly universal enjoyment of maps in general, most individual maps are of primarily local interest. This has implications for the pricing of maps and the valuing of collections, which we consider here.

Markets

There are two markets in which maps are bought and sold: the dealer market and the auction market. To a degree, each of these can be segmented. The rarest and most expensive maps, such as early modern maps of Europe, the Americas, and the world, are the province of a select group of dealers and of the major auction houses. These dealers and auction houses also offer city maps

[5]Bird's-eye views are prints of towns and cities represented as though viewed obliquely from a balloon. They were especially popular in 19th-century America, and after years of neglect, they have become treasured and expensive.

and other local maps that are of especial distinction. At the other end of the scale, maps that are of lesser quality or distinction, such as maps extracted from fairly common atlases and that are of interest primarily to antiquarians and collectors of things connected with smaller regions, are the province of a larger and more miscellaneous set of dealers, most of whom sell other collectibles besides maps, though there are also small specialty map dealers, and smaller, sometimes regional auction houses. And there are dealers and auction houses intermediate in size and cachet.

Dealers participate in the auction market as both principals and agents, and therefore maps pass fluidly from one market to the other. Indeed, all participants (dealers, auction houses, buyers, sellers, and the objects of their interest, the maps) appear in both markets, with the exception that the auction houses do not participate in the dealer market. Dealers will even sell at auction.[6]

A challenge for an analyst of these markets is to create an economic model that explains why both markets exist and how a map ends up in one market or the other. Of course, in any day, month, year, or decade, a copy of any given map is likely to turn up only in one market or the other, if at all, but this is insufficient to explain the contemporaneous existence of both markets in long-run equilibrium.

One possible explanation for their parallel existence is that the dealer market provides instant liquidity for the seller (at a cost, as we discuss later), whereas the auction market allows the seller to realize the best possible price (again, as we discuss later), as long as the two most eager buyers are participating at the time a particular item comes up for auction. (The dealer provides instant liquidity if she purchases the map, not if she takes it on consignment.) The dealer has to be compensated for the possibility that a map will have to be held in inventory longer than she would like. Liquidity, however, is not an entirely satisfactory explanation. Auctions occur frequently, and if not in the same venue, then in other, sometimes easily accessible ones, for both the grandest and the most modest auction houses and therefore provide reasonable liquidity. The largest auction houses can provide more publicity than even fairly large dealers, and items can be left on consignment. So, except in the case of the most urgent need for cash, illiquidity in the auction market should not pose a serious problem for the seller.

Another possible explanation is that the dealer is providing a service to the buyer. Consider that anyone with sufficient time can learn, for example, to do his own plumbing or even investment management; most individuals, however, lack the time or inclination to do so and therefore hire experienced professionals. Just so does a collector make use of the services of knowledgeable dealers, who not only advise on purchases but can act as tutors and agents. (Of course, some collectors develop sufficient knowledge in their own specialties that they may eventually know more than any dealer and may even become dealers.)

[6]Manasek (1998), p. 103.

Further, dealers form a network, and any one dealer can use this network to help a buyer find a particular item.

Dealers can use this network also to provide a service to the seller of an especially valuable map by taking it on consignment. This is a fairly common arrangement. It is even possible for a dealer who places an item this way to provide a better return to the seller (after transaction costs) than the seller would realize by disposing of the item at auction. Together, these services to buyers and sellers make a strong argument for the continued existence of the dealer market in the presence of the auction market. The argument does not, however, explain why or how a seller chooses one market over the other, and therefore the argument is incomplete in describing the comparative advantages of the two markets.

A third explanation is an expansion of the second. Informational efficiency provided by dealers may partly explain the existence of the dealer market when auction houses can often have lower bid-ask spreads. Not all sellers are sufficiently knowledgeable to sell their maps through an auction house that will receive the highest possible bids, and less valuable maps that are of mainly local appeal may not be accepted by large auction houses. Knowledgeable dealers may take advantage of small, regional auctions to buy maps for inventory at low prices, though this advantage is diminishing as the Internet broadens the accessibility of these auctions. They are less likely to buy for inventory at the auctions run by Sotheby's, Christie's, and other major auction houses, though they may. But this explanation depends almost entirely on the possibility of there being sellers with insufficient knowledge, which is a slender premise.

In general, there is a great amount of informational efficiency about the history and significance of maps, though not their prices. There are many reference works and histories of cartography. The larger auction houses employ specialists who can provide background information on a map almost as readily as a specialist dealer, and the buyers of maps are likely to be on the mailing lists of both the major dealers and the major auction houses that specialize in their niches in map collection. A dealer, however, can often put a map directly to a known collector without that collector necessarily having sought out that particular map. In this way, the dealer may provide information efficiency that is advantageous to the buyer, though not necessarily the seller.

We still require a complete, satisfactory, and testable explanation for the existence of both the dealer and auction markets for maps. Even without an explanation, though, there is a lesson for the collector: She should buy like a dealer (if she has the time and knowledge) and sell either by consigning to a dealer or by committing to an auction house that offers the best publicity. For example, in buying like a dealer, an astute collector of lesser-known maps will likely find better values in regional auctions, where the other bidders are more likely to be dealers acting as principals and therefore willing to pay only such amounts as will allow them their usual margin on resale.

Although the question of why the two markets exist in parallel is an interesting one in the abstract, the lack of an explanatory model is not a serious hindrance to understanding the pricing of maps and the economic returns to their owners. A model might, however, aid a map owner in deciding how to sell a map. It might also lay the foundation for the development of new institutions for decreasing the bid-ask spread in the market for collectible maps.

It is possible that the Internet will provide a completely new market for maps: peer-to-peer exchanges for collectors. Such exchanges would not require dealers and would, presumably, result in a sharp drop in transaction costs.[7] But this has not yet happened.

Prices

As we consider the prices of maps, we should bear in mind two propositions that will be justified later: Many if not most true historical prices of maps are unobservable, and published prices represent an upper limit on what the true prices were. The first proposition limits the possibilities for any quantitative analysis that can be done with historical prices. The second proposition vitiates the economic, let alone the statistical, significance of any results that may be found.

> On the matter of the determination of prices, Dr. Manasek's account is worth quoting at length: *In practice, a map is worth what the seller can get for it. This sounds simplistic, but the consequences of this argument are important. There are some maps that trade in a fairly narrow price range that really is a consensus price. These are maps that have wide appeal and which are bought and sold frequently enough to create an almost public market. For the scarcer, or more unusual, or little-known stuff, a specific seller and buyer create a market for each transaction. ... The price of an individual map is based on many things, most importantly knowledge about the map and its place in cartographic history. [Italics by the author.]*[8]

We return to the issue of valuation later.

The one unified source for historical map price data is the *Antique Map Price Record*, begun by David C. Jolly, now issued annually on CD-ROM by Jeremy Pool and as of 2009 in its 24th edition. Each issue incorporates all the data of its predecessors. This is not, however, a record of all published map prices everywhere. For one thing, it includes few maps sold on eBay, which has become a significant auction venue for less expensive but worthy maps (and where some bargains can be found). It does, however, include prices from the major auction houses and dealers' catalogues. It is packaged with its own database management software, and it is designed to be a reference for looking up historical prices, not a research tool for econometric analysis.

[7] I owe this suggestion to Michael Buehler.
[8] Manasek (1998), p. 107.

Except for the very rarest and most historically significant examples, maps generally command lower prices than large numbers of rare books. This generalization is difficult to quantify or prove, but another way of putting it is that a collector can possibly build a significant map collection for less money than is often needed to build a significant collection of, say, rare books, oil paintings, or clocks and watches. Dr. Manasek, writing in 1998, says, "There are wonderful maps, maps that are interesting, attractive and important, that are available *for under a hundred dollars*" (italics in the original).[9] It is difficult to say more precisely how the prices of maps compare with those of prints and books. The very rarest of maps can command prices comparable to those of the very rarest of prints, but at the lower end of the price scale, a collector might be able to build up a significant collection of maps of a particular locale while spending no more than $100 to $5000 for each map.

Price data are sparse. The 2008 edition of the *Antique Map Price Record* contains a total of 120,687 records from around the world, which seems at first to be a large number of observations, but these are the records of 26 years of prices. There are 23,144 maps (or atlases) with prices of at least $1000, 5405 with prices of at least $5000, 2652 with prices of at least $10,000, 516 with prices of at least $50,000, 236 with prices of at least $100,000, and four (all from 2006 and later) with prices of at least $1 million. (These are the published prices or their dollar equivalents, with no adjustment for inflation, and may represent different copies of the same map or the same copy at different times; there may also be some duplicate records.) These numbers are evidence supporting the view that map collecting may be a less expensive hobby than indulging in other fine collectibles.

Published prices realized by maps sold at auction can be considered accurate, though the buyer's premium should, of course, be added to the hammer price to represent the true price paid by the buyer.[10]

The estimates in auction catalogues can be highly unreliable. There are two widespread and opposite beliefs about them: that auction houses consciously underestimate the sale prices to make the items look more affordable and thereby to entice bidders, and that they inflate the estimates to attract consignors. Regardless of whether either of these beliefs is true (or both are true for different auctions), the auction estimates are seldom systematically more accurate than the order of magnitude of the realized price. A would-be bidder who is knowledgeable will not be misled by the auction house estimates, and a researcher can safely ignore them, especially because the realized prices will be published.

Dealers' prices as published in their catalogues can be misleading. Most dealers are open to negotiation, at least for some maps and on some occasions. The prices in their catalogues can therefore be considered only upper bounds

[9]Manasek (1998), pp. 15–16.

[10]Auction prices published in the *Antique Map Price Record* include the buyer's premium.

on the true sale prices. Although not as inaccurate as auction house estimates, dealer's published prices may overstate the actual sale prices by large percentages, though experience suggests that most discounts (if any) from the published prices will be no more than 10%, maybe 15% for clients with the most clout.

Furthermore, if a dealer knows an eager and ready buyer for a map that he acquires, he has little or no reason to list the map in a published catalogue. In such a case, the agreed price of the map is never published. A map may be sold at a book fair or map fair or over the Internet before there is time to list it in a printed catalogue. Catalogues are expensive to produce (at least in time committed by the dealer and often in financial cost), and dealers issue them at broad intervals, so it is often the case that sales occur between publications. Some dealers are forgoing printed catalogues altogether and are publishing their inventory solely on the Internet. This makes asking prices more readily available at any given moment, but the information is transient because the record of the price vanishes when the dealer updates his site. Consequently, the available price record of map sales, both in the *Antique Map Price Record* and in dealers' catalogues, is a sparse representation of the actual historical transactions.

Cash Flows

We consider the economic returns to map ownership separately from prices, looking first at cash flows and then at price appreciation.

There are likely to be cash flows generated by the ownership of maps, but these are all negative. The negative cash flows are payments for conservation and restoration, presentation, storage, appraisal, and insurance. Insurance (and sometimes appraisal), being a continuing expense and based on a percentage of value, will significantly reduce the return realized on the sale of a map in any price range. The other cash flows may be less significant in relation to the price of the most expensive maps (say, \$50,000 or \$100,000 and up), but they will have a large impact on the returns realized upon sale of less expensive maps.

Dealers in the most expensive maps and even maps in the middle price range (in the value of a few thousand or tens of thousands of dollars or pounds) will often have paid for any necessary or desirable conservation and restoration work so that the maps will appear in the best possible light. Less expensive maps and even some in the middle price range, however, may be sold in a state that makes such work desirable, especially if the buyer wants to display the map. Such work includes cleaning, repair, and deacidification (or buffering). Nineteenth-century wall maps may have their coat of crackling yellow varnish removed and may require new linen backing.

Although some of the materials used in the conservation work (for cleaning and deacidification) may be expensive, most of the expense of conservation and restoration is for the skilled labor that such work requires. Trained and experienced paper conservators are few. The work could easily cost a couple of thousand dollars or pounds, though it could be less. For a map that was purchased for, say, $5000, this represents, as a percentage of price, a huge (though one-time) negative cash flow. It also means that even a map that was purchased at a bargain price with all faults may, after restoration, turn out not to be quite the bargain it first appeared to be. Such work is nonetheless desirable, not only because it improves the map's appearance and incidentally increases its longevity but also because it makes the map more saleable, which is why dealers frequently undertake the expense in the first place. (The cost of this work to the dealer may also be less than it would be to an individual collector because the dealer can guarantee a continuous flow of business to the conservator.)

Many map owners want to display their purchases. The cost of skilled framing of a large map, with "museum glass," could also, depending on the size of the map, run up to $1000 or more. Again, for a map that is not among the most expensive, this will significantly reduce the financial return, and unlike the conservation work, which makes the map more saleable, the framing has no effect whatsoever on price. Maps are seldom sold with frames, not merely because taste in frames varies and an existing frame has the potential to put off prospective buyers, but also because the dealer or the auction house will want to inspect the map itself thoroughly, and the mat and frame prevent close scrutiny of both surfaces of the map in their entirety. In short, the cost of displaying a map, which may be a significant percentage of the cost of purchase, is not recoverable upon sale.

Storage can also represent a large one-time cost, though because this cost can be spread over many maps, it may not be significant as a percentage of the cost of any one map. If the maps are not to be displayed, they should be stored flat in archival conditions. Cabinets with large, shallow drawers are not hard to find but can require a certain amount of floor space. All the same, given that all except relief maps (and atlases) are completely flat, maps require less space and are easier to store than nearly any other kind of collectible other than stamps, coins, and medals. Archival folios or binders can be purchased or made to order. Most collectors of any kind of object almost inevitably find that their collections rapidly outgrow the space originally allocated to them. In consequence, the possibility of having to purchase a larger home or to build additional space onto an existing home is at least worth a thought. Few collectors, though, will likely choose to install the precise controls for temperature and humidity that are virtually a requirement for institutional map and book collections.

Transaction Costs

There are virtually no data, not even anecdotes, for the size of the bid–ask spread for maps in the dealer market. Dr. Manasek, in his otherwise comprehensive account of buying and selling maps, passes over this quickly and vaguely. He argues that the experienced dealer will pay whatever he has to as long as he believes he can resell the map at a profit and that the size of the markup does not matter.[11] This viewpoint, however, ignores the likelihood that the dealer is better informed than the seller about the value of the map in the market as well as the cost of the dealer's time. I believe that most dealers have some idea of the size of the margin they would like to realize upon sale of a map.

To ask a dealer about his gross margin is equivalent to asking him how much he earns; you cannot ask. Furthermore, for the dealer to reveal his gross margin would undercut his position when he is negotiating either the purchase or the sale of a map. Indeed, any single dealer can only speculate about the margins of others. Only those collectors with considerable experience selling maps to dealers will have information that they might willingly share on spreads that they have observed. Having said this, however, I will offer a lightly informed guess: A dealer will often buy a map for about 20% to 30% of the price at which he expects to sell it. Quite possibly the margin is less, even as little as 10%, on the most expensive and saleable maps, where the monetary value of the margin can be very large or there is a near certainty that the maps can be quickly sold.

The truth in Dr. Manasek's statement lies in the certainty that the dealer will set the price of a map as high as he thinks he can, consistent with his objective of selling it in a reasonable span of time. But he is likely to have a gross margin in mind when he is negotiating a purchase. I have recently observed another printed item in the collectibles market sell at auction for $396 (including the buyer's premium) to a dealer who then offered it for $1200 and sold it to a second dealer, and I believe it was this second dealer who offered me the same copy of the item for $1750, all within the span of five months. (The first dealer probably discounted the item by $100 or $200 when he sold it to the second dealer.) One can hardly underestimate the effect of this bid-ask spread on the return that a map owner can realize when selling a map. This means, of course, that a map whose apparent nominal price, that is, the asking price, does not change between purchase and sale will realize a large negative return, even before reckoning in the negative cash flows. (At least it will escape the capital gains tax.)

The transaction costs for a collector who is selling may include appraisal of the map or the collection. If the map is sold through a dealer rather than an auction, there will normally be the huge bid-ask spread we have just considered as the dealer's margin. Depending on the venue where the map is sold and whether there is a gain, the seller may have to pay a capital gains tax. In the United States, the capital gains tax rate on collectibles is 28% and is unlikely to change. For the buyer of the map, transaction costs, again depending on the venue of the sale, may include sales tax or VAT. If the map is purchased at auction, the transaction cost for the buyer is primarily the premium above the

[11] Manasek (1998), p. 114.

hammer price, and this can range from 10% (at a small, regional auction) to 25% (at Sotheby's or Christie's). There can also be costs associated with travel to the auction, if the buyer wants to inspect the map before the auction, or with the retention of a dealer as agent. In the auction market, there can be transaction costs, too, for the seller, who may be charged a commission and sometimes may also be charged for storage and other incidental costs.

Dealers in the rarest maps want to buy only items of the highest quality, not bargains that require a significant investment in restoration. But consistent with that, they will, of course, want to pay as little as possible so that they can ask the most that at least one eager buyer will be willing to pay. The spread, however, is likely not pure profit. The dealer may have to pay for conservation and restoration, possibly for authentication and other costs associated with researching the history of the map, and, of course, marketing. Besides this, however, the dealer is assuming risk. Although the dealer should know the market for the map, it may remain in his inventory far longer than he would like. He will only very reluctantly lower the price, because there is always the possibility (anticipated when the dealer bought the map) that a buyer will eventually come along who is willing to pay the original asking price. Moreover, as noted earlier, maps are among the least expensive collectibles to store, so the inventory costs for the dealer are low. Naturally, the dealer will be more open to negotiation if the map has been in inventory for a long time.

The implication of this last point is that, in the field of map collecting (and of collectibles generally), the bid-ask spread should decrease as liquidity[12] decreases, which is the opposite of what one observes in markets for securities, which, unlike maps, are fungible. But we have already noted that with the most valuable and liquid maps, the dealer decreases his margin; this means that the bid-ask spread may narrow at both ends of the range of liquidity. These spreads are, however, mostly unobservable because, as we saw earlier when considering prices, the published and therefore observable dealer price is only an upper limit on the true purchase price paid by the map collector.

The market impact of large-scale trading in maps can be a transaction cost, as it is in the trading of financial securities. This has been observed more in the purchases than in the sales of collectors. Observers believe that several collectors who have had spells of voluminous buying, like David Rumsey,[13] have driven up prices. Like large institutional buyers of securities, they have engaged in strategies to minimize their market impact, such as buying anonymously through dealers acting as intermediaries (which is entirely legal and ethical). Some of the most expensive cartographic items bought in the last few years were atlases sold at Sotheby's London auctions of the Wardington collection (October 18, 2005, and October 10, 2006). An American collector bought the

[12]If we define *liquidity* here as the length of time between a purchase and sale.

[13]The David Rumsey Historical Map Collection boasts more than 17,400 maps whose images may be viewed at *www.davidrumsey.com*.

very top-end items in these auctions. He did this anonymously through dealers, and his identity is still not widely known, but his deep pockets have nonetheless had an effect on the very high end of this market. There are also claims by some that W. Graham Arader III, an American and perhaps the most successful of map dealers (at least financially), has somehow managed, in his more than three decades in the business, to drive up demand and prices.[14] These are particular observations or impressions, but there are insufficient data for statistical validation, and the last claim, in particular, will probably be forever unproven.

Primary Valuation Factors

Let us now consider the factors that determine the prices of maps.

In valuing stocks and shares, we use valuation models synchronically, to estimate the variations among asset values at a point in time, and we use "risk" models diachronically, to estimate the variability of asset values over time. Both kinds of models are built of explanatory factors. It is often the case in the quantitative analysis of stocks and shares that there is overlap between the set of factors used for valuation and the set of factors used to explain variation in prices over time, also known as *risk*. (Among economists, it is a fundamental proposition that return is associated with risk.)

If we think of maps in the same way that we think of financial assets, it is worth considering whether factors can be found that could be built into precise, numeric valuation and risk models for maps, given the limitations of the pricing data. I will keep my discussion at a broad, conceptual level, looking first at the valuation factors and then at the risk factors and correlations among the factors. Because I hope that it may one day prove possible to build a numerical pricing model for maps, I will consider separately two groups of factors: those with which, just maybe, it would be possible to build such models, and then those for which there will never be a substitute for the judgment of an expert. I discuss this latter group in the section "Other Factors Affecting Valuation." For many maps, these latter factors may overwhelm the quantifiable factors in determining prices.

All the valuation factors can be considered risk factors, too. In a later section, when considering risk, I will add two factors not considered in valuation.

As in the case of stocks and shares, variations in prices among maps at any one time and over time are the result of differences among factors that are presumably both systematic and unsystematic. (Again, I ignore inflation.) Although our difficulties in measuring prices and the sparseness of the data will make these factors difficult to quantify, there is little doubt about what they are.

[14] I owe nearly the whole of the discussion in this paragraph to Jeremy Pool; private communication, July 30, 2008.

The primary and possibly quantifiable systematic factors determining valuation (or price) consist of three endogenous variables: size, condition, and age (or date); and a large set of exogenous factors, each of which is a location that a map may represent.[15]

Condition requires no justification for inclusion in our model. As with books, condition may be described as "fine," "near fine," "very good," "good," and so on. Although these words reflect subjective judgments by the dealer or auction house, these judgments take into consideration how a likely buyer would also judge an item so described, because a buyer who feels that he has been misled by the description will be aggrieved and can damage the dealer's or the auction house's reputation. There is, however, no industry-wide agreement on how to evaluate and rate map condition. (In this respect, maps differ from other collectibles, such as stamps and coins.)[16] Condition takes into consideration not just damage but also the quality of repairs and whether the map has contemporary or later coloring. The researcher could in theory identify a set of maps where in each instance there is a map in, say, a first edition, first issue, and in fine condition, and then the same map in lesser condition, and thereby measure how much condition, in isolation, tends to affect price.

Size matters because, generally speaking, a large map will sell for more than a small map. Larger maps are able to include more detail, which tends to increase their historical interest and aesthetic value. The effect is not linear, but there is a difference in detail and interest between, for example, a county map published as a page in a county history or in a periodical and a map of the same county published in an atlas or on a sheet that is a meter wide.

Age in itself is not a very valuable quality for a map, though older maps tend to be more valuable than newer ones. (Beginning collectors commonly and mistakenly assume that anything old is *ipso facto* valuable.) Age, however, is more easily quantified than scarcity, for which it may be a proxy, though the relationship is not deterministic. Age is also a proxy for another relevant concern: the time the map was produced and its historical significance. For example, a map of Boston, Massachusetts, from 1776 is valuable not merely because it is two and a third centuries old, but because it was created at an important historical moment, has associations with that moment, and conveys information about that history.

Location matters, and although it is intrinsic to a map, I describe it as an exogenous factor because it is the fortunes of the place represented that help to set the price. For example, in recent years, as the economies of Ireland and Russia have boomed, or at least produced very wealthy individuals with a taste for collecting, maps, like art and other collectibles linked to these countries, have reportedly undergone considerable price appreciation. Dr. Manasek gives

[15]*cf.* Manasek (1998), pp. 109–111.
[16]Jeremy Pool, private communication, July 30, 2008.

further examples dating from the early 1990s, Turkey, and Arabia.[17] Even within a single country, at least one as large as the United States, the value of maps may vary with region so that maps of more prosperous regions, like New York City, are more valuable than maps of, say, Iowa. (Location would, in a practical and numerical valuation model, be a series of what econometricians call *dummy variables*.)

In determining prices, one has to be sensitive to the complex interplay among these valuation factors and the ones described in the following section. For example, I once paid a considerable sum for a map with wormholes. One might, therefore, consider its condition to be poor, but it was evidently extremely rare; neither the dealer nor I had ever before seen this map or any reference to it, and there are few copies listed in WorldCat (the unified online catalogue of research libraries), so it seemed unlikely that I would find a better copy if I waited. It was also handsomely executed and offered much of historical interest. This example demonstrates that the use of these valuation factors is not simply a matter of assigning a score for each one to a map and summing the scores; rather, in the manner of most quantitative stock valuation models, the map valuation model is a system of weighted averages of the scores, with some hard-to-measure idiosyncratic valuation considerations.

Is it worthwhile to build a quantifiable model for pricing maps? Right now, it is probably not possible, given the quality and total quantity of data, let alone the quantity of contemporaneous observations. All the same, an attempt might be made, for better or worse, to see if anything can be made to fit. This would create a framework for thinking further about map pricing. This is not a mere matter of intellectual curiosity; it may have practical benefits. A better understanding of how prices vary across the several factors could permit the construction of a matrix pricing model, like those used for thinly traded bonds, that could create guidelines for the pricing of maps for the market. This would permit more objective valuation of collections, and other interesting possibilities would follow from this, such as the construction of an index of sale prices. The ideal, and probably unattainable index, would be like the S&P/Case-Shiller Home Price Indices or the Mei Moses Art Indices, where the constituents are the prices of specific properties or paintings at the times of successive sales. I am not suggesting the replacement of the judgment of dealers, auction house specialists, and buyers with valuation models, but rather aiding them.

Other Factors Affecting Valuation

Beyond the main factors affecting map prices, there are other factors that cannot be neatly systematized or quantified and that will affect some maps but not others.

One factor that almost certainly cannot be quantified with the existing data is the variation of scarcity and desirability with edition, issue, or state. For

17 Manasek (1998), p. 109.

example, the famous Foster or Hubbard map of New England (1677) exists in two nearly contemporaneous editions, with the Boston one rarer and more valuable than the London edition and therefore commanding a much higher price. No model would capture this distinction for all maps. Those who are valuing the map simply have to know this information. And there are no copies of the Boston edition in the *Antique Map Price Record*.[18] For other maps, there may be no difference in value among editions, let alone issues of the same edition.

We have already considered age as a proxy for scarcity, but scarcity needs to be considered with greater sensitivity. It naturally affects map price, but there is little information to be had about how common any map or any given edition, state, or issue of a map is. Old maps probably had print runs comparable to those of old books (especially when published in atlases), but there was, of course, a large degree of variability in the print runs of books, and there surely was for maps, too. Collectors, dealers, and auction specialists will form their own impressions of scarcity based on their experience, and I have found on a number of occasions that my impression (or experience) differs widely from that of a dealer or another collector. Moreover, that a map is not scarce does not imply that it will be inexpensive. It is not difficult, for example, to find fine copies of Cellarius's maps of the heavens, but they still cost in the thousands of dollars.

Does scarcity increase over time? Scarcity is related to time in that it might be quantified as the number of copies of an item that become available (or are sold) in a given span of time. One might think that, as human population grows, so does its subset of map collectors, thereby increasing demand relative to the fixed supply, and maps also disappear permanently into institutional collections or vanish through inadvertent loss or destruction. Thus should scarcity increase, and there is a common belief in the trade that it is increasing. But these arguments are too simple. Much depends on local conditions and changing tastes. Even the disappearance of maps into institutional collections cannot be assumed. In coming years, institutions may deaccession some maps to reduce near-duplication or to reorder their collections and to raise funds for other purchases.[19]

In one area, scarcity may follow a curious pattern. The "breaking" of illustrated books is firmly deprecated by serious collectors,[20] but nonetheless, there is a long history of dealers breaking atlases because they could earn more by selling the constituent maps than by selling the complete books. The supply of copies of any single atlas is limited, however, and as the copies of an atlas are broken, so that atlas becomes increasingly scarce. It only stands to reason, then,

[18]The *Antique Map Price Record*, Vol. 24 (2009), will contain the record of the sale of a copy of the London edition of the Foster map for an asking price of $175,000.

[19]I owe this hypothesis to Michael Buehler.

[20]"I was a Visigoth," said W. Graham Arader, a leading map dealer, of his earlier engagement in this practice; "A Rival Is Charged, and a Map Dealer Wants to Say, 'I Told You So,'" *New York Times*, October 10, 2005.

that atlases will become more valuable as copies of them are broken, thereby making it less likely that the surviving copies will be broken. This, in turn, will make the constituent maps increasingly scarce, and therefore more valuable.[21] It is believed, but not proven, that this gives rise in the marketplace to oscillations in the relative values of atlases and the maps that constitute them, and that there are phases in the breaking of atlases.

In describing age as a primary factor, I explained that it was a proxy for two more subtle and less quantifiable factors, of which scarcity was one. The other was historical context. This factor is often more important than scarcity. I am told, for example, that currently, maps connected with the American Revolution are much in demand, and it is possible that maps connected with the American Civil War may not be far behind. In addition, the first map of a place is generally much more valuable than subsequent maps.

Publication history may also be a valuation factor. This is a way of describing a combination of publisher and place of publication. I am told that, at least in the United States, American imprints, especially of the 18th century, currently command a premium over British imprints of the same period, which in turn command a premium over French imprints.[22] This may not, however, be a factor distinct from historical context, which we have already considered.

Two matters that quite naturally affect value are the authenticity and the provenance of a map. While this should go without saying, there are unquestionably forgeries (that is, reproductions that are intended to pass as originals) in the map market. I have heard the claim that there are many of them, but this seems to be very much a minority view. Also, some maps being sold may be of dubious provenance, which is a polite way of saying that they may have been stolen. In recent years, there have been a couple of well-publicized instances, in one of which a very well-known dealer in the rarest maps, E. Forbes Smiley III, was selling maps that he had himself stolen, possibly back to the institutions that he had unburdened of them. (He admitted the thefts in court, was convicted, sentenced to serve time, and ordered to pay restitution.) Although this was, of course, an exceptional case, it may give the collector of more valuable maps good reason to buy only from reputable dealers and auction houses (thereby passing up possible bargains) and to pay to have the maps appraised by an expert. If map prices continue to increase, as they seem recently to have been doing for those that are regarded as being the most valuable, one might reasonably expect that theft will become an increasing concern for buyers and for institutional owners that lack the resources for the best security. But if word gets around that a particular map's provenance is suspect, it probably will be incapable of sale through established dealers or auction houses.

[21]Manasek (1998), p. 106.
[22]I owe this suggestion to Michael Buehler; private communication, August 11, 2008.

Price Appreciation

The owner of a map or a collection of maps naturally hopes that it will appreciate in value, even though we have just argued that cash flows may negate much if not all of the price appreciation and transaction costs may be enormous. Increasing value may not be the primary concern for the collector, whose motivations are usually other than mercenary, but it may be the primary concern of his heirs. The buyer of a map will, all the same, often form a judgment of its probability of price appreciation.

Price appreciation of maps can arise from several causes, which have analogues in discussion of the valuation of financial securities. (We will ignore inflation and consider price appreciation only in real terms.)

As in most areas of investing, the greatest returns can be earned by investors who buy assets that have been overlooked by other participants in the market. Unlike, say, investors in stocks, however, the buyers of maps cannot use rigorous valuation methods to reckon bargains, as all the foregoing discussion ought to have demonstrated.

One possibility for taking advantage of undervaluation is that of finding a map that appears to be underpriced when consideration is taken of similar maps that are evaluated across similar dimensions (subject, edition, condition, and so forth). If there are several nearly identical maps on the market at the same time or in a short span of time, then, obviously, the map with the lowest price is the best value with the most possibility of price appreciation. This is a simple matter of mispricing, which seldom occurs with financial securities but is somewhat more likely to occur in the map market because informational efficiency with respect to prices is less than for publicly traded financial securities. With the widespread use of the Internet, pricing efficiency is presumably greater than it was. Dr. Manasek's maxim that "a map is worth what the seller can get for it" militates against pricing inefficiency, but it does make the collector, not the seller, who is likely more knowledgeable, ultimately more responsible for setting the price.

A second, more subtle version of undervaluation arises from the possibility that a map collector who is also a connoisseur will be able to anticipate a rise in value. This is predicated on that ethereal quality, a fine sense of taste, as well as an appreciation of where other collectors may soon be looking. As always in investing, skill may be undistinguishable from good luck. I have lately been collecting in a cartographic specialty (which I prefer not to publicize) that, given its aesthetic and intellectual value, seems to me to be undervalued. Sometimes (although not with the present example), it may be possible to imagine an event or a cultural shift that would trigger a rapid appreciation—in both senses of the word—of the maps' value. As with financial securities, the market is the ultimate arbiter of value, and these items could remain inexpensive forever.

A third way that a collector might buy low and sell high is by betting successfully on a change in the premium paid for one of the factors that determine map values. The two factors whose premium movements a collector might be able to anticipate are the geographical region represented by a map and the mapmaker. The region might become economically more successful, so that its inhabitants, with more disposable income, start to buy its rare maps and bid up their prices. And a particular mapmaker may become fashionable.

A fourth (and final) possibility for market revaluation is the intentional manipulation of the market in ways that parallel two factors we have already considered: the market impact of trades and changing tastes or interests. Given the small size of the separate niches within the overall market for collectible maps, it is entirely conceivable that a collector could corner a particular niche. This would be the same as the intentional maximization of the market impact of trading, though I do not know of any instances of this. A collector could also "talk up" the importance of the niche in which she collects. I sometimes wonder if I have inadvertently affected the prices of part of my collection by publishing and lecturing on those maps. Though I have not yet sensed any change in price, I have seen myself cited in dealers' catalogues. (Because I am still collecting in this area, I would rather not drive up demand for these maps.)

Perhaps inseparable from observed revaluation upward in the price of a map is the possibility that winners of maps in auctions are no less cursed than winners in other kinds of auctions. Because dealers' published prices are only upper limits of what the true prices may be, the magnitude of the winner's curse in a map auction may be difficult to determine with the tools of econometrics. And unless the self-same map is sold in a short span of time in both the dealer's market and the auction market, it may be impossible to ascribe any difference in price to the winner's curse, because even small differences in the condition of two copies of the same issue of the same map can account for big differences in price. Moreover, even if the same copy of a map is sold in both markets in a short span of time and there is a big difference between the two prices, the investigator will have to eliminate the possibility that the price difference is attributable to a new discovery about the map (perhaps a previously undetected flaw or a previously unknown association of the map with a person or event) between the two sales.

For a given map, past price is probably the best predictor of future price, given the existence of the *Antique Map Price Record* and other less comprehensive and more dated records of past prices, published in, for example, Jonathan Potter's *Collecting Antique Maps* (Potter 2001), or even old auction dealers' catalogues saved by buyers and dealers. Dr. Manasek warns against the use of historical prices by both buyers and sellers, because, he says, an old map price is no more useful for valuing a map than an old stock price is for valuing a stock. In this, he is mistaken. There is a difference between, on the one hand, predicting the price of a map and, on the other hand, valuing one for sale or purchase. Investment professionals know that historical prices of securities are useful for purposes other than valuation. Moreover, because, unlike securities, maps have no future earnings to be forecast and valued, past prices can be and likely are often used as a guide or indicator for buyer and seller alike. It seems unlikely, though, that there is any detectable serial correlation among returns to maps.

One often hears accounts of tremendous returns realized on the sale of maps. In evaluating such anecdotal accounts of returns, one should be careful to note whether the returns cited are holding-period returns or compound rates of return. In my experience, these anecdotes invariably refer to holding-period returns and are therefore of little or no use, even for framing expectations.

Risks and Correlations

The variability in the prices of maps over time, that is, what an investment professional deems *risk*, is determined mostly by the same set of factors that determine the value of a map. The factors themselves may be priced differently as time passes, and the extent to which a given map is exposed to the factors may change over time.

For example, scarcity is a factor in valuing maps, and it may also be able to explain the variability of the price of a map over time. The premium paid for a degree of scarcity, considered a valuable quality in its own right, may not change over time, because scarcity will always make a map more valuable, all else being equal, but the degree to which a given map is scarce may change. We have already considered how the scarcity of a map might change. New examples may come to light, making it more common, or examples may disappear into institutional libraries, making it more scarce.

The factors whose pricing is most likely to change over time are the regions or subjects represented. The greatest single differentiator of maps from other collectibles from the standpoint of investing is, as we have already noted, that an overwhelming number of maps are intimately linked to specific locations. Consequently, the prices of maps ought to be correlated with economic fortunes of the regions that they represent, because relatively few are of global appeal. So, in contrast with scarcity (as a factor), where the factor itself is likely not to be priced differently over time but the exposure of a map to that factor may change, regional association, as a factor, may be priced differently over time, whereas a map's exposure to it remains constant. We have already discussed the use of regional factors in valuation, but of course, the fortunes of regions vary over time, as in the cited examples of Ireland and Russia. Similarly, one might expect the prices of maps of Texas to vary with the price of oil. Broadly, one might look into the possibility of correlating the prices of maps with prices of homes in the region, and whether there is a lag that might predict a rise in map prices. For the most part, though, these boomlets in map prices cannot easily be confirmed from the *Antique Map Price Record.*

These regional factors may be cities, regions, countries, or other defined geographical entities. The exceptions are world maps (and perhaps maps of continents) and celestial maps. Some collections may span regions. For example, there has lately been some interest in (and a new book about) transit maps from around the world (Ovenden, 2007). Some people collect maps that are printed on postcards. Possibly there are collectors of maps of mountains around the world, or of road maps from around the world, or the works of a particular mapmaker (though mapmakers tend to specialize in regions). Some may collect maps purely for their aesthetic value. But on the whole, collections are built of maps of particular geographical entities, such as the United States, or Scotland, or Ukraine, or Washington, D.C., or Paris, or the Holy Land.

This is not to say that collectors of local maps always live in the localities that the maps represent. They often do so, but commonly, especially in the United States, they may collect maps related to their places of national origin, with an American of Italian descent, for example, collecting maps of his family's native region in Italy. One of the finest collections of maps of Ukraine was built by a Ukrainian exile, Bohdan Krawciw, and now resides at Harvard University (Seegel, 2008).

Another consequence of the local ties of map collecting is that a collector whose maps represent a region far away from his home may find it difficult to get the best price for his collection without returning it to its home region. It is a platitude among map dealers, at least American ones, that every dealer has a drawer full of maps of France.[23] All the same, an American collector of Italian maps could probably sell within the United States without paying a penalty for the displacement of venue from the country depicted.

Geographic concentration can cut two ways in affecting risk. One way is the elimination of currency risk. So, for example, a U.K.-based collector of maps of London will be well situated, in having little exposure to currency risk in building his collection. But this lack of diversification can also lead to wide variations in the value of a collection over time. For example, if the Irish economy were to go into an protracted recession, a collection of Irish maps, held in Ireland, would likely decline sharply in value, whereas economic turmoil would be unlikely to affect the value of a collection of celestial maps wherever that collection is held. If one is collecting maps for any reason other than investing, it would be foolish to diversify the collection geographically merely to reduce economic risk. A collector who does span geographic regions should recognize his good fortune.

Maps of the Holy Land are probably the only exception to the proposition that maps of a locality are exposed to that region's economic risk. There are significant collectors of maps of the Holy Land who live in the region, but most collectors of these maps are scattered throughout the world. These maps are in great demand regardless of the economic fortunes of the Middle East or any other country or region.

[23]Manasek (1998), p. 100.

If, however, a collector in financial distress must sell part of his collection to raise cash, it is therefore quite possible that (if his distress is connected with the economic fortunes of his home region) he will be selling into a falling market. Maps are real assets, but they are probably not a good hedge for anything.

Price may also be a risk factor. Casual observation suggests that for maps, as for other collectibles, the items with the highest prices tend to appreciate more (increasing dispersion of prices over time). As Dr. Manasek says, "Quality counts,"[24] and a high price may be a quantifiable representation of high quality, even though what may seem a high price for one map may be a low price for an entirely different map. We can be fairly sure, though, that a map that sold for $1 million recently was not selling for $1000 10 years earlier. This evanescent characteristic called *quality* is probably highly correlated with condition and scarcity, but it is difficult to identify it with any specific determinable factor other than price. Price, however, is one of the two risk factors that cannot also be a valuation factor; if it were, the valuation model would be tautologous. It seems plausible to hypothesize that in a falling market for collectibles, the quality premium will shrink.

One might consider market risk, too, as an explanation of the varying prices of maps over time. The collectivity of various maps that are sold is so heterogeneous, even from year to year, let alone month to month, that the true "map market" factor is unobservable. Rather, therefore, than taking the market for maps as a whole as a factor in pricing individual maps, it would probably be more reasonable to consider the entire market for collectibles to be the market and to take this as the market risk factor, though no index of it yet exists. One might suppose that a rising or falling market for collectibles in general will affect to some extent the prices of individual maps, at the very least because maps are constituents of that market. Like price, market risk is not useful as a valuation factor. There may or may not be variation among maps in their exposure to this factor.

Conclusion

This chapter has not said whether old maps are a good investment, although it has implied that they are not. It has not assayed past returns. The reason for this hesitation is not just the paucity of exiting data but also its limited reliability. Nonetheless, we have suggested a structured way of thinking about how maps might be valued as well as avenues of research that could lead not just to better information on historical returns to map ownership, but also to regularizing the valuation of maps in the future. It would be presumptuous to claim that the factors for valuing maps recounted here are new; they are, on the

[24]Ibid., p. 108.

contrary, the ways dealers, auction houses, and collectors have been valuing maps for many years. What is novel is the systematization of the valuation and risk factors in a way similar to that by which quantitative security analysts look at securities.

It may, however, be a mistake to consider the returns to map ownership in comparison to other investment vehicles. Collectors buy maps for their intrinsic qualities and historical associations, not for price appreciation. Even if the returns to ownership are negative (because of the large transaction costs and negative cash flows), the financial returns are inevitably better than those that arise from other uses of discretionary income, such as fine food, cigars, and luxury vacations, not to mention other real assets that depreciate to a salvage value that is little more than nothing. Antique maps will always represent a store of financial value, can give pleasure continuously, and offer the satisfaction of ownership of part of our cultural and intellectual history.

Acknowledgment The author thanks Michael L. Buehler, proprietor of Boston Rare Maps, and Jeremy Pool, proprietor of MapRecord Publications, for their extensive comments on an early draft of this chapter, which have improved it immeasurably.

References

Manasek, F. J. (1998) *Collecting Old Maps*, Terra Nova Press.

Ovenden, M. (2007) *Transit Maps of the World*, Penguin.

Pepys (1972) *The Diary of Samuel Pepys, Vol. 7: 1666*, R. Latham and W. Matthews (eds.), University of California Press.

Pool, J. (2008) *Antique Map Price Record, Vol. 23: 1983–2008*, Map Record Publications, CD-ROM.

Potter, J. (2001) *Collecting Antique Maps: An Introduction to the History of Cartography*, Jonathan Potter Ltd.

Seegel, S. (2008) *The Life and Maps of Bohdan Krawciw*, Harvard Ukrainian Research Institute.

10 Collecting and Investing in Stamps

Stephen Satchell and J. F. W. Auld

-Trinity College Cambridge; British Stamp Trade

Introduction

This chapter investigates the possibilities of investing in stamps. We would say at the outset that investment comes in two different forms. First, there is investment for investment's sake, whereby stamps are part of what are known as *alternative assets*. The second version of investing is the increase in value that comes as a by-product of collecting. This chapter discusses both. The approach that we take is that of financial economics. We assume that the reader has some familiarity with the subject, but we try to provide definitions where appropriate, to make the chapter as self-contained as possible. Before we deal with these issues, let's look at a brief description of stamps and the hobby of philately.

The origin of the term *philately* has been attributed to Georges Herpin, a French writer on stamp collecting. The term is formed from the Greek words *philos* (friend) and *ateleia* (exempt from charge, or *franked*). This describes a lover of postmarks rather than a lover of stamps; an alternative is *timbrophily*, a term rarely if ever used.

A Very Brief History of Philately

The first postage stamps were issued in Great Britain in 1840. They were the penny black and the twopenny blue, issued on May 6, 1840. Contrary to popular belief, these stamps were never especially rare. (Printing figures for the penny black indicate that 55 million were printed, and tens of thousands have survived to this day.) However, the demand for these iconic items remains extremely strong and the price has more or less increased through time.

Stamp collecting can be dated to the 1850s or possibly earlier. Gelber claims that "Within a year of England's first issue of postage stamps in 1840, women and schoolboys began collecting them." It is not clear whether this form of

Collectible Investments for the High Net Worth Investor

collecting had any relationship to modern collecting, since there were only four different stamps in existence by the date Gelber quotes (1841). It might be that early stamps were simply used in a decorative capacity, augmenting the Victorian use of scrap to make aesthetic and patriotic patterns. Very quickly, most countries issued stamps for themselves and their colonies. Various attempts at global regulation followed, such as the founding of the Universal Postal Union (1874). The hobby spread at a tremendous rate and became a near-compulsory activity for children, especially boys. It was seen as a worthwhile activity, improving the child's knowledge of geography, and was always seen as an activity that created value.

The discovery of rarities by "the man in the street" helped create the belief that lurking in every collection was a potentially valuable item. It is worth referring the reader to a poem in Gelber (1992, p. 764) that captures this aspect of philately as well as the self-delusive nature of some of the evaluation of profits. Collecting has had a nationalistic and imperialistic aspect to it; this has been an important part of its appeal across all social classes. Thematic collecting has also had great appeal.

Within the British Empire, the interest of King George V and King George VI in philately gave it a social gloss and gave birth to the saying "Philately, the king of hobbies and the hobby of kings." Within the United States, President Franklin D. Roosevelt also collected. The hobby probably reached a peak in the 1960s and 1970s, fueled by high inflation and the fact that stamps kept pace with it. A subsequent decline in values and a switch in young people's interests have dramatically reduced interest in the hobby. It has now become a pastime for the well-off rather than a mass movement. Excessive issuance, not just by third-world regimes but also by the British Post Office, has helped accelerate the decline.

The Economics of Philately

A typical investment item such as a share can be seen as consisting of two components. The first of these is the *capital gains process*, which measures the change in value/price of the asset. The second is the *dividend process*, which is the flow of money that accrues to the owner of the asset. When this analysis is applied to commodities, it changes slightly. Although the capital gains concept may stay the same, for goods that are consumed it can change. So, if the good is a bottle of vintage champagne, the consumption of the champagne produces a dividend to the owner, but the capital gains process terminates at the value zero, unless the empty bottle or cork have some positive value. For stamps, the story is different; the dividends are made up of the psychological pleasures of ownership, but the enjoyment of these pleasures has no impact on the capital gains process unless one becomes so fond of the stamp that one damages it through excessive handling.

At this stage, we can see that the distinction between collecting and investing can be at least partially analyzed in terms of consumption and capital gains. We argue that to concentrate only on investment and not to gain any utility from ownership is probably rather pointless because it will understate the value of the investment. If we can attach some monetary value to the happiness associated with ownership, collecting stamps becomes a serious investment.

To evaluate whether stamps constitute a good investment, it is necessary to discuss stamp prices. Economists have written many books on what constitutes a price; the notion we might consider for a liquid commodity might be the market-clearing price or the price determined in a willing buyer/willing seller context.

There are three basic concepts of price used in philately. The first is dealers' buy and sell lists. These give no notion of market impact or volume, since no dealer would guarantee to buy or sell an unlimited quantity of a stamp at the listed price. These lists tend to be specialized for a particular country or type of stamp. Taking a typical example, Mr. D. White, of the Dunedin Stamp Centre, maintains a list for New Zealand stamps (2007). In this, he lists different stamps by quality, so, for example we have the 1898 five-shilling red listed as unmounted mint, mint, very fine used, and fine used; the prices being 1750, 750, 600, and 400 New Zealand dollars, respectively. There is no specific list for buying and there is no indication as to how many copies you could buy at these prices.

The second source of prices is catalogues. There are a number of these, of which the leading ones are Stanley Gibbons (British), Scotts (United States), Michel (German), and Yvert (French). All these catalogues provide prices for all stamps in the world, so they are global in this particular sense. The prices in the various catalogues are not equal due to different perceptions of rarity and exchange rate effects. These catalogues are indicators of value and do not represent selling prices, with the exception of Stanley Gibbons (SG), which maintains a stock in its shop in the Strand, London and which sells stamps at its catalogue prices. So, for example, SG lists the 1898 five-shilling New Zealand stamp at £200 mint and £350 used (2007). These prices presumably correspond to the mint and very fine used in the list offered by the Dunedin Stamp Centre.

The importance of catalogue values is that they are widely used as a means of valuation. So, for example, a collection can be described as follows: "Italian colonies, Libya, comprehensive mint collection on stock sheets, superb condition, catalogues, Stanley Gibbons, £3000+, price, £800." This description tells the would-be buyer what the collection catalogues at and what price the vendor would accept. The buyer has to assess what proportion of catalogue Italian colonies are worth and what the condition of the stamps is. Though the vendor has described the stamps as superb, this description may not be reliable. Generally, many investors use catalogue value as a summary statistic for the value of the collection or single stamp. This method, however, is fraught with problems.

Some stamps are worth a tiny fraction of catalogue; some stamps are worth far more than catalogue; some stamps are worth catalogue. As discussed earlier, different catalogues can give different prices; vendors will choose the highest, purchasers will choose the lowest.

The third source of prices is auction realizations. As we discuss later in the document, it is often not clear what these actually mean, because different lots can have different treatment in terms of sales tax and commission. Nevertheless, these prices are in some sense the most useful because they do contain hard information about transactions.

The Psychology of Philately

Philatelists exhibit all the characteristics normally associated with collectors. Most stamp collectors are obsessive in their behavior, and much of their purchasing is done in a frenzy rather than through rational decision making. As a market, the stamp market is likely to be much more behavioral than the stock market. Collecting has been described by Belk (1995a, p. 67) as "the process of actively, selectively, and passionately acquiring and possessing things removed from ordinary use and perceived as part of a set of nonidentical objects or experiences." Elsewhere, Belk (1995b, ii) describes collecting as a form of materialism. The term *materialism* here refers to the belief that the possession of collectibles will lead to happiness. This, apparently, is an *ex-ante* belief rather than an *ex-post* experience, since he also quotes some survey evidence pointing to a correlation between materialism and unhappiness.

It should be the case that an investor who is immune to the Circe's voice of philately should enjoy a comparative advantage in trading. Indeed, the most successful traders we have met are those who are neutral to stamps or even despise them. Generally, being both a collector and a trader is not profit maximizing but rather utility maximizing.

It is this interface that can have appeal to high net worth investing. After all, many of the high net worth community have displayed the same obsession in the collecting of money/wealth. It would require only a small amount of psychological adjustment to transfer that obsession from one medium to another.

The Finance of Philately

There are a number of separate issues involved in thinking about stamps as financial commodities. We list them here in no particular order:

- Heterogeneity
- Indexation
- Transaction costs
- Market depth
- Authenticity

- Condition
- Country exposures and emerging markets
- Investing in modern material

Heterogeneity

To focus the following discussion we consider a penny black, but actually the discussion is quite general and applies to virtually all stamps, with the exception of some modern material.

If we wanted to talk about the price of a penny black, we would begin to realize just how complicated such a seemingly simple concept can be. There are extremely fine gradations of value attached to the condition of a stamp, even if that stamp were some sort of base or *numeraire* penny black. On consulting the Stanley Gibbons stamp catalogue (2008, p. 5), we see that the cheapest price for a used stamp is £275, whereas the cheapest price for an unused stamp is £8500. However, there is a list of other prices going upward, depending on the shade of black and the plate number. This is to do with the printing of the stamp. There is also a large range of prices to do with varieties on the stamp and to do with different postmarks. So, for example, different colors of postmark will increase the value, as will different numeric or town postmarks. Early use, such as being used on the first day of issue, or late use will also affect the stamp's value. The prices quoted are for fine stamps, which means that the stamp should not be rubbed or blurred; the stamp should have clear margins round the edges and not be cut into; the postmark should be reasonably clear; and the stamp should not be torn, creased, toned, bent, or thinned.

If the stamp has an exceptionally fresh appearance, wide margins, and a beautiful postmark, it could, in principle, be worth many times the list price in the catalogue. For most stamps that have some sort of minor defect, the value will be much less than the listed price. (We discuss condition elsewhere in this section.) Without a fairly high degree of expertise and experience, it is almost impossible to give accurate valuations for stamps in these circumstances. This makes amateur participation highly risky, but it also has the economic benefit of creating markets with heterogeneous beliefs. Broadly speaking, if goods are heterogeneous, markets will often be quite liquid because differing opinions of worth lead to more actual trading.

Indexation

One of the key requirements for institutional investment is the creation of an index. This becomes very problematic if the commodity class to be indexed is extremely heterogeneous, which is what we argue here. There are a number of possible ways to create an index. Perhaps the most appealing is the weighted repeat sales methodology, which we describe next. (Readers not interested in mathematical exposition may want to avoid the next several pages.) The intuition behind this concept is that if we could track particular stamps that sell in public auctions from time to time, we should be able to get a fairly accurate measure of stamp price change. These methods have been applied to house prices, but they suffer from the difficulties associated with quality changes. Thus, if a house has an extra bedroom added, or if the neighborhood is spoiled by an influx of social undesirables, repeat sales methodology has trouble accommodating such changes, especially since either many of them are unobservable or there are issues of data quality. Stamps, like many other collectibles, do not have these problems. In fact, famous philatelic pieces have very well-documented histories. Their ownership/provenance and the times they have been sold and resold are well documented in many cases. It is possible that a stamp might have been damaged in its time with a particular owner, but this is uncommon.

In this approach, we first characterize individual stamp prices as arising from two components, one of which is the market index, and the other is a random component modeled as a log normal diffusion process. These calculations are based on the logarithm of the price and involve notions of stochastic calculus. This concept, familiar to graduates of financial economics, involves some quantitative complexities. (Mathematical details are provided in the appendix to this chapter.)

If we return now to our example of the penny black, we could consider significant penny blacks with known pedigree; these would usually have current values in excess of £1000. They could have all the variety we discussed earlier. They could be on or off cover, mint or used. They may have exotic postmarks. In building this index, we would be inferring a rate of return to something loosely called *penny blackness*.

If we repeated this process for something quite different—say, Chinese stamps—the steps would be essentially the same. However, now the index would represent some sort of Chinese stamp market average and would be sensitive to what we include or exclude. Suppose we had a penny black on a cover that had been sent to China; we would imagine that such an item would be of stupendous value and be of great interest to Chinese collectors. However, a frenzied bidding war in a Shanghai auction could then have a significant impact on the penny-black index.

Such indices already exist; Stanley Gibbons, a well-established firm, has a number of repeat sale indices based on the most frequently traded and liquid stamps. SG provides one for British stamps and another for British Commonwealth stamps. Without getting into too much detail about the particulars, SG chooses a list of stamps and follows them, rather than choosing unique stamps. So, for example, this could be a £5 Zululand stamp in mint condition, and then the index gets updated whenever one of the several hundred of these stamps in existence is traded. This is in contrast to following the fortunes of a unique stamp.

The difficulty with this procedure is that it is hard to control for quality; even for a mint stamp, factors can influence quality, as we discussed earlier.

Furthermore, exactly what cost assumptions are involved? As we will see later in the chapter, there are numerous ways of incurring transaction costs. Most repeat sales indices ignore costs altogether, which, for property traded every 20 years with 3% transaction costs, might be acceptable. More important, there is a sample selection problem in creating indices based on a list of stamps that is a subset of the whole universe of stamps. Typically, but not always, the stamps that are liquid are the ones whose prices are going up, so picking your subset on the basis of liquidity is likely to show a high return when you back-test your index. This return will exaggerate the return you get from a portfolio of randomly selected stamps. Of course, your investment advisor would hopefully guide you into holding stamps that are positively correlated with the index, if you believe that the index can represent some measure of stamp value. Although one can accept that, broadly, a repeat sales index will measure value, the return inferred from it will not match the return you might expect to get from your stamp portfolio.

Transaction Costs

Buying and selling stamps is extremely expensive and requires some thought as to the best way to proceed. We base the following discussion on our knowledge of the U.K. market; different opportunities could exist elsewhere. It might be thought that auctions would allow collectors to realize the best value due to competition among buyers. Whether this is so or not, auctions charge a significant commission. This is difficult to calculate, since there are numerous separate components. Auctions may charge a rate on sales, possibly 10 to 15%. There may be lotting fees, unsold charges, minimum commission, and insurance, not to mention value-added tax (VAT), a sales tax that could apply to some of the above. However, unknown to the vendor, there is usually a buyer's premium of 10 to 15% (plus VAT), which will apply to the "hammer price." Adding all this up, the difference between what the buyer pays and the vendor receives is very likely to be of the order of 25% or more.

Further problems arise because auctions are effectively unregulated, and there are many small (and sometimes large) auctions run by unscrupulous people. Vendors should be careful to check the auction's credentials; look for the principals of the auction to have membership in professional associations such as the Philatelic Traders Society (in Great Britain), the American Stamp Dealers Association, or the Australian Philatelic Trade Association. It is not uncommon in small auctions for the vendor not to be paid the full amount, or for the auctioneer, having discovered something valuable, to buy the lot directly or indirectly through an accomplice and then resell it at a much higher price. It is fair to say, but impossible to prove, that rings exist for some auctions whereby dealers coordinate their bids to avoid bidding against each other. All of this is not a criticism of the auction process; it is simply a warning that in dealing in auctions, one should deal with someone with a good reputation.

One way for an auction to eliminate rings is to make sure that reserves for the stamps are high enough to make such activity unprofitable. However, if an auction makes its reserves too high, would-be buyers will be deterred and might go elsewhere; there is always a tension between these two considerations.

An alternative to selling by auction is to sell by private treaty. In this arrangement, the dealer sells on your behalf and takes a commission, typically of the order of 15 to 20%. The difficulty with this is that if you don't know what the lot is worth, the dealer can undervalue it dramatically, sell it to his (stamp dealers are predominantly male) accomplice, and then charge you 20% for doing it!

The advantage of selling privately is that you can sell a large collection without the need to break it up. In addition, prior to the sale you can negotiate the minimum price you would take for the collection.

Another procedure is to take a table at a stamp fair and sell your stamps directly to the purchaser. If the fair is well attended, the cost of the table not too high, and you have a significant volume of stamps to sell, transaction costs may be as little as 3 to 4%. However, this introduces some uncertainty into the transaction costs; you might sell nothing, pay £500 for the table, and have some of your stock stolen. It is also likely that if you have little experience, your best material will sell and you will be left with overpriced dregs.

Finally, there is direct selling through the Internet or through advertising in newspapers or specialized publications. The Internet in particular is an excellent mechanism for getting very high prices for scarce but illiquid items. There might be only 15 collectors in the world for Hawaiian beer tax stamps; they could live in 15 separate countries. There is no common physical place for them to purchase these rare items. If you have one of these stamps and place it in an Internet auction, it is not uncommon for the price to go many times over the reserve. Paradoxically, standard material, a modern definitive set, for example, does not seem to attract any sort of premium on the Internet. However, beware—often rare items fetch much less on the Net than in a major conventional auction.

Market Depth

Market depth is a term used in finance to capture the elasticity of demand or supply. It is defined in many ways, but intuitively, it can be thought of as the extent to which you can buy or sell a commodity without influencing the price. It is closely related to the concept of liquidity, although not exactly the same.

The reason that market depth is particularly relevant to stamp markets is that it represents a way whereby private investors can profit. Stamp dealers are typically undercapitalized; they tend to carry a relatively small stock and do not have large quantities of each item. Their rationale is that this would tie up money that would be better used buying new material. Consequently, if a lot of 100 copies of the same stamp comes up for sale, the stamp will be heavily discounted unless it is something extremely liquid (such as a penny black or some other classic). This discussion does not focus on the top end of the market but concerns the many stamps held by collectors that might be worth up to £100 each. The lot of 100 stamps represents an investment opportunity for the private investor, since she can put the 100 copies in storage and, assuming that she has been able to find some way of selling stamps at less than a prohibitive commission, can sell them over a longer period at a higher price. In economic terms, the investor is receiving a premium for providing liquidity to the stamp market.

The shortage of liquidity in stamp markets does provide short-term opportunities for investors. Dealers are invariably short of money, and many have a rather finite list of clients. Once they have sold a particular stamp to their clients, they may find it difficult to dispose of a second copy of that stamp. Consequently, they can be persuaded to dispose of their residual stock at a substantial discount. What may not be able to be sold in one location or to one person, you may sell very well elsewhere.

Authenticity

Until comparatively recently it would be fair to say that most stamp forgeries were of 19th-century origin and relatively crude. In addition, reprints were made from original printing plates.

In the 20th century, most forgeries were the result of repairs and additions. Skillful craftsmen can add stamps to covers, add rare postmarks, repair perforations, apply fresh gum, and so on. One of the authors has seen one seemingly good rare stamp made from no less than five damaged stamps. The forgery was invisible without an ultraviolet lamp. If you want to assess rare stamps on your own, you might find that the purchase of an ultraviolet lamp will pay for itself very quickly. When purchasing rare stamps, it is always worth buying from an established source who will usually guarantee material for a given period of time. Investors might want to obtain a certificate of authenticity from one of the expert committees. In Britain these are the Royal Philatelic Society, the British Philatelic Association, or David Brandon. In the United States the most well known organizations of experts are the American Philatelic Society and the Philatelic Foundation.

Certain stamps are virtually impossible to sell without a certificate. Any reputable dealer would be happy to obtain one on your behalf. If buying in auction, it is normal to ask for "an extension"; this is an extension of the time before the vendor is paid, to give time for a certificate to be obtained. Usually, if the stamp turns out to be fraudulent, the vendor will have to reimburse the purchaser for the certificate. Prices for such certificates consist of a flat fee and/or a proportion of the catalogue value of the stamp. This is always compensated by the increase in market value.

The past few years have seen an increase in forged overprints and cancellations using modern technology. Often these are sold at "bargain" prices on Internet auction sites.

Condition

Condition is absolutely paramount. Stamps, as with all collectibles, must have eye appeal. We discussed the penny black earlier; within the past 12 months, one of the authors has seen examples without any specific cancellation or variety fetch between £10 and £2000! Note that the £10 example had a chunk missing. However, a good example of this stamp would retail at £100 to £200. The £2000 example was a remarkable stamp nonetheless. In 1840, perforations had literally not been invented. Stamps were cut from the sheet with scissors or a razor. This was done haphazardly and thus resulted in most stamps having their design cut into at some point and the margins being small and irregular. Our particular £2000 stamp had such big margins that it had parts of the adjoining stamps attached. Its postmark was an upright Maltese Cross in a rich shade of red. It was the most eye-catching example of its kind and deserving of its high price. It was literally one example in 10,000 and is likely to appreciate far more than the average penny black.

There is only one example in philately in which poor condition is more desirable, and that is the *crash cover*. These are envelopes retrieved from aircraft, zeppelin, and other air disasters. The more charred and water stained they are, the better! Again, though, eye appeal is absolutely relevant.

Country Exposures and Emerging Markets

One aspect in which investing in stamps allows one to mimic conventional financial investments is what is called *global asset allocation*. As international investors, we may want to hold a portfolio of assets reflecting both the distributional global wealth and areas where we believe growth is likely to occur. It is widely believed in investment circles that Southeast Asia, in particular China and India, has important long-term investment potential. Taking China as an example, there are a number of problems with indirect investment, such as buying shares, because many of these shares have restrictions on foreign ownership. In addition, it seems to be the case that local traders enjoy huge informational advantages over overseas investors. It is possible to hold Chinese exchange-traded funds (ETFs), which can be bought on U.S. stock exchanges or over the counter, but these hold a relatively small number of stocks. These stocks are common to the majority of foreign investors and constitute the *investible universe*. The lack of diversification tends to make these forms of investment susceptible to herding and panics.

An alternative *direct investment*, such as starting a business in China, would require knowledge of the law, discovery of investment opportunities, and the acquisition of a whole range of skills, which might not be warranted if one only wants to invest less than £100,000.

We now consider the possibility of investing £100,000 in Chinese stamps. This turns out to be very feasible. The stamps can be bought outside China. Economic growth in China and an increased demand for Chinese stamps from Chinese collectors have led to a substantial increase in prices over the last 30 years. Since the printing figures of much of the earlier material are not especially high, it seems likely that prices will continue to rise. Investing in modern material, as described later in this chapter, is, as always, problematic due to the high printing figures. Notwithstanding that, miniature sheets and certain year stamps that were not excessively printed seem to be very solid investments. In this context, the U.K.- or U.S.-based investor has no particular informational disadvantage over the local dealer. The one source of worry is that as the Chinese market opens up, occasionally there will be spectacular finds that can lead to a flood in the market with respect to the particular issue found. Locally one might be aware of this, but it can take a long time before overseas buyers can assess private holdings.

There is another side to international stamp investment that explains some of the spectacular rises in prices. In situations in which a government forbids citizens to take money out of a country or where there is a perceived threat of nationalization of private assets, individuals have been known to buy stamps with a view to selling them overseas in the event of a bad political outcome. Two examples in the past 40 years are Zimbabwean (Rhodesian) stamps and Hong Kong stamps. The value of both of these countries' stamps went up at exceptional rates as a result of the political situations in their countries.

Curiously, there was an interesting secondary effect whereby U.K. and other collectors were attracted by the rise in value, and so collecting outside the countries in question went up as well. This helped sustain the value of the older stamps after the political events had run their course. However, the modern material from 1965 in the case of Rhodesia/Zimbabwe was used due to exchange controls to take money out of the country; there are therefore large quantities available. To a lesser extent this also applies to South Africa. With Hong Kong, a different set of circumstances applied: Prior to 1997 a mania took place for buying stamps in huge quantities from the post office. Unfortunately the speculators forgot that these stamps ceased to be postally valid on July 1, 1997!

Investing in Modern Material

The most common form of stamp investment turns out to be the worst. There are still millions of people who systematically buy all their country's new issues and first-day covers, presentation packs, and booklets. The postal authorities have responded to this enthusiasm by printing more and more at higher and higher cost to the collector. The collectors feel obliged to continue buying because there is some curious belief that incompleteness in a collection leads to a loss in some ill-defined sense. The sums of money that people can spend this way over a 20-year period can be surprisingly large, of the orders of many thousands of pounds. What is such an investment worth? Based on British figures, we can give a fairly clear answer to this question. The prices we quote are current trade prices, that is, what a stamp dealer who specializes in this material might pay. Of course, there could be some errors or rarities in this accumulation, although typically it is not the case. Mint stamps that you would have paid £100 for from the post office would be bought by the specialist for £65. However, if you sell to an intermediary, you may well receive less than that amount. Middle-period, first-day covers fetch about 10 pence each. Modern ones, which have a face value of perhaps £1.50, fetch about 30 pence. Predecimal mint for the period 1970 back to the mid-1960s is more or less worthless. So suppose I had invested £10,000 over the past 35 years on new-issue material. It is quite possible that I would get back about £4000. When we amortise the £10,000 investment appropriately, we could well be facing an 80% loss. Almost no other available investment does so badly, nor is there much uncertainty about the loss; as long as large numbers of people follow the strategy and as long as post offices maximize their profits with respect to it, it is very likely to perform extremely badly.

Setting Up a Hedge Fund to Provide Stamps for Clients

This idea has been mooted on a number of occasions. How might it work? Presumably, a knowledgeable buyer would go to auctions and dealers and purchase material. The bias of most of the stamp market would be toward high-quality material. The authors are divided on the merits of this; one author feels that if everybody thinks something is a good idea, it probably is not.

The stamps purchased would then be allocated to the investors, depending on their stated preferences. Indeed, investors could provide want lists detailing individual stamps, periods, themes, and countries.

This idea seems appealing, but there are a number of difficulties. Most existing hedge funds probably don't have the distributional structure to do this type of thing. It might be better in the context of a high net worth office. It is not clear to us whether the owners should have access, as this could lead to all sorts of fraudulent activity. Owners could take out valuable stamps, replacing them with cheaper stamps, and then demand reparation from the fund when the collection finally went to market at some future date. However, if collectors could have no access to the collections, then much of the psychological pleasure of collecting would be lost. This effectively reduces the value of the collection to the collector.

Finally, there are the usual issues of storage and insurance. If the fund retains physical possession of the stamps, they must be stored securely in a dry, cool environment; they also need to be insured. None of this is beyond the abilities of financial institutions to organize, but, unless it is done efficiently and at a large scale, it could well add significantly to the transaction costs of the investor.

Conclusion

We have described stamp collecting and the pros and cons of using it as an investment process. As with all collecting, expertise is needed in valuation, and transaction costs are extremely high. To treat stamps solely as an investment item, without taking into account the psychological pleasures of ownership and accumulation, limits the attractiveness of such an enterprise. However, the really successful investments in stamps have been made by those who have formed highly specialized collections of particular countries or areas. They have become highly knowledgeable and have often undertaken original research in post office and printers' archives and produced a handbook on their areas. Their named collections are then sold by auction, and often items fetch a premium price because of the provenance of being from a named collection. An example known to one of the authors was of a collection formed by a London solicitor, which fetched in excess of £1 million.

References

Belk, R. W. (1995a) *Collecting in a Consumer Society*, Routledge.

—— (1995b) Collecting as Luxury Consumption: Effects on Individuals and Households, p. ii.

Case, B., H. Pollakowski, and S. Wachter (1991) On Choosing Among House Price Index Methodologies, *AREUEA Journal* 19(3):286–307

Dunedin Stamp Centre (2007) Price List, 29th ed.; available at *www.dunedinstamps.co.nz*.

Gelber, S. M. (1992) The Historical Dynamics of Stamp Collecting, *Comparative Studies in Society and History* 34(4):742–769.

Shiller, R. J. (1991) Arithmetic Repeat Sales Price Estimators, *Journal of Housing Economics*, 110–126.

Stanley Gibbons Stamp Catalogue (2008) *Commonwealth and British Empire Stamps, 1840–1970*, 110th ed., Stanley Gibbons Ltd.

Appendix
The Mathematics of Building a Stamp Index

In this approach, we first characterize individual stamp prices as arising from a stochastic process in which the (log) price level is represented by a market index and the dispersion, and the volatility of values around the market average are modeled as a log normal diffusion process. We claim no originality in what follows. The explanation follows closely that of Case et al. (1991) and Shiller (1991). The broad approach can be thought of as a repeat sales index with variable intertransaction time.

In our model, the parameter beta is the term that we want to identify/estimate. The panel model is that:

$$\ln(P_{it}) = \beta_t + H_{it} + N_{it}$$

where P_{it} is the price of an individual stamp i at time t; β_t is a market price index; H_{it} is a Gaussian random walk; and N_{it} is white noise.

This implies that the total percentage change in price for stamp i transacting in time periods s and t is given by

$$\Delta V_i = \ln(P_{it}) - \ln(P_{is}) = \beta_t - \beta_s + H_{it} - H_{is} + N_{it} - N_{is} \quad (1)$$

The assumption that stamp prices obey a Gaussian diffusion and additional assumptions about the error process are summarized as follows:

$$E[H_{it} - H_{is}] = 0$$

$$E\left[(H_{it} - H_{is})^2\right] = A(t - s)$$

$$E[N_{it}] = 0$$

$$E[H_{it} N_{js}] = 0$$

$$E[N_{it}^2] = C$$

for all i and j and $t > s$. The market price index β_t represents the average behavior of stamp values in a given market and remains unrestricted. An example might be British stamps. The Gaussian random walk H_{it} describes how variation in individual stamp price around the market index causes stamp prices to disperse over time. One important assumption is that the variances of H_{it} are assumed to be proportional to the length of time between repeat transactions. The white-noise term N_{it} represents cross-sectional dispersion in housing values. The N_{it} are assumed to be uncorrelated over time and across properties.

More generally, the difference in the natural log of the price of stamp i that is observed to transact at any two dates can be expressed as:

$$\Delta V_i = \sum_{j=0}^{j} \ln(P_{ij}) D_{ij}$$

where D_{ij} is a dummy variable that equals 1 if the price of stamp i was observed for a second time at time j, −1 if the price of stamp i was observed for the first time at time j, and 0 otherwise. We can substitute, and this yields:

$$\Delta Vi = \sum_{j=0}^{j} (\beta j + Hij + Nij) D_{ij}$$

$$\Delta Vi = \sum_{j=0}^{j} \beta_j D_{ij} + \varepsilon_i$$

This equation can be estimated using ordinary least squares (OLS) and parameters for the market index β_t are obtained. Notice that the variance of the error term ε_i is not constant over time. The variance of the error term will vary with the length of time between repeat transactions and can be estimated; hence, a more efficient estimate of β_t can be obtained by using a generalized least-squares (GLS) procedure. The estimated variance of the error term from the first-stage OLS regression of equation (1) on a sample of repeat transactions is used to construct estimates of the squared deviations (d_i^2) of observed stamp prices around the estimated market index. Note that:

$$\ln(P_{it}^e) = \ln(P_{is}) + (\beta_t^e - \beta_s)$$

where the predicted price in period t is the original price plus expected market appreciation. The squared deviations are given by:

$$d_i^2 = [\ln(P_{it}) - \ln(P_{it}^e)]^2 = [\ln(P_{it}) - \ln(P_{is}) - \beta_t^e + \beta_s]^2$$

Using assumptions of the stamp price process, it can be shown that:

$$E[d_i^2] = A(t-s) + 2C$$

A second-stage regression of d_i^2 on $(t - s)$ and a constant term provide consistent estimates of A and C, and we can then form the predicted values of the squared deviations $E[d_i^2]$. Using this, we can derive the GLS estimates (third stage) of the β_t parameters by carrying out the following regression:

$$\frac{\Delta V_i}{\sqrt{E[d_i^2]}} = \sum_{j=0}^{j} \beta_j \frac{D_{ij}}{\sqrt{E[d_i^2]}} + \frac{\varepsilon_i}{\sqrt{E[d_i^2]}}$$

This will return estimates of the various betas. Index numbers for periods t = 1, 2, 3, ..., T are given by $I_t = 100 \times e^{\beta_t^*}$, where β_t^* are the GLS parameter estimates. If the restriction $\beta_1 = 0$ is imposed in estimation, then $I_1 = 100$. In practice, we usually constrain the predicted values of d_i^2 to be nonnegative, since the estimates of C could lead to negative squared deviations. One solution is to assume that N_{it} is a constant for each stamp N_i. The second-stage OLS regression now becomes:

$$E[d_i^2] = A(t - s)$$

From the definition of WRS above, we can see that the weighting scheme is based on equally weighted time interval adjustments. The weighting factor $\sqrt{E[d_i^2]}$ is only determined by the time difference between repeat transactions, where prices with longer time intervals are weighted downward. Repeat sales with the same time interval are equally weighted. Note also that since we are discussing log prices, we could form indices using exponential calculating; thus it is the geometric mean of stamp prices.

11 Wine: An Alternative Investment

Alan Brown

-Schroder Investment Management

Introduction

At first sight, wine has many attractions as a possible alternative investment.[1]

As a wine gets older, it naturally gets rarer, potentially fueling rising prices through contracting supply. Of course, this process has its limits because every wine eventually goes over the hill, but for the finest wines this might not be until they are 80-plus years old or, in the case of top sauternes and ports, over a century. For example, a single case of Cheval Blanc 1947 was sold at Christie's in 2007, 60 years on, for £75,000.

Second, the worldwide population of individuals with more than $5 million of investible wealth is growing very rapidly. Wealthy individuals are the natural buyers of fine wine. At the same time, although the production of wine worldwide can grow quite easily, the production of truly fine wine, although not quite finite, is severely constrained. Taken together, this provides for a favorable supply/demand dynamic at the top end of the market.

Finally, compared to other alternative investments, wine has one other unique advantage: If the price performance of the asset is not what you hoped for or if you simply change your mind, you have a free option. You can always uncork it and simply enjoy a sublime drink!

On the face of it, evidence from the marketplace would seem to back up this viewpoint. The Liv-ex 100 Fine Wine Index reported an average annual increase of 16.3% p.a. between its launch in July 2001 and the end of June 2008. This easily beats most other assets over the same time period.

However, the picture is never quite so straightforward. Transaction costs in fine wine are very high, at around 10 to 15% between bid and offer. So too are insurance and storage costs at somewhere around £9 a case p.a. Given high bid offer spreads, an investor's holding period is likely to be long before he will net a decent return, and long holding periods compound storage and insurance costs.

[1]*Note:* This chapter is an introduction to the following previously published one, "Bordeaux Wine Vintage Quality and the Weather," by Orley Ashenfelter, David Ashmore, and Robert LaLonde.

Collectible Investments for the High Net Worth Investor

As with any market, prices do not move in a straight line. The three years from 2005–2007 witnessed spectacular increases, but the path has been anything but smooth. Two examples will suffice to demonstrate.

The 1997 first growths were first offered in London *en primeur* at around £1,200 a case. By 2003 the price had fallen to around £700 a case in the aftermath of the Iraq war, the decline in the dollar, and the equity bear market. As of July 2008, if you want to buy the 1997s, the first growths are commanding between about £1,500 and £1,800 a case (with Lafite commanding a premium price of around £2,400).

Consider now the effect of the bid offer spread and holding costs:

Purchase *en primeur* in 1998	£1,200
Storage costs at £9.00 p.a.	90
Sell in 2008*	1,620
Profit	**£330**

*Assuming a 10% bid offer spread.

That turns out to be an IRR of just 2.4% p.a.! And for most of that period an investor would have been looking at unrealized losses.

In early 2009, Cheval Blanc 1995 commands about £2,500 per case. An investor could have bought it as recently as 2003 for £1,200 a case, which equates to a much healthier IRR of 12.8% p.a.:

Purchase 2003	£1,200
Storage costs at £9.00 p.a.	45
Sell in 2008*	2,250
Profit	**£1,005**

*Assuming a 10% bid offer spread.

The message is hardly surprising. Transaction costs and timing matter. So does knowledge about the likely prospects for each vintage and for each chateau. And an understanding of the behavior of the negociants responsible for selling much of the wines of Bordeaux is essential if one is to avoid the hype so often attached to the wine market. Chapter 12 by Orley Ashenfelter and coauthors helps to take some of the mystery (but none of the pleasure!) out of wine buying. It does this by exploring two critical dimensions: the terroir and how history can tell us a great deal about the individual properties of Bordeaux, and the weather and its profound and quite understandable impact on each vintage. Although not claiming to provide all the answers, the chapter clearly explains much of the mystery of the wine market.

The reader might conclude that a venture into the wine market is indeed warranted, but true lovers of wine will hope that this is driven more from an appreciation of the contents of the bottle than the financial rewards of owning it!

12 Bordeaux Wine Vintage Quality and the Weather

Orley Ashenfelter, David Ashmore, and Robert Lalonde

-Princeton University; *Liquid Assets: The International Guide to Fine Wines*; University of Chicago

Nor let thy vineyard bend toward the sun when setting.

—*Virgil*

In this chapter we show that the quality of the vintage for red Bordeaux wines, as judged by the prices of mature wines, can be predicted by the weather during the growing season that produced the wines. Red Bordeaux wines have been produced in the same place and in much the same way for hundreds of years. When young, the wines from the best vineyards are astringent, and many people find them unpleasant to consume. As these wines age, they lose their astringency, and many people find them very pleasant to consume. Because Bordeaux wines taste better when they are older, there is an incentive to store the young wines until they are mature. As a result, there is an active market in young wines (similar to "new issues" in the securities markets) and an active market in older wines (similar to the secondary markets in securities).

Surprisingly, the weather information that is so useful in predicting the prices of the mature wines plays little or no role in setting the prices of the young wines. We show that young wines are usually overpriced relative to what we would predict based on the weather and the price of the old wines. As the young wines age, however, their prices usually converge to our predictions. This implies that "bad" vintages are overpriced when they are young and that "good" vintages may sometimes be underpriced when they are young. Rational buyers should avoid bad vintages when they are young, but they may sometimes wish to purchase good vintages.

Although the evidence suggests that the market for older wines is relatively efficient, it implies that the market for younger wines is very inefficient. Why don't the purchasers of young wines wait and buy them when they are mature? Why do purchasers ignore the weather that produced the vintage in making

Collectible Investments for the High Net Worth Investor

their decisions? Although there are no simple answers to these questions, we discuss one possible explanation in the final section.

Vineyards

It has long been known that the best vineyards in Europe are usually located near a large body of water (to delay spring frosts, prolong fall ripening, and to reduce diurnal temperature fluctuations), on a slope with a southern exposure to the sun (to enhance ripening), and in soil with good drainage (to overcome the dilution of the fruit that accompanies fall rains). The aspects of the weather during the growing season for which a good vineyard site compensates are precisely those that, when absent, produce the growing seasons that make good vintages. An interesting research project would be to determine how much of the differences in the prices fetched by the various Bordeaux chateaux may be attributed to vineyard site characteristics.

Vineyards and Vintages

The best wines of Bordeaux are made from grapes grown on specific plots of land, and the wine is named after the property (or chateau) where the grapes are grown. In fact, knowledge of the chateau and vintage provides most of the information about the quality of the wine; that is, if we imagine 10 vintages and six chateaux, there are, in principle, 60 different wines of different quality. Knowing the reputations of the six chateaux and the 10 vintages, however, is sufficient to determine the quality of all 60 wines; that is, good vintages produce good wines in all vineyards, and the best wines in each vintage are usually produced by the best vineyards (see "Vineyards").

Although this point is sometimes denied by those who produce the wines, and especially by those who sell the young wines, it is easy to establish its truth by reference to the prices of the mature wines. To demonstrate the point, Table 12.1 indicates the 1990–1991 market price in London of six Bordeaux chateaux from the 10 vintages from 1960 to 1969. These chateaux were selected because they are large producers and their wines appear frequently in the secondary (auction) markets. (A blank in the table indicates that the wine has not appeared in the market during the time period. Lower-quality vintages are typically the first to leave the market.) The vintages from 1960 to 1969 are selected because, by the 1990s, these wines are fully mature and there is little remaining uncertainty about their quality.

From Table 12.1 it is obvious that knowledge of the row means and the column means is sufficient to predict most of the prices in the table. (The explained variance from a regression of the logarithm of the price on chateau and vintage dummies is over 90%.) A ranking of the chateaux in order of quality based on their prices would be Latour, Lafite, Cheval Blanc, Pichon-

Table 12.1 London Auction Prices for Selected Mature Red Bordeaux Wines, 1990–1991

	Chateaux (Vineyards)						
Vintage	Lafite	Latour	Cheval Blanc	Cos d'Estournel	Montrose	Pichon Lalande	Average
1960	494	464	486	—	—	—	479
1961*	4335	5432	3534	1170	1125	1579	4884
1962*	889	1064	821	521	456	281	977
1963	340	471	—	251	—	—	406
1964*	649	1114	1125	315	350	410	882
1965	190	424	—	—	—	258	307
1966*	1274	1537	1260	546	482	734	1406
1967*	374	530	441	213	236	243	452
1968	223	365	274	—	—	—	294
1969	251	319	—	123	84	152	285
Average	1504	1935	1436	553	530	649	—

Note: Column averages are calculated only for vintages indicated by an asterisk (*), where a market price exists for every chateau. Row averages are calculated using only Chateau Lafite and Chateau Latour, where prices are available for all vintages. Sterling prices are converted to dollars at the exchange rate on November 30, 1992. (Figures listed are per a dozen bottles in US$.)

Source: Average prices from *Liquid Assets: The International Guide to Fine Wines,* Issue 8 (October 1991) and Issue 9 (December 1992).

Lalande, Cos d'Estournel, and Montrose. In fact, as Edmund Penning-Rowsell pointed out in his classic book *The Wines of Bordeaux* (1985), the famous 1855 classification of the chateaux of Bordeaux into quality grades was based on a similar assessment by price alone. Surprisingly, the 1855 classification ranks these chateaux in only a slightly different order—Lafite, Latour, Pichon-Lalande, Cos d'Estournel, and Montrose. (Cheval Blanc was not ranked in 1855.) Likewise, a ranking of the quality of the vintages based on price alone would be 1961, 1966, 1962, 1964, and 1967. The remaining vintages (1960, 1963, 1965, 1968, and 1969) would be ranked inferior to these five, but, perhaps because of this fact, many of the wines from these inferior vintages are no longer sold in the secondary market.

Real Rate of Return to Holding Bordeaux Wine

It is natural to ask why the prices of mature wines from a single chateau, made in the same way from grapes grown in the same place by the same winemaker, would differ so dramatically from vintage to vintage, as is indicated by Table 12.1. There are two obvious explanations for this vintage variability. First, the older wines have been held longer, and so they must bear a normal rate of return. This fact alone would make the older wines more expensive than the younger ones. Second, the quality of the wines of different vintages may vary because the quality of the grapes used to make the wines varies.

Figure 12.1 provides a test of the hypothesis that the prices of the wines vary because of their age. In this figure (and throughout the remainder of the chapter), we use as a measure of the price of a vintage an index based on the wines of several chateaux. The chateaux are deliberately selected to represent the most expensive wines (Lafite, Latour, Margaux, and Cheval Blanc) as well as a selection of wines that are less expensive (Ducru Beaucaillou, Leoville Las Cases, Palmer, Pichon Lalande, Beychevelle, Cos d'Estournel, Giscours, Gruaud-Larose, and Lynch-Bages). We construct the index of vintage price from a regression of the logarithm of the price from several thousand auction sales on dummy variables indicating the chateau and the vintages. (The precise composition of the sample has very little effect on the results.) The regression coefficients for the vintage dummies are then used to construct the vintage index. This provides a simple way to construct a vintage index in the presence of an unbalanced sample design. (We compute the antilogarithm of these coefficients and then express the price relative to the index price for 1961. This is merely a convenient normalization and affects only the intercept in the regressions reported later.)

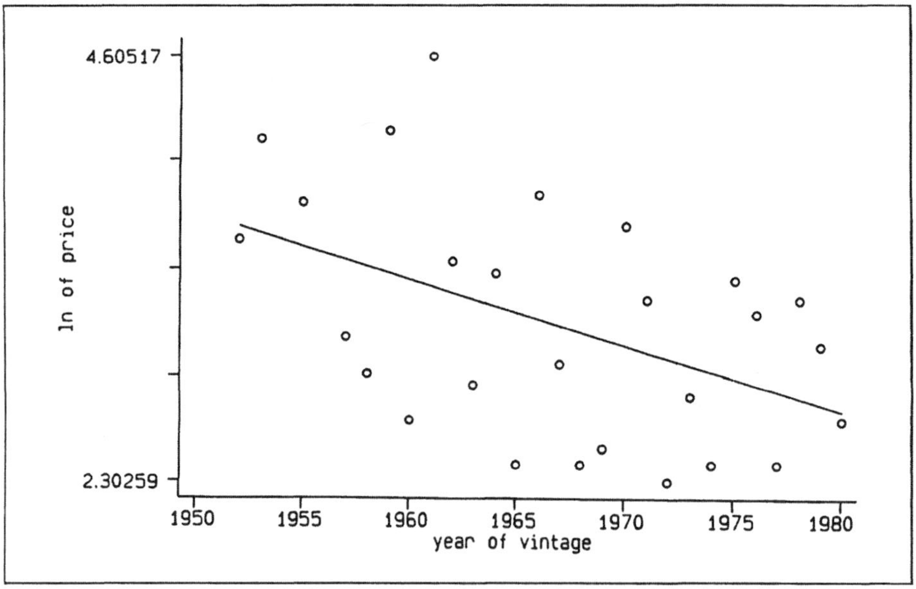

Figure 12.1 Red Bordeaux wines, prices relative to 1961 vintage year

California's Climate for Growing Grapes

The desirability of California's climate for grape growing, and the reasons for it were well known in the 19th century. In his report to the California legislature, A. Haraszthy wrote (p. 143) in 1862 that

> *The California climate is eminently adapted for the culture of grape-vines. The oldest inhabitants [of California] have no recollection of a failure in the crops of grapes. The production is fabulous; and there is no doubt in my mind that before long there will be localities discovered which will furnish as noble wines as Hungary, Spain, France, or Germany ever have produced. In California, site is not so material as in European countries, especially where, during the summer season, a good deal of rain falls. California, having an even temperature, is warm and without rains in summer.*

Figure 12.1 is a scatter diagram of the logarithm of the price of the wines of a vintage against the vintage year. (The vintages of 1954 and 1956 are not plotted because these wines are now rarely sold. These two vintages are generally considered to be the poorest in their decade.) It is apparent from the diagram that there is a negatively inclined relationship. The slope of the regression line through these points is –.035. This is an estimate of (the negative of) what economists sometimes call the *real product rate of return* to holding Bordeaux wines. A "real product rate of return" is a number such that its reciprocal indicates how many bottles of wine one would have to keep in the cellar to be able to consume one bottle per year in perpetuity. These data indicate that it would be necessary to have about 28 bottles in a perpetual cellar that was intended to support the consumption of one bottle per year. With a cellar of this size, the proceeds from the sale of the older vintages would be just sufficient to restock the cellar and provide the consumption of one bottle. Because it is denominated in bottles of wine rather than dollars, this measure does not tell us what the return to holding wine denominated in generalized purchasing power (money) is.

We have analyzed the relationship between the (log) price of Bordeaux wine and its age for many individual chateaux. So long as the sample includes at least 20 vintages, we invariably obtain a negative slope to this relationship of between –.02 and –.04. It is notable that the study of the various vintages of wine provides so reliable and simple a measure of the real rate of return. As we shall see, most of the remaining variation in the price of the wine of different vintages is due to variation from vintage to vintage in the weather that produced the grapes.

Vintages and the Weather

It is well known that the quality of any fruit, in general, depends on the weather during the growing season that produced the fruit. What is not so widely understood is that in some localities the weather will vary dramatically from one year to the next. In California, for example, it never rains in the summer, and it is always warm in the summer. There is a simple reason for this. In California, a high-pressure weather system settles each summer over the California coast and produces a warm, dry growing season for the grapes planted there (see "California's Climate for Growing Grapes"). In Bordeaux, this sometimes happens—but usually it does not. Great vintages for Bordeaux wines correspond to the years in which August and September are dry, the growing season is warm, and the previous winter has been wet.

Figure 12.2 establishes that it is hot, dry summers that produce the vintages in which the mature wines obtain the higher prices. This figure displays for each vintage the summer temperature from low to high as you move from left to right, and the harvest rain from low to high as you move from top to bottom. Vintages that sell for an above-average price are displayed with black triangles, and vintages that sell for a below-average price are displayed in open squares. If the weather is the key determinant of wine quality, then the dark points should be in the northeast quadrant of the diagram and the light points should be in the southwest quadrant of the diagram. It is apparent that this is precisely the case. Even anomalies, like the 1973 vintage, tend to corroborate the fact that the weather determines the quality of the wines. The wines of this vintage, which are of somewhat above-average quality, have always sold at relatively low prices; insiders know that they are often bargains.

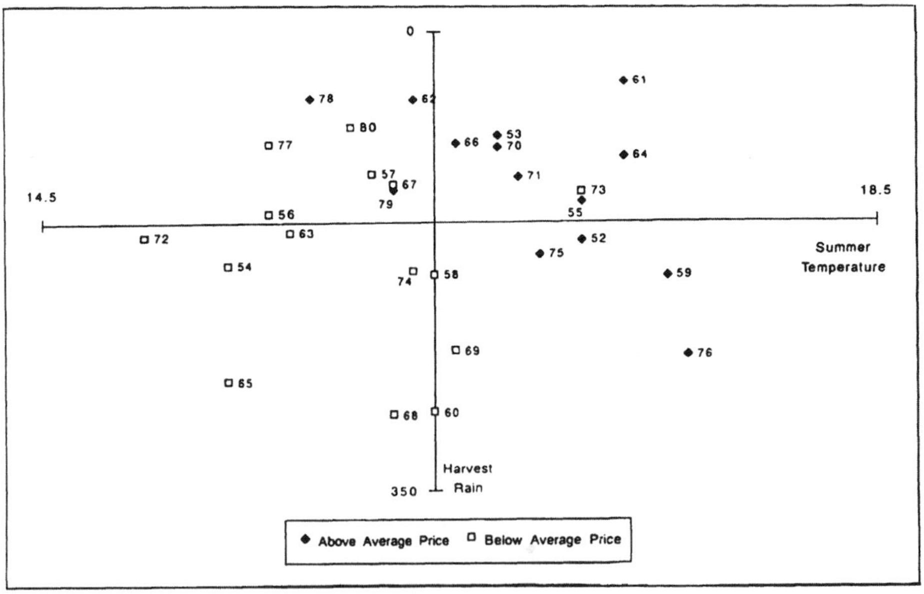

Figure 12.2 Bordeaux: Summer temperature and harvest rain related to price, 1952–1980

Table 12.2 contains a regression of the (log) price of the vintage on the age of the vintage and the weather variables indicated. In practice, the weather variables are almost uncorrelated with each other and with the age of the vintage. As a result, the regression equation is remarkably robust to the addition of other variables. The second column of the table contains the basic "Bordeaux equation," and the third column shows the effect on the regression of adding the temperature in September as an additional variable. It is obvious that this variable does not have a statistically significant coefficient, and, indeed, in further experimentation we have not found any other statistically significant variables to add to the regression.

It is possible, of course, to predict the relative price at which the new vintage should be sold as soon as the growing season is complete. In fact, we have been doing this for several years and publishing the results in the newsletter *Liquid Assets: The International Guide to Fine Wines*. The basic idea for these predictions is displayed in Figure 12.3. Here we have added to Figure 12.2 the data for the vintages from 1981 to 1992. Two things are immediately apparent from the figure. First, all but one of these recent vintages (1986) was produced by a growing season that was warmer than what is historically "normal." It is no accident that many Europeans believe global warming may already be here! This unusual run of extraordinary weather has almost certainly resulted in a huge quantity of excellent but immature red Bordeaux wine.

Second, the weather that created the vintages of 1989 and 1990 appears to be quite exceptional by any standard. Is it appropriate to predict that the wines

Table 12.2 Regressions of the (Logarithm of) Price of Different Vintages of a Portfolio of Bordeaux Chateau Wines on Weather Variables

Independent Variables			
Age of vintage	0.0354 (0.0137)	0.0238 (0.00717)	0.0240 (.00747)
Average temperature over growing season (April–September)		0.616 (0.0952)	0.608 (0.116)
Rain in September and August		−0.00386 (0.00081)	−0.00380 (0.000950)
Rain in the months preceding the vintage (October–March)		0.001173 (0.000482)	0.00115 0.000505)
Average temperature in September			0.00765 (0.0565)
R^2	0.212	0.828	0.828
Root mean squared error	0.575	0.287	0.293

Note: All regressions use as data the vintages of 1952–1980, excluding the 1954 and 1956 vintages, which are now rarely sold; all regressions contain an intercept, which is not reported; the data (and a readme file) are also available by anonymous FTP in the pub/wine directory of irs.princeton.edu. Standard errors are in parentheses.

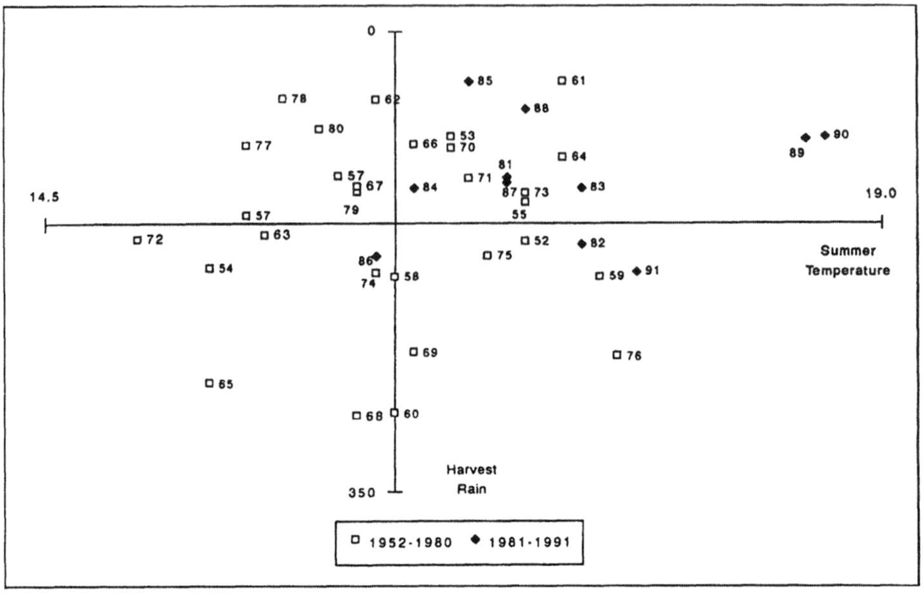

Figure 12.3 Bordeaux: Summer temperature and harvest rain related to price, 1952–1991

of these vintages will be of outstanding quality when the temperature that produced them is so far outside the normal range? Before making the prediction for 1989, we did, in fact, turn to Lincoln Moses (of Stanford University) for informal advice. Moses suggested two informal tests: (1) Would the last major "out-of-sample" prediction have been correct? The idea here is to use the past to indirectly test the ability of the relationship to stretch beyond the available data. In fact, the last major out-of-sample prediction for which all uncertainty has been resolved is the vintage of 1961, which had the lowest August–September rainfall in Bordeaux history. Just as the unusual weather predicted, the market (see Table 12.1), and most wine lovers, have come to consider this an outstanding vintage. (2) Is the warmth of the 1989 and 1990 growing seasons in Bordeaux greater than the normal warmth in other places where similar grapes are grown? The idea here is to determine whether the temperature in Bordeaux is abnormal by comparison with grape-growing regions that may be even warmer. In fact, the temperature in 1989 or 1990 in Bordeaux was no higher than the average temperature in the Barossa Valley of South Australia or the Napa Valley in California, places where high-quality red wines are made from similar grape types.

Based on these two informal tests, we are convinced that both the 1989 and 1990 vintages in Bordeaux are likely to be outstanding. Many wine writers have made the same predictions in the trade magazines. Of course, it is still too early to determine whether the wines will fulfill their promise.

Market Inefficiency

It is natural to inquire as to the prices at which the wines listed in Table 12.1 were sold when the wines were first offered on the market. In particular, were the relative prices of the young wines good forecasts of the relative prices the mature wines now fetch? It is difficult to answer this question because the young wines were all sold in different time periods and at prices that are not generally known. Instead, we have explored a closely related question: Were the relative prices of the vintages when they were first sold in the auction market good forecasts of the relative prices of the mature wines? Were the prices of the young wines, viewed as forecasts of the prices of the mature wines, as good as the predictions made using the data on the weather alone?

Table 12.3 reveals the answer to both of these questions. In this table we have listed, for each calendar year from 1971 to 1989, the price of the portfolio of wines from each vintage relative to the price of the portfolio of wines from the 1961, 1962, 1964, and 1966 vintages. The benchmark vintage portfolio is a simple average of the 1961, 1962, 1964, and 1966 vintage indexes. The second column gives the value of the benchmark portfolio in pounds sterling in the year indicated and provides a general measure of the overall inflation in wine prices in the London auction markets. The entries for each of the vintages in the remaining columns are simply ratios of the prices of the wines in each vintage to the benchmark portfolio in column 1 of the table. The 1961, 1962, 1964, and 1966 vintages were selected for the benchmark because the weather data in Figure 12.2 predict they would be good, and the wines from these vintages are, no doubt as a consequence, still widely traded. The vintages that are studied in the table include all those between 1961 and 1972. Listed in the bottom row of the table is the predicted relative price of the vintage as taken from the "Bordeaux equation" in Table 12.2.

The data in Table 12.3 confirm two remarkable facts. First, most of these older vintages began their lives in the auction markets at prices that are far above what they will ultimately fetch. For example, the bottom row of the table indicates that, based on the weather, the wines of a vintage like 1967 would have been expected to sell for about one-half the price of an average of the wines from the 1961, 1962, 1964, and 1966 vintages. In fact, the wines entered the auction markets in 1972 at about 50% more than expected and slowly drifted down in relative price over the years. Second, the predicted prices from the "Bordeaux equation," which is fit from an entirely different set of data, are remarkably good indicators of the prices at which the mature wines will ultimately trade.

The Response of the Wine Press

The mere mention of the use of statistical analyses to analyze the quality of wine vintages has sent the wine trade press into a frenzy. The leader in the *New*

Table 12.3 Price per Case of a Portfolio of Bordeaux Chateaux, 1961–1972, Relative to the Price of the Portfolio for the Vintages of 1961, 1962, 1964, and 1966

		Vintage											
Year of Sale	Benchmark Portfolio[a]	1961	1962	1963	1964	1965	1966	1967	1968	1969	1970	1971	1972
1971	£54	1.66	0.79	0.41	0.76	—	0.79	—	—	—	—	—	—
1972	£97	1.58	0.76	0.26	0.70	0.27	0.96	0.77	—	0.75	—	—	—
1973	£119	1.62	0.71	0.28	0.74	0.24	0.93	0.62	0.28	0.70	0.83	—	—
1974	£85	1.31	0.77	0.39	0.84	—	1.08	0.78	0.30	0.70	0.88	—	0.30
1975	£76	1.65	0.77	0.29	0.78	0.35	0.80	0.57	0.31	0.41	0.84	0.61	0.44
1976	£109	1.67	0.83	0.30	0.65	0.29	0.85	0.51	0.23	0.36	0.69	0.54	—
1977	£165	1.67	0.83	0.26	0.63	0.26	0.87	0.50	0.23	0.36	0.70	0.51	0.32
1978	£215	1.67	0.76	0.26	0.65	0.18	0.91	0.45	0.25	0.31	0.70	0.53	0.25
1979	£274	1.61	0.73	0.20	0.66	0.23	1.00	0.49	0.24	0.29	0.71	0.50	0.23
1981	£296	1.75	0.62	0.22	0.70	0.04	0.93	0.47	0.25	0.29	0.82	0.52	0.22
1982	£420	1.80	0.71	0.15	0.60	0.18	0.89	0.39	0.17	0.24	0.77	0.55	0.19
1983	£586	1.77	0.53	0.10	0.59	0.18	1.11	0.36	0.18	0.21	0.91	0.48	0.20
1985	£952	2.19	0.53	0.12	0.50	0.21	0.78	0.30	0.11	0.14	0.68	0.46	0.13
1986	£888	2.10	0.56	0.25	0.54	0.17	0.80	0.30	0.15	0.19	0.65	0.46	0.14
1987	£901	2.11	0.56	—	0.53	—	0.80	0.32	0.19	0.20	0.64	0.49	0.18
1988	£854	2.01	0.56	0.21	0.61	0.14	0.82	0.34	0.23	0.20	0.67	0.58	0.17
1989	£1,048	2.09	0.61	0.28	0.53	0.19	0.77	0.27	0.24	0.18	0.66	0.43	0.15
Predicted price[b]	—	1.74	0.72	0.29	0.76	0.16	0.78	0.49	0.21	0.29	0.60	0.53	0.14

Note: A portfolio (for a vintage) consists of the wines from 15 leading chateaux. The chateaux used are the same for all vintages. The "benchmark" portfolio consists of the portfolio of leading chateaux and wine from the vintages of 1961, 1962, 1964, and 1966.

[a]Absolute price of benchmark portfolios.

[b]Predicted relative price from the "Bordeaux equation."

York Times (March 4, 1995) was "Wine Equation Puts Some Noses Out of Joint," which may have been an understatement. Robert Parker, Jr., generally regarded as the most influential wine critic in America, calls the approach "a Neanderthal way of looking at wine." Britain's *Wine* magazine said of the use of multiple regression analysis to predict wine quality that "the formula's self-evident silliness invited disrespect." Some of the reactions in the wine press imply condemnation of the entire approach for reasons that most statisticians will find humorous. For example, *The Wine Spectator* said, "the theory depends for its persuasiveness on the match between vintage quality as predicted by climate data, and vintage price on the auction market. But the predictions come exactly true only three times in the 27 vintages since 1961 that he's calculated, even though the formula was specifically designed to fit price data that already existed. The predicted prices are both under and over the actual prices." Apparently the presence of imperfect predictions in the regression equation causes consternation, even if "they are both under and over the actual prices."

One interesting way to see the inefficiency in this market is to compare the prices of the vintages of 1962, 1964, 1967, and 1969 in calendar year 1972. As the weather data in Figure 12.2 indicate, and the prediction in the bottom row of Table 12.3 confirms, we should have expected (in 1972) that the 1962 and 1964 vintages would sell for considerably more than the vintages of both 1967 and 1969. In fact, in 1972 these four vintages fetched nearly identical prices, in sharp contrast to what the weather would have indicated. By around 1979, the prices of the 1969s and 1967s had fallen to around what would have been predicted from the weather.

It is apparent from Table 12.3 that most vintages are overpriced when the wines are first offered on the auction market and that this state of affairs often persists for 10 years or more following the year of the vintage. The overpricing of the vintages is especially apparent for those vintages that, from the weather, we would predict are the poorest. This suggests that, in large measure, the ability of the weather to predict the quality of the wines is ignored by the early purchasers of the wines.

An interesting recent example of this phenomenon is the 1986 vintage. As Figure 12.3 indicates, this is a vintage that, based on the weather, we should expect to be "average." Compared to the other vintages of the last decade, this vintage should fetch a considerably lower price. In fact, the vintage was launched with great fanfare as among the finest two vintages of the decade. The wines were sold at similar and sometimes higher prices to initial buyers than the wines of the other vintages of the past decade. The enthusiasm for these wines has dampened somewhat because they have not fetched auction prices higher than those of the other vintages in the decade. We should expect that, in due course, the prices of these wines will decline relative to the prices of most of the other vintages of the 1980s.

Conclusion

Why does the market for immature red Bordeaux wines appear to be so inefficient when the market for mature wines appears to be so efficient? We think there may be several related explanations. The current Bordeaux marketing system has the character of an agricultural income stabilization system, and this may be its purpose. Complete income stabilization for the growers would require that the price of the young wines be inversely related to the quantity produced and independent of the quality. Although the actual pricing of young Bordeaux wines falls short of this ideal, it is clearly closer to it than would occur if purchasers used the information available from the weather for determining the quality of the wines. The producers do attempt to raise prices when crops are small, despite the evidence that the quantity of the wines (determined by the weather in the spring) is generally unrelated to the quality of the wines. Moreover, it is common for the proprietors to claim that each vintage is a good one, independent of the weather that produced it. Indeed, there is no obvious incentive for an individual proprietor to ever claim anything else!

A more fundamental question arises about the motives of the early purchasers of the wines. Why have they ignored the evidence that the weather during a grape-growing season is a fundamental and easily measured determinant of the quality of the mature wines? Will they continue to do so as the evidence for the predictability of the quality of new vintages accumulates?

Additional Reading

Haraszthy, A. (1862) *Grape Culture, Wines, and Wine-making*, Harper.

Liquid Assets: The International Guide to Fine Wines, Orley Ashenfelter (ed.), various issues.

Penning-Rowsell, E. (1985) *The Wines of Bordeaux*, 5th ed., The Wine Appreciation Guild.

13 Collecting Classic Cars

David Barzilay

-Freelance Journalist and Writer

The Development of Classic Car Collecting

To many, the motor car was the most earth-changing device of the 20th century and the one that has had the most impact in a relatively short space of time.

The 20th century saw huge technological change—from just a handful of motor cars at the beginning to most families owning one by the end. Right from the start there were both drivers and engineers who wanted to get the best from the new machines, to go ever faster, to provide greater comfort, and to make machinery that would be ever more reliable. It was a golden age in which human and machine came together in a symbiotic relationship that has lasted to this day.

In the early days manufacturers were desperate to prove that their machines were the best, the most reliable, and the fastest. Above all they wanted to catch the public imagination. They knew right from the start that machines that won the early endurance trials and races would be the ones the public would purchase. It was these races and endurance trials that developed a competitive spirit among manufacturers and that meant, right from the start, that the motor car would be at the forefront of innovation.

Initially, the car was a tool, a new means of getting from point A to B quicker than by previously established means. It soon developed into what today we would call a "must-have" item. The problem, of course, was that initially most people could not afford to own one. That didn't stop hundreds of people going to watch the initial races that were held in the United Kingdom, Europe, and the United States. There were some horrendous accidents, but that didn't stop millions of people following early motorsport and falling in love with the motor car and the men who drove them.

As the machines developed and manufacturers became more and more competitive, the need for speed, and speed records, evolved. It meant that many famous motoring pioneers were to go down in history chasing the increasingly shifting goalposts. But like the cars themselves, these heroes were seen as an essential part of selling cars. They were feted by manufacturers and suppliers

Collectible Investments for the High Net Worth Investor

of oil and petrol companies, who attracted them with the very earliest kind of sponsorship deals. The men and women who were driving the fastest cars were becoming the pop heroes of the age, and the machines that they drove were the icons of the day.

The challenge of speed dominated, and groups of people like the Bentley Boys raced supercharged Bentleys at Le Mans in France and Brooklands in the United Kingdom. Developments made on the racing and speed circuits were being passed on to a growing number of car manufacturers, many of whom, like Henry Ford, were developing cars that could be afforded by most people rather than an elite group.

But it was these cars driven by the elite that, in the heady period between the end of the First World War and the beginning of the Second World War, ultimately set the scene for later collecting. They were the cars that were involved in the Golden Age of the motorcar, where records were broken on almost a daily basis from a race, speed, and manufacturing perspective.

The way the car was to look was developed during this period. The quest for ever-higher speeds was joined by a quest for cutting-edge design, with manufacturers and coach builders employing the top designers of the day to come up with bodywork that reflected modern trends for speed and luxury. At the top end of the market you could order a Rolls-Royce and have a body built by a variety of coach builders. They all vied for customers, producing a wide selection of stunning motor cars.

Car manufacturers opened lavish showrooms to show off their wares. Motor shows were held to entice the public, with the rich and famous ordering specialist bodies and vehicles with the latest innovations and materials of the day. The market was splitting into two: the lavish cars that set the pace in terms of looks and design, and the more utilitarian vehicles that could be owned by an increasing number of people.

Then the world was plunged into the Second World War. The technology that had been used in developing the car and pushing it to its limits was put to use to develop tanks, armored cars, and a variety of military vehicles. Many of the more well-built marques such as Rolls-Royce and Bentley were pressed into service as staff cars, troop carriers, and ambulances.

At the end of the conflict, the world was on a technological high, but the Golden Age of motoring had been lost. Mass production was becoming the norm, and some people who had experienced the heyday of motoring were wondering what had happened to the great cars. Some people started to track down the cars that they had remembered—the Bentleys of the 1920s and 1930s, the early Aston Martins, Ferraris, and Alfa Romeos.

For others it was the earlier vehicles that came to the fore. It was still possible to buy cars from the very early days of motoring for a few pounds and restore them for events such as the annual London to Brighton Veteran Car Run. It was these early collectors and the events in which they were involved that set the scene for what was to follow. *Genevieve*, a film about a restored

Darracq on the London to Brighton Run, became a British movie blockbuster of its day and has now taken on almost cult status.

But to many, the cars were still simply old cars. They were not classified until Britain's Vintage Sports Car Club came up with a clarification that defined *veteran cars* as those built before 1905, *Edwardian cars* as those built before 1919, and *vintage cars* as those built before 1931. The cars were sold in small ads in local papers; there were very few auction houses, although auctioneers such as Coys of Kensington in London, had been selling interesting cars to a growing band of enthusiasts over the years.

By the early 1970s, the cars that people had remembered from the Golden Age interwar period were coming of age, and to simply label and sell them as "old cars" was no longer working. There was a sudden realization that these cars would never be built again; furthermore, some of them had not been built in great numbers in the first place. Many had disappeared, had been scrapped, or were beyond repair. Those that were left were starting to become collectible and more valuable as a growing band of people set about finding the cars and restoring those that needed it.

The Bentleys, Aston Martins, and other similar marques were fairly obvious, but it was soon realized that there were many other famous marques, some of which had simply stopped manufacturing and gone out of existence and that might become even more collectible. These included Auburn, Bugatti (which later had a renaissance), Cord OM, and others. In addition, manufacturers, such as Ferrari and Maserati, realized that they were manufacturing collectible cars that were limited to a small run of any particular model and therefore kept their exclusivity. Some, like the California Spyder, were made in very small numbers, making this, and cars like it, even more collectible. They were in many respects what was called a *limited edition*, and many of these cars would become collectible. This is particularly true of the vehicles that were made in the late 1940s, 1950s, and early 1960s, not only by Ferrari but also by manufacturers such as Cistalia, Maserati, OSCA, and Lamborghini when they started to manufacture cars in the early 1960s.

It was still the age of style and design before the age of the mass-manufactured car took over in the 1970s, in all but the most expensive models, when safety, environmental issues, and pen-pushing bureaucrats often dictated design. Suddenly, owning a classic car looked an awful lot more attractive than it had in the past, and the cars were starting to go up in value by leaps and bounds. Owning a classic car suddenly appealed to a new group of people who wanted to have fun and to own something that would never be produced again, and if they could make some money along the way, so much the better. They wanted to drive and own something that wasn't just seen as a mass-produced piece of steel but instead exuded style and made a statement.

The collecting of classic cars really started to take off in the early 1970s, but it wasn't until the early 1980s that it started to become big business. It soon became apparent that buying and selling classic cars could make money. Those who realized what was going on were laying down the conditions. Original condition and provenance as to a car's history were paramount. If the car had been restored, a history file on what had been done, with accompanying photographs, was essential. Specification also started to become more important, with the larger engines and power outputs commanding the higher prices. Those who had simply started collecting cars because they loved owning them realized that they had a growing market value and perhaps they were a better investment than stocks and shares.

It was the Americans who first came to Europe looking for cars to invest in, as they had earlier done for antiques, and they set about shipping pristine examples back home. Next came collectors from the oil-rich Middle Eastern countries. Today it is emerging countries like Russia and China, whose newly rich want to be part of an elite band of high-end car collectors and investors. China is even in the process of setting up its own classic car museum, and the newly rich are regularly seen at auctions and with dealers in the West.

In the 1970s and 1980s, more and more classic car magazines were set up in both Europe and America. Initially, it was those prewar cars that set the pace at sales and auctions, but then the supercars of the 1950s and 1960s came into their own and the market blossomed. Classic car auctions and sales became a regular feature and began to dictate the market values. The number of dealers specializing in classic cars also grew.

Cars were seen as a good investment and started to become an important part of some people's portfolios, which, until then, had contained stocks, art, and real estate. But it was all to come to a shuddering halt in 1989, when the last recession hit. The demand for classic cars, even those at the top end of the market, quickly fell. Those who could afford to do so stayed in, and of course the traditional collector, who purchased a car not just for investment proposes but for fun, was not about to sell his cherished possession unless he really needed to. The big auction houses, like Coys, Bonhams, and Christie's, simply saw the recession as a glitch and pointed out that, like stocks and shares, the value of cars could go down as well as up.

Many also pointed out that, like property, cars were a long-term, not a short-term, investment. They said that quality was most important, and once again, that those early marques such as Bentley and Aston Martin and the supercars from the 1950s and 1960s were the best bet and indeed were the cars that would bounce back, and that was certainly the case. It was still true that those cars with an interesting provenance, racing history, or extreme rarity would always be in demand, even if the price fluctuated, and that is still true.

As this book went to press and a worldwide recession was starting to bite, it appeared that the classic car market would be hit once again. It also appeared that those who had money were selling shares and putting money into gold, art, antiques and, once again, high-end motor cars. It remains to be seen whether these cars will retain the value that they had in the past.

Classic Car Collectors

There are lots of reasons why people collect cars. It might be that a collector wants to buy a car associated with his or her childhood. He or she might have fallen in love with a particular marque of car or might simply see certain cars as a long-term investment. There is no one type of classic car collector. If a person has a passion for motoring and the car, they can get the collecting bug. You might not be able to afford to own a Hispano Suiza, but you can probably own some sort of classic piece of motoring history, from the enthusiast with his Austin 7 or his Ford Escort RS200 to the international billionaire with a collection of competition Maseratis.

The point is that car collecting is accessible to virtually everyone at some level. The man who purchased his Mk.1 Ford Escort from a neighbor down the road is just as proud of it as is the owner of the £8 million Ferrari. They share the same dreams, the same aspirations of maintaining the car and showing it to other like-minded enthusiasts. They will probably be amateur experts in their field and more than likely will be members of the relevant owners or enthusiasts clubs. Mainly, they have taken the plunge and acted on their passion.

How many times when you have been driving down the road have you seen coming the other way that classic Alvis, Delahaye, or Mercedes-Benz you have always dreamed of owning but never done anything about? You have probably thought about how great it would be to climb into your 1940s Jaguar Roadster, put on your flying helmet, adjust your goggles, and set off, just as it was done in the day—but then reality kicks in and you think about the expense of it all and what it is going to mean to the tax man. Although it could be fun, the fact is that it could cost a great deal of money!

Owning, storing, and maintaining a classic car is not cheap, particularly if the vehicle needs to be restored. But the rewards in terms of both fun and financial return can be high if you carefully choose the type of car that you buy, with an eye on what cars are going up in value, and look at the whole thing from a long-term perspective. The important thing to remember is that whatever classic car you choose to invest in, it will never be manufactured again, so in theory these cars, if they are well looked after, are always going to go up in value. There are only a certain number available, and in the United Kingdom and Europe and around the rest of the world there are many collectors and investors who are constantly looking for the car of their dreams or to contribute to the collection that they already have.

Cars as the Collectible Investment

To many collectors, putting money into classics is part of a wider portfolio of investments, which could include property and shares. For others, this commitment is the only investment that they are ever likely to make, apart from the one that most of us make—owning our own home.

Like any other investment, the amount of money that you can invest will dictate the type or the quality of the car you can aim for, but unlike some other investments, you can always make the choice of buying a car that is not in pristine condition but is restorable. In other words, there are choices in achieving your goal. You don't have to get a vehicle that is in concours d'elegance condition and is going to cost you a lot of money; you can buy cars at different levels of restoration and then work on them yourselves. This, of course, will depend on your level of expertise, but to many collectors, the fact that they have purchased the classic car of their dreams and that they can spend a few hours at the weekend bringing it back to its former glory is all part of the fun.

Alternatively, and if you do your sums right, you can buy a car that needs to be restored and give it to an expert company to work on it for you. Basically you need to work out how much the car is going to cost to buy, how much it is going to cost to restore, and then determine whether both those costs exceed the value of the car when it is complete. When some people do the sums, they don't quite add up. However, they take the view that they will have a great car to take to events and enjoy over a period of time. The difference between what they have spent buying and restoring the car will eventually catch up, and they will have had many happy hours of classic motoring in the meantime.

Finding Classic Cars

Many collectors quite rightly scour catalogues from auction houses such as Coys, search the Internet, buy classic car magazines, look at used car advertisements in newspapers, and contact the owners clubs. Coys has been finding cars for clients since 1919. Set up by W. E. Coy, the company has had a significant presence in motoring since the end of the First World War. The business opened in Queens Gate Mews in London to dispense petrol to discerning motorists and important local clients, including those from Buckingham Palace. The business evolved, always with the emphasis on sporting and quality cars. It became a pioneering organization specializing in showroom sales and eventually auctions for the most desirable collectors cars.

Other collectors turn detective and spend a great deal of time tracking down cars that have resided in barns, sheds, or buildings for many years. They spend hours visiting locations where a classic might be hidden or researching rumors about cars that were put into storage years before. This dedication has turned to gold for many collectors, particularly in the United States, where many classics were put into scrap yards that have simply been added to over the years or, when the owners of cars passed away, their relatives simply pushed the car into a barn or shed, only for it to be discovered much later.

There have been some great examples of cars being found, and many of them have been unearthed (sometimes literally) simply due to the dedication of the collector who heard a rumor that a certain person put a car into storage in 1955 and that it might still be there. Collectors have been known to spend years trying to find a particular vehicle they had heard was hidden away in the 1950s or 1960s, and then almost as long negotiating with the owner to buy the vehicle, which—although it might not be in prime condition—is part of the family history and will not be let go easily. In these instances and depending on the model of the car, substantial rewards can be gained from bringing something that is extremely rare back to life.

Cars like this, often called *barn finds*, still turn up today. In 2007 Coys offered for sale at auction, with no reserve, a Ferrari 246 Dino that had resided in a barn in Northamptonshire, north of London, for 30 years. Interest was intense because it meant that someone would have the chance of buying a desirable car and carrying out a ground-up restoration to their own specification. They would have a complete record of what many call a "nut and bolt" restoration. When the car was ultimately sold, the pictures of the car in the state in which it was found, its restoration, and its newfound glory would be a very important historical document to accompany the car for the rest of its days, proving its provenance and in turn guaranteeing that the seller would always receive the best market price.

Cars are sold in various conditions from the barn finds mentioned earlier, where a car has just been driven into a barn or a garage and left to deteriorate over the years, to cars that have simply not been treated very well and need some TLC to bring them back to condition up to those that are in 100-point concours d'elegance condition. Over the years, some amazing cars have been found under hayricks, in bricked-up garages, in old barns, and at the back of quite well-known petrol filling stations. Many of these have been sent to auction and in a wide variety of conditions.

There are three main routes to finding the car of your dreams: the auction house, a private seller, and the dealer or expert. They all have advantages and disadvantages.

The Auction House

Since the beginning of the 1980s, a variety of auction houses, such as Coys, Bonhams, and Christie's, have dealt in classic cars. Most of them are based in the United Kingdom or the United States, although many of them now have subsidiary offices in most countries. Auction houses do offer a virtually unlimited number of possibilities. To this day, it is still feasible to go to an auction house and walk off with a bargain if you have done your research and you know what you are doing.

"Sleeping gems" can be found at an auction, but you have to do your research and know what cars are selling for what prices, what might be worth buying and restoring, and indeed what cars might be bought in one marketplace and then sold in another for a profit. A good example of this is the American muscle car. Finding a good example in the United States for a reasonable price is proving harder and harder. It used to be that U.K. American muscle car enthusiasts would buy cars at auction in the United States and ship them to the United Kingdom. Now very often, important American cars are purchased in the United Kingdom and shipped back to the United States.

Cars are offered at auction for a variety of reasons. For example, a collector wants to make a quick sale. The collector does not want to restore a car, which he or she might have to do if it is to be sold to a private buyer or a dealer. The important thing to remember is that gems do turn up at auction, and this is why many classic car dealers buy at auction and make a very good living from it. An auction gives everyone, whether a dealer or a private individual, an equal opportunity to get involved and get a good deal. However, you need to carefully look at all the paperwork. You need to go over the car yourself to be assured that it has no hidden problems. It might be sensible to take an expert with you, and of course this applies to other methods of purchase as well. There is a comeback: If the car that you have purchased at auction is not as it was described in the catalogue, you do have recourse with the auction house. It is down to the buyer, however, to assure himself that the car matches the description.

Private Sales

Private sales can be very fraught and are often difficult to conclude. There is always a meeting between the seller, who wants to get as much as he can for the car, and the buyer, who wants to buy it as cheaply as possible. There is always a vested interest; be assured that the private seller will always have the stomach for a fight. Be prepared to disagree, too; sellers will very often come up with unusual and unsustainable claims. If the claims later turn out to be fraudulent, there is not a lot than you can do once the sale has gone through; there is little recourse afterward. Go and look at the vehicle, think about it, and give it a thorough going over. Do not be afraid to take a flashlight and magnet with you.

A private sale can be one of the most pressurized car buying and selling environments. Having said that, with a private sale you get a very good insight into where the car has come from and its history. You also get a very good impression of how the car has been looked after. You don't often get that insight at auction.

Dealing with the Motor Trade

If you are buying from a dealer or a company that specializes in classic car sales, you will be negotiating on a car that has been well considered and described. Specialist car dealers and companies that deal exclusively in selling cars for the collector have a reputation to maintain, one that they cannot afford to lose. The car will have had some degree of preparation. The cars that are sold in this way will often be of a high standard, with a corresponding premium over and above their perceived market value. The company or dealer will have put in a great deal of time researching the car and making sure that any claims that are made about its provenance are correct. More often than not, you will be paying for a nice environment and a good experience. Companies and dealers who specialize in high-end classic cars are experts in their field and know what they are talking about, and you will pay for this expertise. Peace of mind does come at a price—a price that is often worth paying. You will have to decide to accept or not what the dealer or company tells you and make a judgment based on the available information.

In summary, auctions are exciting; you can take a chance and make a lot of money. Remember that if you are bidding against a classic car company or dealer, it is sometimes worth making that extra bid, because they will have to sell on at a profit and so need to mentally build in their margin. Private sales can raise a lot of problems, but dealing with someone face to face is a question of personal judgment, and you will get a feel for where the car has come from and how it has been looked after—but remember, there is little recourse after a sale. Buying from a dealer or classic car company means that the car will be properly documented and maintained as well as properly prepared, and you will have recourse to action if you have purchased a car that turns out to be something other than described. However, you will generally have to pay for the privilege.

Tips for Buying the Car of Your Dreams

One of the first tips in buying the classic car of your dreams is to identify how much you have to spend and whether you are going to use that money to buy a fully restored and functioning car or whether you will buy one that requires some work. Restorations are expensive; it is always advisable to buy once all the work has taken place, if possible. You then need to decide whether you can accomplish the work that is required. Some work is just cosmetic and can be carried out by most of us over time, or you could employ a professional.

Perhaps a good analogy for all of this is the current Aston Martin market. If you have always aspired to be James Bond and want to buy an Aston Martin DB5, depending on the particular model and condition of the car, it could cost you between £140,000 and £180,000 for a fully restored concours d'elegance model. On the other hand, a reasonable model with only some cosmetic work would set you back just £120,000, and one that requires a major overhaul could be picked up for as little as £80,000. It depends on the car and how much work is to be done.

So, finally, here are some financial tips on buying a classic car. There's some good news: If you do buy the car of our dreams, you live in the United Kingdom, and it goes up in value, you will not have to pay capital gains tax on any profit that you make. Her Majesty's Revenue and Customs designates classic cars as "wasting assets," which don't attract capital gains. Every country is different, however, and tax and financial regulations change all the time, so if you are thinking of investing in classic cars as part of your portfolio, take local financial advice on how much to spend and what is worth doing. Remember, go for quality if you are looking for the long-term investment.

There are well-trodden paths to follow if you are intending to collect classic cars, particularly if you are doing it from an investment perspective. Look at what has happened in the past and go for the "gilt-edged" cars. Stick with the legends and the cars that have always gone up in value. Don't try to be clever and second-guess the market. Do your research. If you buy a poor car on the basis that it might go up in value or become a collectible marque in the future, it might all go terribly wrong. On the other hand, if you want to buy a car at the lower end because that is all you can afford on the basis that it will become a collectible car of the future and might go up in value, then—if you can store it—go for it. But these are not the cars that should be purchased as part of an investment portfolio.

At the top of the collecting list is Ferrari. Ferrari has achieved the best prices for collectors and investors over the years. They have become extremely collectible because they embody so many collecting attributes. There is the history of the company and its motor-racing heritage. The company enjoyed victories; particularly in the early days, when it was not easy to win, they triumphed over everyone. Ferrari embodies Italian flair and exotic spirit, especially because not many of them are made and because there is an almost religious enthusiasm for the brand, perhaps more so than for any other marque.

But having taken into account the quality issues, your decision is really based on the car that you want to own, whether an Austin-Healey, Bristol, Porsche, or Lagonda. This is an important part of the equation, especially if the car is a one-off purchase and you want to drive it and not let it just sit in a garage.

There is another factor to take into account. In the early days of collecting there was a huge push to restore cars and get them back to pristine condition, and in some instances this was done when there was no reason to do it. It is important to remember that the totally unrestored original car is now seen in the same way as the totally restored car was a few years ago, and in many cases the unrestored car in totally original condition will now fetch far more money. More and more collectors are looking for these cars, which, of course, are few and far between, making them even more valuable. They are a good collecting and investment bet.

However, if you are going to go down that road, check that the vehicle has a continuous history. If it hasn't, try to find out why it hasn't. There could be a perfectly good reason why it disappeared from view for 10 years. Check that the car has matching engine and chassis numbers, although in the case of, say, a racing Bugatti, it might be that the engine was replaced 50 years ago when it blew up in a race. It is important that you can establish this history, especially if you are considering high-end competition machinery. Check that the car has the right documentation, has the correct specification, and has the right sort of engine. Every car will have a story; it is whether it has the *right* story that is key. If the car comes with a good history file, a paper chain will tell you whether the car has been looked after and properly serviced over the years. It will also enable you to check the mileage on the speedometer against the relevant paperwork, service history, and so on.

If you have checked a car's antecedence, it is up to you to check its condition; if you are not an expert in this area, it is often worthwhile to take someone with you who is and who can assess the car for you. These people are most easily found by contacting the relevant owners club. Every make of car has its foibles and idiosyncrasies; experts in particular marques will know exactly what these are and if they are worth worrying about.

Conclusion

Collecting cars can be a lot of fun. A great deal of money can be made, too, but at the end of the day, it is the same as with any investment: The value of classic cars can go down as well as up. However, investing in classic cars can offer much enjoyment along the way. Some people do just put the car that they buy from an investment perspective into a heated, dehumidified garage, where it is left to accrue in value, perhaps being allowed out for a run on a dry day in the summer. Others want to experience their classic and are not concerned that they will be adding miles, wear, and tear as they do so. They want to drive the car as it would have been driven, and they want people to see it. This is, after all, what they were built for.

Because of people like these, there has been a resurgence in famous retrospective events such as the Goodwood 12/12, the Vernasca Silver Flag, and the 1000-mile Mille-Miglia, which takes place in Italy every May and that features more than 350 classic cars worth many millions of pounds battling it out.

The choice is up to you.

Index

D

FSC
www.fsc.org
MIX
Papier | Fördert gute Waldnutzung
FSC® C083411

Kolibri 360 GmbH
Ferdinand-Jühlke-Straße 7
99095 Erfurt, Deutschland
produktsicherheit@kolibri360.de